THE COLOR BLACK

ENSLAVEMENT AND ERASURE IN IRAN

BEETA BAGHOOLIZADEH

Duke University Press *Durham and London* 2024

Printed in the United States of America on acid-free paper ∞
Project Editor: Liz Smith
Designed by Matthew Tauch
Typeset in Alegreya and Anybody by Westchester Publishing Services

Library of Congress Cataloging-in-Publication Data
Names: Baghoolizadeh, Beeta, author.
Title: The color black : enslavement and erasure in Iran /
Beeta Baghoolizadeh.
Description: Durham : Duke University Press, 2024. |
Includes bibliographical references and index.
Identifiers: LCCN 2023026786 (print)
LCCN 2023026787 (ebook)
ISBN 9781478030249 (paperback)
ISBN 9781478026013 (hardcover)
ISBN 9781478059257 (ebook)
Subjects: LCSH: Slavery—Iran—History—19th century. |
Slavery—Iran—History—20th century. | Racism against Black
people—Iran—History—19th century. | Racism against Black
people—Iran—History—20th century. | Black people—Iran—
Social conditions—19th century. | Black people—Iran—Social
conditions—20th century. | BISAC: SOCIAL SCIENCE / Ethnic
Studies / Middle Eastern Studies | SOCIAL SCIENCE / Black
Studies (Global)
Classification: LCC HT1286 .B344 2024 (print) | LCC HT1286 (ebook) |
DDC 306.3/62095509034—dc23/eng/20231117
LC record available at https://lccn.loc.gov/2023026786
LC ebook record available at https://lccn.loc.gov/2023026787

THIS PUBLICATION IS MADE POSSIBLE IN PART BY THE BARR FERREE
FOUNDATION FUND FOR PUBLICATIONS, DEPARTMENT OF ART AND
ARCHAEOLOGY, PRINCETON UNIVERSITY.

PUBLICATION OF THIS BOOK IS SUPPORTED BY DUKE UNIVERSITY
PRESS'S SCHOLARS OF COLOR FIRST BOOK FUND.

THE COLOR BLACK

DEDICATED TO THE ONES WHO
LIGHT UP
MY HEART AND MY SKY

CONTENTS

ILLUSTRATIONS

NOTE ON TRANSLITERATION

Throughout the text, I have used a transliteration system most commonly used in English by lay Persian speakers, with specific emphasis on the standardized Tehrani dialect. For example, I have opted for *Golestan* or *Haji Naneh* instead of *Gulistān* or *Hājī Nanih*, for the ease of the reader. Although it is uncommon to capitalize regional ethnic and racial labels in their transliteration into English, such as *Habashi* or *Siyah*, I have opted to do so to recognize these labels and identities.

For citations in the notes and bibliography, I have followed a simplified version of the *International Journal of Middle East Studies* (*IJMES*) system for the transliteration of Persian-language book titles and articles in citations. Diacritical markers for consonants have been omitted, with the exception of ' for *hamza* and ' for *'ayn*. I have kept this for the sake of researchers and scholars who use this system regularly.

NOTE ON PHOTOGRAPHY

This book argues that enslavement and abolition were defined by processes of forced visibility and forced invisibility in Iran. Forced visibility involved, in part, the photography of enslaved people against their consent, which I discuss at length throughout the book. I have reprinted some of these photographs to demonstrate the mechanisms and dynamics involved in the forced visibility.

With a few exceptions, I have prioritized publishing photographs that have already been in circulation, to redescribe their context and content. This is especially pertinent, as some of these photographs have contributed to the erasure of this history and its violence. Because they do not conform to some individuals' preconceived ideas of what enslavement looks like, these photographs have, in some instances, been used to promote an idea of a generous form of enslavement or to explain enslavement away altogether.

In an effort to be deliberate about the circulation and reproduction of these photographs, I considered making the editorial choice to blur the photographs, share tracings, or elide them altogether and offer detailed descriptions instead. But because Black and Afro-Iranians regularly face the denial of their histories and existence, both within Iran and in the Iranian diaspora, I have decided against the censoring or removal of these photographs to prevent contributing to these large-scale erasures. Instead, I have included some of these photographs to combat the voyeurism, correct the narrative, and reject the erasure of this history. I thank the Collective for Black Iranians for sharing their insight as I navigated making this decision.

ACKNOWLEDGMENTS

I will begin my thanks backward, with an apology: whatever I write here will not be enough. The research for this book began with a simple question, and I'm grateful to all those who have helped me try to answer it in this book.

My first thanks go to Eve Troutt Powell. I remember when I first walked up to Eve to tell her that I wanted to research slavery and race in the Iranian context. "Is that a deal?" she asked. It was, I said (and we shook on it). I know that this book would not exist were it not for that conversation and handshake. I'm grateful to her as my adviser, and to Kathleen Brown and Jamal Elias as the supportive pillars of my dissertation committee, who saw me through my doctoral work and beyond. I loved how dynamic my committee was and feel lucky that they were the ones to oversee my training.

The Penn History and Africana Studies Departments provided me with an intellectual home that shaped my approach to history and historiography. I was fortunate to have benefited from a number of faculty at Penn in addition to my committee, including Cheikh Babou, Anthea Butler, Camille Charles, Paul Cobb, Ali Dinar, Peter Holquist, Firoozeh Kashani-Sabet, Joseph Lowry, Benjamin Nathans, Amy Offner, Kathy Peiss, Karen Redrobe, Barbara Savage, Teren Sevea, Ramya Sreenivasan, and Beth Wenger.

Bucknell's Departments of History and Critical Black Studies provided me with both support and independence in pursuing my research and teaching, a rare and special gift for an assistant professor at a liberal arts college. I'm grateful to my colleagues from Bucknell, including Paul Barba, Nicholas Brady, Claire Campbell, David Del Testa, Sanjay Dharmavaram, Mehmet Dosemeci, John Enyeart, Cymone Fourshey, Jay Goodale, Nicholas Jones, Jennifer Kosmin, Bret Leraul, Elizabeth Loss, Khalil Saucier, Jennifer Thomson, Jonathan Torres, Jaye Austin Williams, and

Nikki Young. It is impossible for me to think about life in Lewisburg without immediately thinking of Talha Ali, Artemio Cardenas, Owais Gilani, and Esra Kose, who created the coziest COVID-safe pod with us that I will forever look back on with love.

I appreciate the intellectual community that I have found at my current academic home at the Mossavar-Rahmani Center for Iran and Persian Gulf Studies at Princeton University thanks to Behrooz Ghamari-Tabrizi, including Sheida Dayani, Sheragim Jenabzadeh, Naveed Mansoori, Milad Odabaei, Negar Razavi, Maral Sahebjame, Deborah Schlein, Daniel Sheffield, Lindsey Stephenson, and Marzieh Tofighi Darian. I am also grateful to colleagues for welcoming me to New York, including Manan Ahmed, Amy Chazkel, Najam Haidar, Mana Kia, Durba Mitra, Celia Naylor, and Rhiannon Stephens.

I consider myself lucky to have so many colleagues in Africana Studies, History, Iranian Studies, Media Studies, and Middle East Studies who have supported me and engaged with my work. Many of these individuals deserve their own sentence detailing the ways they have made my life infinitely better through their mentorship, guidance, laughter, and memories that I cherish deeply but will not share here: Kamran Aghaie, Shaherzad Ahmadi, Blake Atwood, Narges Bajoghli, Ali Behdad, Nimrod Ben Zeev, Aomar Boum, Ayelet Brinn, Alexis Broderick, Kristen Brustad, Ezgi Cakmak, Houchang Chehabi, Belle Cheves, Manuela Coppola, Elizabeth Della Zazzera, Rayya El Zein, Lacy Feigh, Laura Fish, James Gelvin, Chris Gratien, Sarah Gualtieri, Zeynep Devrim Gursel, Timur Hammond, Jae Han, Amanda Hannoosh Steinberg, Kevan Harris, Fuchsia Hart, Katie Hickerson, Persis Karim, Arang Keshavarzian, Mikiya Koyagi, Daniel Lowe, Alex Lubin, Neda Maghbouleh, Amy Malek, Afshin Marashi, Rasul Miller, Mostafa Minawi, Ali Mirsepassi, Sharon Mizbani, Ciruce Movahedi-Lankarani, Peter Miller, Taylor Moore, Arzoo Osanloo, Erin Pettigrew, Babak Rahimi, Samiha Rahman, Sara Rahnama, Samira Rajabi, Kelsey Rice, Christopher Rose, Jim Ryan, Sahar Sadeghi, Cyrus Schayegh, Mira Xenia Schwerda, Alex Shams, Nur Sobers-Khan, Lior Sternfeld, Jill Stinchcomb, Camille Suárez, Chris Alen Sula, Tehseen Thaver, Paraska Tolan-Szkilnik, Luke Yarbrough, Noor Zehra Zaidi, and Rustin Zarkar. I'm especially thankful to Amy Motlagh for her support and her mentorship.

Several people read and generously gave feedback on drafts of the manuscript, either in part or in full. Camron Amin, Michael Gomez, and Reza Zia Ebrahimi gave insightful comments at a book manuscript workshop organized by Beverly Tsacoyianis and the Women Historians of the Middle East (WHOME). The Race and the Middle East / North Africa Mellon-Sawyer Seminar at CUNY, led by Beth Baron and Mandana Limbert, invited me to workshop the first chapter of the book with their community, including Nahid Mozaffari, Kristina Richardson, and Zavier Wingham, among others. As a Regional Faculty Fellow at the Wolf Humanities Center, I received comments on chapter 2 from the rest of the fellows under Karen Redrobe and Ramya Sreenivasan's leadership. Reem Bailony, Alma Heckman, Pauline Lewis, and Anoush Suni read outlines and chapter drafts in the early writing stages. Sahba Shayani provided detailed comments on chapter 6 from multiple continents. I thank Meghan Drury for editing drafts of the manuscript. Priscillia Kounkou Hoveyda read the manuscript closely and shared her honest thoughts on the narrative, for which I am deeply grateful. She and other members of the Collective for Black Iranians, including Alex Eskandarkhah, Pardis Nkoy, Parisa Nkoy, and Chyna Dumas, also gave feedback on the inclusion of photographs.

I thank Priscillia and the Collective for Black Iranians for their support of my work as the collective's resident historian, where I worked closely with artists, especially Kimia Fatehi and Mina Jafari, to illustrate episodes from these histories to make them accessible to broader audiences. I thank Twelve Gates Arts, especially Aisha Zia Khan and Atif Sheikh, for disrupting the art world and making space to share these histories. The Collective for Black Iranians also worked with Hoda Katebi and the Because We've Read Book Club, where they hosted a discussion based on excerpts of my dissertation paired with Victoria Princewill's *In the Palace of Flowers*. I am grateful to them for that conversation, which demonstrated the deep need for and interest in this research.

The Social Science Research Council funded fieldwork in Iran, Switzerland, the United Kingdom, and the United States. The Wolf Humanities Center at Penn Regional Faculty Fellowship and the Bard Graduate Center Research Fellowship provided me with time, space, and feedback that helped shape how I approached different parts of the book. Awards from Princeton's Open Publication Fund Program and Mossavar-Rahmani Center for Iran and Persian Gulf Studies contributed funds that will make this book open access in the coming years, and the Barr Ferree Fund made the publication of the photographs possible. I'm indebted to the archivists at the various repositories where I did my fieldwork, especially the archives in Iran, where I consider some of them more friends than professional contacts.

This book would probably still be tucked away in a drafts folder were it not for Elizabeth Ault's infectious encouragement of my research, and I could not have asked for a better editor to work with. Along with Elizabeth, Benjamin Kossak, Jes Malitoris, Chad Miller, James Moore, Chris Robinson, Laura Sell, Liz Smith, Christi Stanforth, and others at Duke took a document saved on my computer and turned it into a real book—thank you all so much.

Old friends also remind me of life outside academia, including Amani Abdallah, Keli Arslancan, Neema Assemi, Atiya Bahmanyar, Pouneh Behin, Amira Elmallah, Marken Greenwood, Weiss Hamid, Jeff Handel, Sama Haneef, Farhat Hanifi, Homaira Hosseini, Amina Husain, Sarah Khanghahi, Diana Kim, Bonnie Krenz, Fareeha Molvi, Zachia Nazarzai, Sabrin Said, Dani Torres, and Machiko Yasuda. I also thank Sara Zia Ebrahimi as both friend and mentor for supporting my research as well as my broader practice. Maya Ortiz has also been a major source of support for our family for the past year. And I know I am not the only one who remembers Liyna every day.

I am grateful to my family for providing me with the space to research and write this book. I wrote the entire manuscript at my family's home, and I'm writing these acknowledgments where I did my revisions, at my in-laws' residence. I thank Jahangir, Parvin, Mohammad, Azam, Behrooz, Behnaz, Mahta, Kian, and Neekta for their love, support, and patience as I constantly snuck away to finish this book. Above all, I thank Delara and Soraya, who have helped me throughout this process: Delara with her sweet doodles on nearly every page of my writing notebook, and Soraya, who learned how to smile a few days before I submitted the final manuscript.

And finally, I'm grateful to Ali, who has read every word I've written and always tells me to write more.

INTRODUCTION

There were many Yaquts. I am not referring to the precious gem, though *yaqut* is the Persian and Arabic word for "ruby." I am referring to the enslaved Black men who were forcibly brought to Iran and renamed Yaqut throughout the nineteenth and early twentieth centuries.[1] The ones whose names only appear briefly in single-page documents among thousands about the slave trade along the Persian Gulf coast.[2] Some were enslaved alongside other men named Almas, or "Diamond."[3] The gemstones reflected the nature of enslavement in the region: while some enslaved people were forced to serve as manual or agricultural laborers along the gulf coastline, many were bought and sold as status symbols in the homes of affluent merchants, royalty, and those with access to power, wealth, and resources.[4] Some of these Yaquts make appearances in this book. Others do not. Some of them were enslaved alongside Black women, many with floral names, such as Golchehreh, Sonbol, and Narges.[5] Some of these women also appear in this book. Others do not. And some of their names are lost to us altogether.

Names are hard to trace, and this book does not try to trace them all. Sometimes names are misleading, contrived, or not even names at all.

———

This book began as a study of nineteenth-century enslavement in Iran, but as Christina Sharpe writes, "Those of us who teach, write, and think about slavery and its afterlives encounter myriad silences and ruptures in time, space, history, ethics, and research as we do our work."[6] I encountered these silences and ruptures at every stage of writing this book: in the sources, in the archives, and in people who preferred to look away.[7] These erasures stretched the focus of my work and pushed me to think about them as extensions of enslavement, which led me to examine enslavement and erasure together.

Despite claims otherwise, the history of enslavement in Iran is a long one, with references to enslaved people as imperial tribute dating as far back as the Achaemenid Empire.[8] For centuries, Iranians enslaved many from around their domains, including the Caucasus, Central Asia, South Asia, and East Africa.[9] During the nineteenth century, elite and wealthy Iranians enslaved people in their domestic spaces as nannies, wet nurses, eunuchs, cooks, and other jobs critical to the maintenance of a healthy household that are often socially undervalued.[10] While some scholars have described their work as "menial" and therefore unimportant, no such word in Persian describes their work as insignificant, except in the tone of these later histories.[11] Instead, these individuals were seen as critical for the preservation of the family and the royal court. They were generally symbols of power and status, not economic slaves, despite some examples of chattel slavery in the South.[12] This book focuses on those held in bondage by royal and wealthy families and argues that their presence and gradual disappearance shaped the discourse of race and racism on a national scale in the modern period.

Just as enslavement was not new during the Qajar period, neither was the term *Siyah*, or "Black." For centuries, *Siyah* had been used to describe various ethnic groups, and the term morphed to accommodate whatever groups were represented in Iran at the time. During the sixteenth and seventeenth centuries, for example, the term *Siyah* typically described enslaved South Asians at the Safavid court.[13] Similarly, in poetry, *Siyah* might have been paired with another term to describe a person—*Zangi-ye Siyah* (the Black Zanzibari) or *Hindu-ye Siyah* (the Black Indian)— regardless of their free or enslaved status.[14] As a term, *Siyah*, or "Black," was malleable. Not only had it referred to different groups across two continents; it had also always been used as an adjective. Not until the mid-nineteenth century did government documents refer to *Siyah*, or the plural *Siyah-ha*, as nouns and identities unto themselves: *Black* and *Blacks*.[15]

Even though Iranians viewed many as categorically enslavable, by the late nineteenth century, a particular language of enslavement arose that racialized East Africans as exclusively Black, and *Black* as equivalent to *enslaved*. This was largely due to geopolitical transformations that changed who was being enslaved in Iran. Once Russians increased their power in the North, and the British colonized South Asia, East Africans were left as the dominant group of enslaved people in Iran. Starting in 1848, the Qajars signed several treaties with the British, each promising to stop the Persian Gulf slave trade. There were several iterations of these treaties, and with each new version, the British pressed for more control over ships in the Persian Gulf, a key waterway. Perhaps some people expected that these treaties would make enslaved people harder to come by in Iran and the institution would then disappear on its own. It didn't exactly happen that way; Iran's Parliament abolished slavery in Iran in 1929.

After 1929, the process of abolition involved an active process of erasure on a national scale, such that a collective amnesia surrounding enslavement persists today. This collective amnesia is multifaceted: just as *enslaved* had come to refer exclusively to Black people, the erasure of enslavement arrived largely with the erasure of Black presence, life, and history in Iran. Together these erasures have allowed for Iranians to purport that they are not racist and that racism has never existed in Iran, resulting in a kind of "white innocence" outlined by Gloria Wekker in her eponymous book on racial politics in the Netherlands.[16] Rather than a humanitarian effort, the abolition of legal enslavement was a project to present Iran as modern and save the nation from embarrassment on the global stage. By the twentieth century, enslavement and Blackness had become so blurred that the erasure of slavery resulted in the erasure of Black freedpeople as well, a forced invisibility in a country where they were now citizens. Black Iranians, who once would have been seen regularly in major cities, became a peripheral population, concentrated in the Persian Gulf coast. In their place, blackface caricatures in theater and comic formats gained popularity in urban centers, further normalizing the erasure of Black people in Iran. Anti-Black caricatures were sanitized and couched in folk traditional rhetoric that hid the legacies of these institutions. The erasure of Iran's history of enslavement even reconfigured simple terms. For example, the term *bardeh*, which referred to an enslaved person, was used in the Manumission Law of 1929. *Bardeh*, however, now refers primarily to enslaved people on US plantations. The tacit shift in connotation allows for the abundance of statements such as "We never had *bardeh*!" The lack of language to discuss this history is a recent problem. Nineteenth-century records show us that not only was there a language for discussing race and enslavement but also that it involved a precise vocabulary that responded to social realities and changes, from the populations being enslaved, to the global efforts toward abolition, even to the debates over who belonged in the family unit. In recent decades, this forced invisibility has fostered the emergence of various documentary projects that claim, tacitly or otherwise, the discovery of Afro-Iranians, many of whom are descendants of freedpeople.[17]

Detractors of the study of enslavement will argue that because "few" people were enslaved in Iran, it is an insignificant topic of research. Unfortunately, the exact number of individuals enslaved in Iran is lost to us. Aside from a handful of records, there is no hard data about the number of people enslaved in Iran, African or otherwise.[18] But contrary to what these detractors might expect, the presence of enslaved East Africans in the homes of wealthy and powerful Iranians had an outsized effect on conceptions of race and shaped Iranian life during the nineteenth and early twentieth centuries, from the structure and responsibilities of family members, to the architecture of their homes, to life in the bazaar, and even appropriate forms of entertainment. Because of their positions of power, these enslaving families were tastemakers for Iranian society, and Iranians from other social classes would have attempted to copy them. As it became less common and ultimately illegal to enslave people in one's home, Iranian life changed dramatically to one that prioritized nuclear families in smaller family homes and justified blackface theater with alternate, revisionist descriptions. The presence of enslaved people—and their disappearance—touched every aspect of Iranian urban life: their presence was significant in Iran.

This book is concerned with the tension between forced visibility and forced invisibility: a recent history of enslavement, one that was wielded for visual displays of power and status, was made to disappear so dramatically that even the most obvious of footprints are explained away. In the first half of the book, "Enslavement," I argue that enslavement in Iran was a process of forced visibility, where enslaved people were ranked by their appearances and used as representatives of the enslaving family in public and visual settings. Enslaved people lacked mobility afforded to other members of the servant class: that is, they were either forcibly migrated to Iran and sold into the homes they worked in, or they were born in those homes and forced to stay. While other servants might have worked in return for room and board, their ability to leave and find other homes or families to work for on their own volition distinguished them from those who were enslaved. And by the late nineteenth century, the Blackness of the individual—their visibility—would have marked them as someone forcibly brought into Iran, and therefore as an enslaved person, despite the presence of free Africans in Iran.

Abolition, which I define here as an erasure of slavery, triggered a forced invisibility of enslavement, formerly enslaved people, and their histories. This collective erasure created a vacuum where blackface caricatures, racial ideologies, and even personal histories received revisionist explanations for their existence to allow for the public erasures to remain. The second half of this book, "Erasure," demonstrates the extent to which the government, society, archives, and the descendants of enslaving families sought to hide, cover, and deny a history of enslavement in Iran in which they were implicated. No erasure, however, is ever complete, and nothing and no one can ever be made fully invisible.

To be clear, this is not a comprehensive study on the history of Black or Afro-Iranians. The history of Black or Afro-Iranians is much more layered, much richer, and spans millennia of exchange, migration, and belonging. This is a modern history of Iran and Iranians, whether they were part of the elite classes who enslaved people or part of the wider public that aspired to be like them, whether they intentionally denied this history or unknowingly perpetuated these erasures.

SHOWING–HIDING

Have you seen this little girl in the photograph (fig. I.1)? She stands tall, looking boldly at the camera. There are others, too, a whole group of children both younger and older than her, and a few adults, smiling patiently or blankly staring while the photographer painstakingly takes their photograph. The photograph was taken some time in the late nineteenth or early twentieth century, when the process took a little longer than what we are used to today. Everyone had to be very still, including this little girl, who stood all the way over to the far left, her bangs curled as they poked out from under her scarf and chador. This little girl is visibly Black; the rest of the household is not.

She was enslaved, likely born into enslavement in the same household she was photographed in. None of the other children in the photograph were enslaved; rather, they were her enslavers, along with their mother sitting in the middle. The individuals in the back were likely servants. The information on the photograph is scant, and nothing tells us directly that she was enslaved.

But if we were to follow Tina Campt's lead to listen to the photo and think through its layers and textures, we can glean more details that show how this photo came to be in the first place.[19] The photo was taken outside: in the upper left corner, a brick wall peeks out from behind a white sheet, undoubtedly hung to give the impression of an indoor photo while still

I.1 A little Black girl and the family that enslaved her. She is remembered in records published by the Majles Library in Tehran and Harvard's *Women's Worlds in Qajar Iran* as either Juju or Suski, neither of which is a name. ("Children of Yamin al-Saltana," *Women's Worlds in Qajar Iran* digital archive, record no. 31e141, http://www.qajarwomen.org/en/items/31e141.html; also in *Asnad-i Banuvan dar durih-yi Mashrutiyyat*, published by the Majles Library. Text from *Women's Worlds in Qajar Iran*.)

taking advantage of the natural light. The sun was so bright that two of the individuals have their hands up to shield their eyes from it. Someone had decided to hang an oil painting in a gilded European-style frame on the wall, but it seems to be a bit crooked, another indication that this was not its permanent spot. Instead, they had hauled it outside to give the viewer the impression of wealth. Some photography studios would have offered backdrops with European-style scenes on them, but the inclusion of a stand-alone painting indicated the family's status: they had their own oil painting and did not need a fake backdrop to cue their cosmopolitanism. In addition to the painting, a single chair had been brought for the matriarch at the center of the photograph. The style of clothing—most of the girls in starched white scarves pinned under their chins, the matriarch distinguished in a gauzy black scarf, the other women in floral chador, and the inclusion of a few double-breasted coats, one worn by a young boy in the front and another by an older man in the back—all indicate that this photo was taken in the late nineteenth or early twentieth century. Not many households could afford photographs at this time, much less highly stylized ones with their oil painting hanging askew in the back. The sort of households who could afford these portraits were usually elite or very wealthy families, the kind that had a live-in staff. The kind that would enslave people in their homes.

While these photographs are unusual across the general populace, they are fairly common and even expected when thinking about these households. These photographs all similarly scaffolded the individuals pictured—the matriarch required a seat. In the presence of a seated matriarch, most of the children would stand close by her to show respect. Servants and enslaved people would be relegated to the margins, visually signaling their deference to the matriarch and her family. The little girl, with her stylized bangs and tightly gripped chador, stood next to the children of the enslaving family—she was too short to be sent to the back. Instead, she would stand to the side, her chador pulled over her head, not wrapped around her waist like the chadors of the other girls.

The members of the enslaving family are all well documented, their relations painstakingly noted in the two places where the photograph is published: the *Women's Worlds in Qajar Iran* digital archive based at Harvard University and an edited volume titled *Sources on Women during the Constitutional Period*, published by the Majles Library in Tehran, reflecting the different yet similar curations of a family-oriented institutional archive and a state archive.[20] The little girl is even left forgotten in the archival label of the photograph: the *Women's Worlds in Qajar Iran* archive calls the photo "Children of Yamin al-Saltanah," while the edited volume from the Majles Library leaves it untitled. Certainly, she was not the daughter of anyone in the photograph or the patriarch named in the archival title; rather, she was enslaved by them.

The captions provide us with further details. These are names ostensibly provided by the contributor, as no image of the verso or scribbled marginalia is provided.[21] As you might expect, their names (and whether we can identify their names at all) reflect their status. The names of the enslaving household all have titles attached to them, either *khanum* or *saltaneh* or *soltan*, honorifics that remind us that they are genteel individuals and connected to the royal family. The names of the servants in the back have been marked as forgotten, partly because they likely worked for the family for a shorter period, as servants cycled through jobs and employers like any other occupation. In chapter 2, I discuss another photo from the same household taken a few years earlier, where these servants are not present but the little Black girl shows up again. But who is this little Black girl? Where were her parents? Were her parents enslaved in the same family but left out of the photograph? Who pulled her to the side of the frame? Or did she already know to pull herself to the margin?

The preservation of her name—or the lack thereof—speaks to the difficulty of studying enslavement and abolition, and how these processes informed constructions of Blackness within the Iranian context. Each published version of the photograph remembers her name differently: in *Women's Worlds in Qajar Iran*, the little girl is listed as Suski. In the Majles Library's edited volume, she is listed as Juju. The two "names" are starkly different. Suski is a diminutive for *susk*, or "cockroach," a racial epithet shrouded in childlike language, a reference to her being very young and Black. By contrast, Juju means "chick," a childish pronunciation of a sweet term of endearment. Neither of these is a name. What was her name? Such a simple fact, lost in two of the most significant physical and digital spaces for the study and preservation of modern Iranian history. Her name cannot be studied or preserved here because her name has been erased, forgotten, removed. Denied.

The shrouding and removal of this history does not begin and end with her name. As with many other historical and archival records, the issue of cushioning language emerges. We researchers not only have to grapple with contradictory names like Suski and Juju; we also grapple with archives that are hesitant to release sensitive documents at all or, instead, move forward and relabel texts to prevent any associations with enslavement.[22] The aversion to identifying individuals as enslaved can be observed in both Persian and English-language archival descriptions, due to an idea that *slavery*, *slave*, *enslavement*, or *enslaved* are unhelpful terms for describing the Iranian phenomenon. Scholars, archivists, and others have suggested that these terms might be misleading for a public unfamiliar with Iran, as they conjure images of US plantation or chattel slavery that do not apply to the Iranian context. The US-centric connotations surrounding the term *slavery*, or even its closest Persian equivalent, *bardeh-dari*, have seeped into Persian as well. Enslaved people are recast as *servants* or *household members*, as if changing the term will lighten its indictment of history. Often archivists or scholars will hide behind the slipperiness of the vocabulary of servitude, picking terms that do not explicitly determine whether or not an individual was paid.

Terms such as *khadameh* or *mostakhdameh* only tell us that the person worked in a domestic capacity; these terms shroud whether they were paid or enslaved. But when we read the photograph with all its layers—a little Black girl, who appears standing to the side of more than one photograph of the same wealthy family, with no clear name but several "nicknames"—we can see that this little girl was born into enslavement, raised in part by the same family who enslaved her.

These negotiations in captions between institutions and within archival records is evident in other documents and texts as well. Texts digitized by the *Women's Worlds in Qajar Iran* are particularly compelling because the archive not only curated materials held by private families, such as figure I.1, but also documents and other paraphernalia held by archival institutions in Iran. For example, a document held at the Yazd branch of the National Archives was embellished by the National Archives with a modern brown border with faux inscriptions all around it, with a label at the bottom that reads, "An Example of a Wedding Contract" (fig. I.2). The decorative border is odd, as it is clearly fake, but more to the point, this is not a wedding contract at all. It lacks any of the necessary elements of a marriage contract. It does not even involve two people who are to be married. The same document, fake border and all, has since been digitized for the *Women's Worlds in Qajar Iran* archive, which has listed it as a "Sale document of a black slave, 1891."[23] But it is not a sale document either.

The document is a testimony of a reconciliation between two individuals regarding the sale of an enslaved Black man named Salman that had already taken place. In it, an individual who claimed he had not received proper compensation for selling Salman delineated the various steps that were taken to rectify the situation, ultimately resulting in a settlement that involved a lump sum of money exchanged to end his complaints. One can see how the researchers at the *Women's Worlds in Qajar Iran* archive might have skimmed quickly and decided to classify it as a sale document.

But the archivists at the National Archives seemed to have only read the last line of the document, where it refers to *sigheh-ye masaleh*, or "a vow of reconciliation." The term *sigheh* is often used in reference to marriage vows, but it is used more expansively here to refer to an agreement or resolution. Whoever decided to add this border seems to have read that word and deemed it enough to justify labeling the entire document a

نمونه‌ای از سند ازدواج

I.2 Not an example of a wedding contract. ("Sale document of a black slave," 1891, *Women's Worlds in Qajar Iran* digital archive, record no. 13122A31, http://www.qajar women.org/en/items/13122A31.html.)

marriage contract—a somewhat incompetent and lazy interpretation. A more cynical read, however, may be that the archive intentionally mislabeled it to avoid having to identify it as a remnant of Iran's enslaving past.

I pursued some of my research at the Majles Library in Tehran, where the directors had approved my research topic after an interview.[24] But the archivist at the reference desk responded to my request for documents on enslavement with, "You must be from overseas, where they had *bardeh*. We never had *bardeh*. Cyrus the Great freed them all. You've been poisoned by the racism of wherever you're from to think that we are like that, too."[25] After some back-and-forth, he shrugged his shoulders and allowed me to submit document requests. I ultimately found the materials I was looking for. In most Iranian archives, however, I could only move forward with my research when I described it using less-charged terms, such as *kaniz* or *gholam*, each of which primarily refer to enslaved women and men but could also take on the connotation of any young or subservient woman or man, regardless of free or unfree status.[26]

Similarly, questions of race and racism and whether these concepts exist at all in Persian have been denied and avoided time and time again because of the lack of clear equivalents in Persian. *Race* is usually translated as *nezhad*, although the term can often refer to lineage or ethnicity as well. *Racism* is typically translated as *nezhad-parasti*—the worship of one's race—although in recent years terms such as *nezhad-setizi* or *nezhad-zadeh*—"race discrimination" or "raced," respectively—have entered Persian and gained traction as well. Although terms like *race*, *racism*, and *racialization* can be useful for a critical analysis, their presence or absence in a language does not preclude whether certain actions, dynamics, vocabularies, and structures are raced, racist, and racializing. Hiding behind the lack of clear equivalents, many scholars and Iranians have made claims along the lines of "Because there is no clear term for 'race' or 'racism' in Persian, it obviously never existed." A notable example of this is found in Behnaz Mirzai's *A History of Slavery and Emancipation in Iran*. Despite having written the first full-length monograph on Iran's history of enslavement, Mirzai argues that conceptions of race were irrelevant in enslavement; she even defines racial slurs as terms of endearment.[27] Mirzai's rejection of a racial framework in her analysis is based on works in general Middle East Studies, including that of Madeline Zilfi. Zilfi's research on the Ottoman harem came with a small caveat: that because the Ottomans enslaved people of different backgrounds and ethnicities, race cannot be considered a factor in their enslavement, as it was an

"Atlantic-derived" category.[28] Ironically, these scholars use enslavement in the Atlantic world as the standard for identifying whether or not certain practices count as slavery instead of acknowledging the horrors of enslavement plainly present in the Iranian and other Middle Eastern cases. In many ways, Zilfi was responding to Bernard Lewis's *Race and Slavery in the Middle East*, which she described as an "ahistorical compilation." In it, Lewis suggested that the constructions of race in the region have been largely unchanging, sanctioned by Islamic law, and wholly racist.[29] His book and its one-dimensional sweeping claims have haunted the field and created a generation of defensive scholars eager to entirely reject race as a salient category in the Middle East. Several scholars, however, have rejected both approaches and asserted the importance of taking race seriously as a dynamic category in the broader Middle East and Indian Ocean world.[30] *The Color Black* joins them in asserting that constructions of race, like any other category of analysis, were shaped by and responsive to social, political, economic, and other changes.[31]

The general reticence to discuss race in Iranian Studies has shifted in recent years. Amy Motlagh's work on the subject has consistently critiqued the general consensus in Iranian Studies, pointing toward how enslavers aggrandized themselves and how celebrated intellectuals such as Simin Daneshvar and Mirza Fath ʿAli Akhundzadeh had a more complicated relationship with race, specifically Blackness, than has been readily acknowledged.[32] The study of whiteness in the Iranian context, however, has received much attention in Iranian Studies, as demonstrated by Reza Zia Ebrahimi in his study of intellectual thought and Aryanism in Iran during the nineteenth and twentieth centuries and Neda Maghbouleh's study of race and racial identifiers used in the Iranian diaspora in the United States.[33]

The Color Black traces the opposing process: as Iranians viewed Africans as more and more Black, they in turn viewed themselves as more and more white. Iranians had once viewed themselves as in between "white" Caucasians and "Black" Africans, but the diminished presence of Caucasians led to the creation of a clear category of *Black* as *enslaved* that was framed by an Iranian whiteness.[34] Ultimately, the emphasis on an Iranian whiteness was used to erase Black Iranians: the same people whose presence rendered others as white would be eclipsed by the racial category altogether.

The change from a racial spectrum to a clear-cut binary was one that developed throughout the nineteenth century. Few other studies of Qajar Iran (r. 1794 to 1925) have incorporated race into their analysis. Those that do examine race, however, have done so based on an assumed Black/white binary, accepting anti-Blackness and the whiteness of Iranians as a foregone conclusion during the Qajar period. This is especially the case with scholarship that deals with visual analyses of photography, namely Pedram Khosronejad's *Qajar African Nannies* and Staci Gem Schweiller's *Liminalities of Gender and Sexuality in Nineteenth-Century Iranian Photography*. Khosronejad, whose published album focuses entirely on enslaved African eunuchs and women, makes no mention of enslaved non-Black individuals and goes so far as to crop the enslaved Caucasians out of his selection of photographs or simply ignore them. Schweiller, whose book focuses on the gendering and sexualization of photographs during the late Qajar period, overlooked enslaved Caucasians, who were sought after explicitly for their sexual appeal. Instead, she focuses entirely on photographs of enslaved Africans, equating whiteness with Iranians. This analysis unintentionally replicates the free/nonfree binary exacerbated by the black-and-white nature of the photographs; it imposes later racial realities back onto the late nineteenth century. And while *The Color Black* focuses on the forced visibility and invisibility of Black people in Iran during the nineteenth and twentieth centuries, it was the distinction between enslaved Caucasians and Africans that so clearly *othered* Black people as equivalent to enslaved in Iran. Caucasians were allowed to assimilate, lean on alternate histories unrelated to enslavement, and ultimately claim a nativized Iranian identity in the multiethnic fabric of the country.[35] A close analysis of photography reveals more such nuances.

The photographs, like the archives that housed them, were always for the benefit of the enslavers. To my knowledge, none of these photographs were ever contributed to an archive by an enslaved person or their families. The archival record of these photographs is one that rests entirely on the memory of the enslaving families' descendants, who differ even among themselves in their accounts of the lives of the enslaved. Perhaps that is why this little girl's name has been recorded as both Suski and Juju: maybe two different individuals, each with a different memory or understanding of the girl's name, gave the photograph to different archives.

Other examples of the unreliability of enslaving narratives abound. Consider, for example, the life of Sonbol Baji, nanny to siblings Haleh and Kamran Afshar. In an article Haleh Afshar wrote about the life of Sonbol Baji, she asserts that Sonbol Baji arrived at the Qajar palace at the age of two and that she was "taken in" by her grandfather, Khabirsaltaneh, sometime between 1918 and 1922 as a "harem trained young lady."[36] Haleh

Afshar implies that Sonbol Baji was freed in her grandfather's home, although she still played the role of a domestic servant. But in Pedram Khosronejad's collection of Qajar-era household portraits, *Qajar African Nannies*, he published a photograph of the Afshar children with Sonbol Baji, courtesy of Kamran Afshar. The description diverges from Haleh's narrative: here Sonbol Baji is said to have been born in the king's harem and "freed in childhood."[37] And while Haleh insists on Sonbol Baji's infinite happiness with her enslavement in the harem, Motlagh has highlighted the photograph as an unintended critique, revealing a somber and even melancholy image of her life.[38]

The revelatory ability of nontextual sources to refute and reject the dominant narrative drew me to include them in this book: I incorporate visual and architectural sources alongside textual ones to subvert the erasures that have permeated Iranian society. While I read testimonies, manumission documents, sale contracts, marriage contracts, letters, memoirs, newspapers, travelogues, dictionaries, poetry, and literature, I made sure to also examine photography, portraiture, art exhibits, films, television programs, circus acts, residential structures, religious architecture, archaeological objects, caricatures, archival catalogs, and illustrations produced in multiple languages and locales. Ultimately, however, many if not all of the sources in this book are filtered through the lens of the enslaving families or other institutional powers. Even testimonies that claim to be written from the perspective of the enslaved are often recorded or translated by government officials. Archives and other repositories assume their audience to be non-Black Iranians who view themselves as inheritors of an elite past, regardless of their own familial affiliation.

When I was researching in Tehran, I asked one of the Majles archivists involved in the volume's publication why the little Black girl's name was listed as Juju and not an actual name. He said that that was the name the person donating the photograph had offered and that the recipients had accepted it. "Better than having no name at all," he suggested.[39] The question arises, Who are these records for? Who benefits from such a name?

DELETED–OBSCURED–CLAIMED–AND WHISPERED

For a shah who desperately wanted to modernize Iran, Reza Shah viewed the ongoing legality of enslavement in the twentieth century as an embarrassment to him and the country. These concerns were not humanitarian in nature but, rather, an effort to catch up and curry favor with the West. Reza Shah wanted everyone to forget anyone was ever enslaved in Iran. He wanted to build and shape the institutions that would forge a modern future for Iran.[40] He destroyed the Golestan Palace harem in the early 1930s and built the Ministry of Finance building in its place.[41] He also established the National Library and Archives of Iran, a space for Iranian history to be preserved.[42]

The modernization project, however, could not escape the ghosts of those once enslaved and even rested on what they had left behind. Reza Shah established the National Archives and Library using the inheritance of an enslaved person.[43] ʿAziz Khan, a royal Caucasian eunuch who had been enslaved in the late nineteenth century, bequeathed his personal library to a charitable endowment in the name of the ruling shah. These were the books that made up the core collection of the National Library when it was first established in the 1930s.

ʿAziz Khan's contribution, which was foundational for the National Archives and Library, was included on the institution's website just a few years ago, and I had saved it when I was writing my dissertation. A more recently updated page on the history of the National Archives on that website, however, no longer mentions ʿAziz Khan or his charitable endowment. We can make guesses as to why it was erased and rewritten, since the newer version also has no reference to Reza Shah. Due to ongoing domestic politics, the current administration remains uninterested in Reza Shah's legacy and removed references to his role in establishing the National Archives and Library. But Reza Shah's contribution to the library was not solely his legacy; it was also that of ʿAziz Khan. ʿAziz Khan has been erased, his foundational donation left unmarked for the public. Notably, ʿAziz Khan's story was not unique. Other eunuchs like him also left their inheritances, big and small, to charitable endowments, as they often had no other choice.[44] How many other institutions benefited from inheritance of those denied inheritors, the property of those considered property?[45]

The organization of the archives themselves deepen these erasures. As Rosie Bsheer has described the selective narratives promoted by archives in Saudi Arabia, "Erasure is not simply a countermeasure to the making of history; it is History."[46] Most archival institutions in Iran do not have a systematic way of organizing files on enslavement or abolition. Or, more pointedly speaking, they choose not to. Instead, these files are interspersed in their collections, either as individual papers or under other groupings.[47] Often, because of the domestic nature of their work, many of the files on enslaved people—regardless of their gender or sex—are filed under the "Women" binders, as is the case in the Golestan Palace Photo Archive. The religious usage of *kaniz* and *gholam* in reference to the Prophet, his daughter Fatima, and the Shi'i imams—Kaniz-e Fatimeh, Gholam 'Ali, and so on, which operate both as names and markers of religious devotion—made it difficult for me to find relevant sources at the Astan-e Qods Archive in the Imam Reza Shrine Complex in Mashhad, Iran. Even more confounding, *bardeh*, the catchall term for "slave," is written the same as *bordeh*, the past participle for "taken" in Persian; their identical spelling makes scanning services less than helpful. Finding sources on enslavement requires the researcher to engage in a meandering process of finding files. The general lack of organization around this topic has led some scholars to assume that there are no sources and that it might be impossible to research, an assumption that exists beyond Iranian Studies as well. Zavier Wingham, who works on Afro-Turks and Ottoman legacies of enslavement, opened the inaugural Middle East Librarians Association Social Justice series in 2020 by saying, "I was told I wouldn't find anything, but I did find something."[48] In the same respect, the recent push toward digitization has made certain files hypervisible, while others are totally obscured, depending on the keywords and tags given to each entry.

The Iranian archives operate in stark contrast to their British counterparts, where there are boxes and boxes of files labeled *Slavery and Antislavery*, many of which focus on the Persian Gulf slave trade. The British Empire prided itself on championing abolition worldwide and routinely used the language of abolition to cloak their imperial efforts.[49] Anyone who has sifted through these files can see that the British regularly prioritized strategic political choices that went against the freeing of enslaved individuals or their well-being. This was chiefly the case in the Persian Gulf as well.[50] Nonetheless, the archival holdings on antislavery are still very much centered within the British archives, whereas in Iran the public erasure of slavery has prevented most of the documents from being organized in a centralized manner.

But documents do exist in Iran, both within the archives and beyond them, as do many photographs. Enslaved people were more likely to be photographed than the "average" Iranian, because enslaved people were often enslaved by wealthy and powerful Iranians who had access to cameras and photography in ways that other Iranians did not. The circulation of images through archives—like that of the little Black girl denied a proper name and her enslavers—is a reminder of how widely photographs have moved around the world.[51]

Archives and museum projects not only obfuscate their collections pertaining to enslavement; in addition, the very structures out of which they operate can contribute to that project of forced visibility and invisibility. The circulation of photographs in and out of archives is not new, nor is it a neutral practice. Temi Odumosu and Jarrett Martin Drake have examined the circulation and holding of photographs of Black individuals in white institutions. Odumosu's "The Crying Child: On Colonial Archives, Digitization, and Ethics of Care in the Cultural Commons" examines reproductions of a photograph of a young Afro-Caribbean child and argues that the labeling practices around these reproductions were another form of taming the other through "the cutting, pasting, and inscription of album production."[52] Drake's article on Tamara Lanier's court case regarding the custody of Delia and Renty's daguerreotypes held at the Harvard Museum is also instructional for understanding this kind of forced visibility.[53] The daguerreotypes show the father and daughter as naked from waist up, taken as proof for Louis Agassiz's theory of polygenesis.[54] Lanier, who has provided evidence of being the direct descendant of Delia and Renty, has asked for custody of the photographs. Harvard has rejected these claims and continues to hold the dehumanizing photographs in their collections, along with that of five others also taken by Louis Agassiz. As Drake has shown, if Harvard were remorseful for their role in the history of enslavement, they could simply return the photographs to Lanier as Delia and Renty's rightful heir and descendant. But to do so would require a shift in archival praxis and would undermine the archival institution as a whole.

Instead, the photographs remain in Harvard's possession and reflect, quite literally, the afterlife of enslavement. Drake highlighted the "blood at the root" of the archive—much like a lynching, the violence of it involved not only the gruesome murder but also that the family and friends of the victim were forced to see the body long after their death. In the same way, the violence of these photographs is not limited to the actual taking of the photograph; it also includes the fact that they are forced to remain in Harvard's museum. Lanier's fight for Delia and Renty's photos has resulted in petitions, protests, and even student demands that the photographs be returned to her. In response to the students, Harvard's president has said that the photographs "belong to history."[55] Because they are relegated to this timeless state of belonging to "history," Delia and Renty are forced to continue performing their forced visibility in their afterlives.

If Simone Browne's *Dark Matters* taught us to rethink the structure of a slave ship as a panopticon structured to surveil those kidnapped and enslaved through the Middle Passage, this book argues that the very structures of urban life and living lent themselves to a similar surveillance of enslaved individuals in Iran. The tight alleys, the labyrinthine bazaar layouts, even the separated public and private spaces of homes meant that enslaving families would have been able to control—and socially benefit from—the visibility of those they had enslaved. Enslaved people, especially those from East Africa, would have been made readily visible at every opportunity possible.[56] Photography, then, operated as the most obvious and lasting extension of this forced visibility. But the circulation of these photographs raises the same issues facing the photographs of Delia and Renty—they are being made accessible without their (or their descendants') consent, extending the life of enslavement into the present day. By contrast, some of these photographs have been wielded toward a forced invisibility, where they have been used to downplay the horrors and violences of enslavement, especially after abolition. The changing nature of these technologies and their contrasting implications in forced visibility/invisibility is unsurprising, as Ruha Benjamin has argued that technologies can both make Blackness hypervisible and ignore it altogether.[57]

The history of enslavement and its aftermath is one that has not been studied fully because of boundaries within the discipline of history. Although the tide is now changing, historians tend to cling to written and textual sources, rendering visual sources secondary or supplemental to their key archival findings. But in this context—where the history of race and racism in Iran rested on a visual language of difference—visual sources are just as important, if not more so, in a serious examination of the racial legacies that undergirded nineteenth-century patterns of enslavement. Photographs reveal a great deal about the visual language of race and enslavement that was only sometimes supplemented with a clear vocabulary. The visuality of this language, and the insistence of those in the academy and the Iranian diaspora that such racial hierarchies do not exist, urged me to look at photographs more closely. Much like how Saidiya Hartman scoured spaces to find traces of a little girl in a photograph, I found myself staring at photographs, trying to figure out more about those still individuals staring back at me.[58] It is in these photographs and other sources that we see the full weight of the forced visibility and invisibility of enslavement and abolition in Iran.

Forced visibility involved, in part, the photography of enslaved people against their consent, which I discuss at length throughout this book. The inclusion of these photographs may be viewed as an extension of this forced visibility. At the same time, eliding the photographs altogether can also contribute to collective erasures, which have prevented scholars and others from addressing this history head-on and have prevented many from knowing their own family histories. It is not uncommon in the Iranian or Iranian diaspora context to see certain photographs or portraits circulate without any acknowledgment of the enslaved Black person in the frame, or, if addressed, presented as though they benefited from a benevolent form of servitude. Even more common are claims made by non-Black Iranians that they "never knew" Black Iranians existed. It is for this reason that I have chosen to include the visuals: to provide a corrective context and mitigate these continued erasures.[59]

The dearth of scholarship on the histories of racism and enslavement in Iran is rooted in both the general erasure of this history at large and scholars themselves. While some scholars have told me that they had never realized Iran had a history of enslavement, the reasons for which I detail in the latter half of the book, many of the scholars who were aware of the history of enslavement in Iran came from enslaving families themselves. These scholars have often shared stories of their grandfathers' or grandmothers' "servants" in passing with me after conference presentations and other spaces, calmly recounting their family history, *Oh, you study slavery, yes, that's interesting. My grandfather had one of those from his trips to Mecca.* These are individuals who have written books and articles themselves in which any references to enslaved people are relegated to footnotes (if ever mentioned at all), avoiding any discussion of the racial dynamics their families benefited from.

The scholarly erasure of this history makes efforts to read it from a Black perspective all the more important, even if they do not yet exist in forms that typically receive a stamp of approval in the ivory tower. Victoria Princewill's historical novel *In the Palace of Flowers* imagines life in Golestan Palace from the point of view of an enslaved Abyssinian woman and eunuch, Jamila and Abimelech, whose lives are shaped not only by their enslavement but also their own searches for freedom.[60] Even more pressing, the work of the Collective for Black Iranians—a transnational organization founded and organized by Black and Afro-Iranians in the

United States, Canada, France, Germany, and Iran—has focused on amplifying and centering Black Iranian voices in stories about the past and present. This organization's work on social media and other platforms has pushed forward the conversation on race and racism from a Black Iranian perspective and rejected the historical erasures that have remained the norm for nearly a century.[61] The collective, which wields creative storytelling in Persian and English, has supported Black and Afro-Iranians in reclaiming their personal histories.[62] As the collective has shifted the conversation and created opportunities to discuss the entangled histories of Blackness and enslavement in Iran, I am sure more family histories will be recovered, and perhaps another historian will be able to write about the transition from enslaved to citizen in the future. As a historian who has worked closely with the collective, I find myself continuously confronted by the need for historical narratives written from a Black Iranian perspective to counter the default positionality of non-Black Iranians, myself included.[63]

ENSLAVEMENT AND ERASURE

The book is split into two parts: "Enslavement" and "Erasure." Part I, "Enslavement" (chapters 1–3), examines the forced visibility of enslaved Black people in Iran. Part II, "Erasure" (chapters 4–6), investigates some of the consequences of the forced invisibility of enslavement and Black people after abolition in 1929.

Part I, "Enslavement," begins with chapter 1, "Geographies of Blackness and Enslavement," which maps out the terrains of enslavability within and around Iran's environs throughout the nineteenth century. This chapter examines the imagined racial geographies that informed architectural structures and urban spaces in the nineteenth century. Opening with the story of Khyzran, a Zanzibari woman who was kidnapped and trafficked into Iran, this chapter examines the different mechanisms that endangered her life, justified her enslavement, and jeopardized her freedom. After enslaved East Africans survived Middle Passages via land and sea, their arrival in Iran was marked by a forced visibility vis-à-vis their enslavement. The dwindling of the Caucasian, Central Asian, and South Asian slave trades left East Africans as the dominant enslaved group. The racialization of East Africans as exclusively *Siyah*, or "Black," as opposed to more nuanced geographic labels, such as *Bombasi*, *Somali*, or *Zangi*, relied on a specific salience of racial visibility. This chapter also calls into question British and Qajar abolitionist efforts of the nineteenth century and how they were deployed for political means. It examines the undulating contours of enslavement and abolition and describes how increased abolition movements came to ultimately converge with the racialization of *Black* as *enslaved*.

Chapter 2, "Limits in Family and Photography," argues that the term *khanevadeh*, or "family," did not carry connotations of intimacy and instead would be better translated as "household." Piecing together single moments from the lives of both free and enslaved Black people in Iran during the late nineteenth and early twentieth centuries, this chapter argues that enslavement remained the dominant social association of visibly Black people in urban centers. Enslaved African domestics served as the face of enslaving families in public spaces. In turn, enslaving households wielded photographs and portraits to further intertwine their images. This chapter is organized around the stories of Yaqut Gholam, Narges, and the little girl whose name has been replaced with Juju/Suski, a mix of free and unfree Black individuals for whom the "family" served as a complicated locus of entrapment, manipulation, loss, and survival. Their lives shed light on the different spaces afforded to Black people in Iran, and the kinds of intimacies they were allowed or banned from enjoying. This chapter highlights the limited notion of the "family" and shows how enslaved people instead sought intimacy and safety in their own found families.

Chapter 3, "Portraits of Eunuchs and Their Afterlives," showcases a case study that links the lives of dying eunuchs at the royal court to the rise of minstrelsy performances within a generation. Naser ed-Din Shah (r. 1848–96) began to memorialize eunuchs at his court through photography and other commissioned memoirs. Most eunuchs were of African ancestry and were among the last ones in Iran, due to ongoing abolition efforts. The royal enslaved eunuchs, I argue, were not simply a status symbol; rather, their very presence was a visual metaphor for the Iranian Crown. Foreign dignitaries, ambassadors, and royal guests, for example, would first meet with the chief eunuch before any member of the royal family. Photographing these eunuchs at such a critical period captured a different face of Iran, as the aging eunuchs were frail and delicate. These photographs served as a complicated site for preserving the memory and agency of eunuchs, as some eunuchs were trained as photographers as well. At the court of Mozaffar ed-Din Shah (r. 1896–1906), the photographs became fodder for court jesters, and blackface minstrelsy took on a very specific form. This chapter highlights the direct connection between enslavement and its legacy of blackface in Iran by examining photographs from the Qajar court, many of them preserved at the Golestan Palace Photo Archive, in tandem with published memoirs and travelogues written by viziers and other court personalities.

Part II, "Erasure," begins with chapter 4, "Histories of a Country That Never Enslaved," and supplies an in-depth analysis of abolition as a process of erasure after the Manumission Law of 1929. Under Reza Shah (r. 1925–41) and his son Mohammad Reza Shah (r. 1941–79), erasure was the guiding principle of abolition, to the extent that entire palace wings were demolished, dictionary definitions of the word *slavery* were carefully rewritten, and ancient Iranian history was reframed entirely. Within decades of the abolition law, Iranians began to adopt an exclusively US-centric understanding of enslavement and its legacies, as well as embracing a nationalist Aryan myth, eliding any reference to Iranian enslavement or Black Iranians on a broad scale in urban centers. This chapter examines how the Manumission Law and the efforts surrounding it were intended not to rectify the harms of enslavement but, rather, to restructure society as if no one had ever been enslaved. While Reza Shah and Mohammad Reza Shah crafted modern images of Iran on the world stage, freedpeople quietly built new lives as Iranian citizens.

Chapter 5, "Origins of Blackface in the Absence of Black People," examines the development of the blackface character, from the court minstrel shows to street performances to print magazines. While entertainment had served as a lifeline for some freed Africans in Iran in the nineteenth and early twentieth centuries, non-Black Iranian actors in blackface, now called *siyah*, or "the black," replaced them after 1929. The development of these minstrel shows into a type of folk theater required their sanitization, and while the framework of the plays replicated all existing references to the enslavement of the *siyah*, alternate rationales and narratives emerged to distance the theatrical genre from the tainted past. As minstrel plays grew more popular, the inclusion of a blackface caricature would catapult satirical magazines, such as *Towfiq* and later *Yaqut*, to a heightened popularity during the 1960s and onward. This chapter charts the canonization of blackface caricatures in public spaces and how their imagery came to displace the presence of Black Iranians.

The sixth chapter, "Memories and a Genre of Distortion," identifies the writings of enslaving families and their descendants as its own specific narrative genre that blurs experiences of enslavement with ideals of benevolence divorced from racist attitudes. Drawing on Trouillot's four phases of history-making, this chapter defines the genre of distortion as one that emphasizes a shared love between enslaver and enslaved, denies the full extent of one's enslavement, and asserts an intimacy that outsiders cannot be expected to understand. This chapter argues that the descendants of the enslavers frame their ancestors as having been infallible and incapable of wronging their enslaved.

The book concludes with the epilogue, "Black Life in the Aftermath of a Forced Invisibility," which moves away from the discussion of enslavement and erasure and looks at Black history, presence, and perspective as a genre of restoration.

PART I
ENSLAVEMENT

On my early research trips to Iran, a few people suggested I look at the life of Anis od-Dowleh. "Oh, slaves—you must mean servants. Have you considered Anis od-Dowleh yet? She was a peasant girl servant at the shah's court, but she soon became the de facto queen of Iran."[1] They suggested that her ascent exemplified how love could transcend class in Iran: she was their very own Cinderella. Even when I explained that I worked on enslavement—on unfree servants and not their free counterparts—they continued to push this idea of love. *Love* could still have transcended enslavement, they insisted. They seemed to believe that Anis od-Dowleh would have still risen to the top as long as she was beloved by the king.[2]

At the archives of Golestan Palace, where Anis od-Dowleh had once ruled over the harem, I came across a photo of two young boys perched on a windowsill.[3] The boys could not have been more than ten years old and were likely closer to five. One boy was Black; the other was likely Caucasian. They were dressed and positioned as stylish royal servants, their hats askew, their laps full. They were both likely enslaved, the Black boy certainly so.

At the top of the photo, Naser ed-Din Shah had noted: "Beloved by Anis od-Dowleh."[4] His caption does not bother remembering their names. Again, the question of love arises. What did her love do for them? What does love mean here? Did they love her back? Did her love free them from enslavement? Did love transcend anything?

The photograph does not answer our questions. Instead, it inscribed their enslaved status. Perhaps she loved them as they were—because they were—enslaved.

Little children. Little *beloveds*.[5]

1 GEOGRAPHIES OF BLACKNESS AND ENSLAVEMENT

The Qajars are not remembered for their detailed accounting, especially when it came to population censuses. During the early years of surveying their subjects, they experimented with different terms and categories.[1] In 1867, Naser ed-Din Shah asked ʿAbd ol-Ghaffar Najm od-Dowleh to carry out a census of Tehran's population. Over fifty-six days, Najm od-Dowleh and his committee counted 147,256 people in the capital city. Their categories were simple: men, women, military personnel, servants, enslaved Black women, and enslaved Black men.

——

In 1856, a young woman named Khyzran was enslaved for a second time.[2] She had already been born into enslavement in Zanzibar, her childhood spent in service to an older man. She found freedom only after his death, having lost thirteen years of her life already. Years later, on her way home from a dance, she was kidnapped and thrown onto a boat under the night sky. The boat headed north, buoyed by the monsoon winds that carried so many against their will to the Persian Gulf, first to Ras al-Khaimah and then to the port city of Lengeh, where she would be sold to a man named Kamal.[3]

We know of Khyzran's story because she ventured away from Kamal's house to seek her freedom. Kamal had left for a trip to his hometown in Basra, and Khyzran took her chance to find independence. She had made a new friend, another enslaved woman who had told her, *Your enslavement is illegal; you should be free.* She knew that the British would intervene on Khyzran's behalf, since Mohammad Shah Qajar had issued a royal decree banning the Persian Gulf slave trade in 1848. Go to the British offices, her friend urged her, and tell them your story. They will free you. Khyzran remembered the explicit orders Kamal had given her before leaving: stay inside and hide from the British. She ignored him and listened to her friend instead.

Khyzran went to the house of Mulla Ahmad, a local employee of the English agent in Lengeh, and asked for her freedom. She explained how she had been brought that season on a boat captained by a certain Feerooz of Ras al-Khaimah. Mulla Ahmad listened and took down her testimony. Only the translated summary of her statement and the subsequent papers shuffled back and forth between the British offices remain in archival boxes today. These papers, their language, and their structure raise more questions than they answer, which I return to later in this chapter.

In his notes, Mulla Ahmad agreed with Khyzran. Per the 1848 decree, her enslavement was illegal, and he arranged for Khyzran to be sent to the freedpeople's depot in Basaidu on Qeshm Island. But before she left for Basaidu, Khyzran appeared on Mulla Ahmad's doorstep again, this time with a boy named Walladee. He had been enslaved and kidnapped into Iran on the same boat as her: if she had been promised her freedom, she argued, so should he. Mulla Ahmad agreed. A few days later, Khyzran and Walladee boarded a boat together again, this time to freedom, to Basaidu, where they would wait to leave the Persian Gulf.

While they waited in Basaidu, surely imagining what their lives could look like again, a notable sheikh from Larestan threatened the British for taking Walladee. He had enslaved Walladee for years, the sheikh claimed, circumventing claims based on the 1848 decree. Despite having accepted Khyzran's testimony on behalf of Walladee, the British were eager to avoid conflict. They forced Walladee back onto a boat again, back into enslavement, back to the sheikh. And they fired Mulla Ahmad, the employee who had granted them their free papers in the first place.[4]

Did Khyzran keep her freedom? We will never know; the archival records end here. Yet we are left wondering how much of these testimonies we can trust to begin with.

A NEW GEOGRAPHY

It is unlikely that Khyzran was one of the individuals counted in Tehran's census. After all, she was enslaved and perhaps freed along the Persian Gulf coastline in the South, and Tehran was nearly a thousand miles away.

The vocabulary that informed the census categories, however, was the same language that deemed her enslavable even as it defined abolitionist rhetoric in Iran. By the time Khyzran had arrived in Iran in 1856, the Persian term *Siyah*—Black—had come to serve as a noun specifically denoting one's skin color and enslavability. Specific regional labels including *Bombasi*, *Somali*, and *Zangi* were abandoned in favor of *Siyah*. Iranians who regarded the visibility of these individuals as a mark of their enslavability described them as either "Black" or "more Black."[5] As a result, someone's Blackness made them both more visible and vulnerable to enslavement (and in turn, abolitionist policies) in the mid- to late nineteenth century.

In this chapter, I discuss how Iranians rhetorically mapped out an imagined geography of Blackness that informed built structures and urban spaces in the late nineteenth century.[6] Drawing on Paul Gilroy's seismic work *The Black Atlantic*, how can we understand the Indian Ocean, East Africa, the Persian Gulf, and Iran as part of a Black Indian Ocean?[7] Although the water has long afforded sailors, merchants, and laborers passage between the southern coast of Iran and the beaches of East Africa, Iranians developed and sustained a narrow, one-directional narrative of enslavement from Africa to elsewhere in this period.[8] Because Blackness was racially *visible*, geographies of Blackness in Iran overlapped with geographies of enslavement, where Iranians built their homes and cities based on this forced visibility. Iranian geographies of Blackness re-created cartographies that were defined through enslavement.

The existing scholarship on enslavement in the Middle East has routinely emphasized that Middle Easterners enslaved people regardless of racial background—that Caucasians, Central Asians, South Asians, and others were as vulnerable to enslavement as East Africans. These same scholars have extrapolated further, arguing that all enslaved people were treated equally and that race played no role in their enslavement.[9] The visibility of East Africans, however, rendered their enslavement categorically different from most other enslaved people, a difference that was reflected in the very language of Tehran's census. Their presence and visibility in city centers became a major feature of their enslavement. By the late nineteenth century, enslaved Caucasians seem to have disappeared from concerns about enslavement, and abolition efforts singularly targeted the Persian Gulf slave trade in the name of enslaved East Africans. Similarly, popular understandings of race in Iran relegate Blackness to the Persian Gulf coastline, even though their presence extended far beyond the littoral into the interior.

The racial visibility of East Africans combined with the British focus on enslaved Black people highlighted their presence further. Because traffickers often smuggled enslaved people through the Persian Gulf, the British focused on abolishing their enslavement, as it served their political interests in the waterway.[10] Caucasians and South Asians had begun to disappear as enslaved populations in Iran. In the early nineteenth century, Iranians enslaved and trafficked people from the Caucasus, Central Asia, South Asia, and East Africa into the plateau. Many of those who survived would eventually be sold to royal or wealthy families, where they would serve as domestic attendants, maintaining the household and managing day-to-day routines of cooking, cleaning, and child-rearing.[11] By the 1830s, traffickers forcibly bringing enslaved people into Iran shifted more toward southern trade routes, as the Treaty of Turkmenchay (1828) marked the growing strength of the Russians and Qajar loss of Caucasian territories, the emancipation of enslaved people in the region, and the driving of Circassians into the Ottoman Empire, where many would be enslaved in the 1850s–60s.[12] As the British colonized South Asia, the enslavement of Indians in Iran decreased as well, instead serving as cheap labor for the British.[13] Various social and religious movements would advocate for abolition during this period. For example, in 1873, Baha'u'llah, prophet of the emerging Baha'i faith in Iran, outlawed enslavement for his followers.[14] The geopolitical realities and the continued legality of enslavement throughout Iran, however, left East Africans as the last significant population of enslaved people in Iran until abolition in 1929.

Under the best weather conditions, the Persian Gulf and the East African coastline were weeks apart by boat.[15] Some boats carried sandalwood trunks and spices alongside enslaved individuals for sale, dispersing their goods and smuggling people into the Persian Gulf and ultimately Iran. It was this traffic, like the boat that carried Khyzran and Walladee, that had caught the attention of the British naval powers, who counted abolitionist efforts for enslaved East Africans among their top priorities in the region. The narrative that the issue of enslavement was limited to the Persian Gulf benefited both the British and the Qajars—the British for their political interests in controlling the gulf, the Qajars for wanting to continue enslaving people in their domestic spaces while deflecting international attention from it.[16] The abolitionist discourse was not taken seriously by elites in Iran, who continued to build homes with massive suites to accommodate the enslaved members of the household. And as we see in Khyzran and Walladee's story, the British operated in their own interests, maintaining the guise of an abolitionist champion while working against the enslaved when convenient.[17] As such, access to the Persian Gulf coast did not define whether the wealthy enslaved individuals in their homes. Rather, Iranians took to buying enslaved individuals on their travels outside Iran on overland routes, including pilgrimages to Mecca. In travelogues written in Persian and English, a racial spectrum of Blackness was mapped onto ethnic and geographic categories that already existed in Iran.[18]

By the time Najm od-Dowleh was asked to conduct a census of Tehran's population in 1867, the presence of enslaved Black people was significant enough to denote their own category. Of the nearly 150,000 people living in Tehran, about 4,000, or 2.5 percent, were identified as Black *gholam* or *kaniz*—enslaved men and women, respectively. These numbers did not include the nearly fourteen thousand free individuals—Black or non-Black—who worked as servants.[19] Nor did it include a category for others enslaved in Tehran during this period—namely, Caucasians, along with Central Asians and others. Only two groups are highlighted as enslaved—enslaved Black men and enslaved Black women.[20] "Black" was not an ethnic group. It was a racial category. How did a population of enslaved Black people grow to be so significant in Tehran that they would be included in a citywide census? Who counted as "Black"? Where did they come from? And how did they figure into abolition efforts?

STRUCTURING ABOLITION

Some twenty years before the Tehran census, on June 12, 1848, a British lieutenant colonel named Francis Farrant, the British chargé d'affaires at the Qajar court, wrote to the grand vizier, Haji Mirza Aghassi, pressuring him for a response to the question of the abolition of the slave trade by sea. "It is a long time since it was promised," Farrant wrote. "I am obliged to demand a clear and decisive answer. . . . If it be the intention of the Persian Government to issue this order, I request to be made acquainted with it today. The British Government are very anxious to know."[21]

Later that day, Mohammad Shah Qajar issued a short, four-sentence royal decree. "Let them not bring any negroes by sea; let them be brought by land," it begins, followed by three sentences that clarify that the shah is pleased with the agreement, but only because of his relationship with Lieutenant Colonel Farrant; "otherwise some trifling discussions still exist between us and the English Government."[22] In the days and months that followed, announcements were sent to the provincial governors to alert them of this new policy, and some of them wrote their own decrees banning the trade of "black slaves and slave girls."[23] Despite the anxieties of the British government regarding the abolition of the slave trade in the Persian Gulf, Farrant's superiors in London would not receive news of the decree or thank the shah until September 6, 1848.[24] But Mohammad Shah Qajar had died the day before, and his son, Naser ed-Din Mirza, was crowned shah. The decree would be forgotten.

The British remained focused on the trafficking of Africans into Iran, as well as the broader Middle East.[25] Despite their expressed focus, however, Vanessa Martin has noted that the number of enslaved Black people who sought help from the British Office in Iran, like Khyzran and Walladee, was less than thirty over the course of forty years.[26] In their messages to the Qajar government, the British seemed to suggest that the end of the slave trade by sea would end enslavement altogether. Colonel Justin Sheil, the British envoy to Persia, wrote to the grand vizier in 1846 arguing that ending the slave trade would end enslavement. Nearly twenty years after the Treaty of Turkmenchay, the presence of enslaved Caucasians had diminished so greatly that Sheil drew on their absence to make his argument: "Because no Georgian slaves are for sale, no one can buy them." The same could be true for East African slaves, he argued.[27]

The Qajar court was not yet convinced that the British were sincerely interested in abolition. In the margins of the missives, Mohammad Shah Qajar noted his suspicions, questioning British motives and their investment in the enslaved Africans. Why were the British so concerned with the Persian Gulf? "There were plenty of hostages in Bukhara and Khiva," he surmised, referring to those enslaved from Persia and trafficked into the Central Asia, "why not discuss them?"[28] Moreover, what had come to be known as the Persian Gulf slave trade was not a singular route but a myriad of networks. People from all over the Indian Ocean world were kidnapped and taken to the various port cities of the Persian Gulf, where they were forced to remain or sent to enslaving families on the interior.

Although the 1848 royal decree was promptly disregarded after Muhammad Shah's death, the British returned to prod the Qajars to enforce the ban. In 1850, Amir Kabir, the vizier to Naser ed-Din Shah, issued an order to the governors of the Persian Gulf ports of Khuzestan and Arabistan stating that "citizens of the High Government are forbidden from bringing *Siyah* from the sea."[29] In other words, Amir Kabir reminded his governors that people were forbidden from trafficking "the Black" into Iran. Although the ban was on enslaved people, and not free East Africans, the status of being enslaved had become so racialized in Iran that the noun alone could communicate Amir Kabir's intention without being misunderstood.

Amir Kabir's 1850 order, however, would not stop the pressures from the British. Those pressures returned in 1851, 1882, and 1890, with different treaties, conventions, and diplomatic conversations in between, all promising to end the Persian Gulf slave trade by giving the British navy increased powers to patrol and intercept boats carrying enslaved people in the waterway.[30] None of these measures, however, would end slavery in Iran. Nor did Iranians believe they would.

VOCABULARIES OF RACISM

Wealthy Iranians felt confident in their ability to continue enslaving people. That was because if they had the means, they would. Although enslaving people from the Caucasus and the Persian Gulf had become legally and logistically more difficult, overland routes still remained active in the traffic of East Africans. Affluent merchants and members of the royal court outmaneuvered the British patrols in the Persian Gulf by purchasing enslaved Africans in Mecca and forcibly bringing them to Iran via alternate routes.[31] In 1886, when Mirza Mohammad Hosayn Farahani had returned from his pilgrimage to Mecca, Naser ed-Din Shah asked him to compose a travelogue of his journey.[32] The travelogue, intended as a guide, included practical information about currencies, climate, and geography.[33] Farahani also included extensive demographic information and a breakdown of the enslaved people in the Meccan bazaar:

> Slave girls and male slaves are plentiful here and relatively inexpensive. There are three enclosed areas in the middle of the bazaar specifically for selling male slaves and slave girls. They put wooden benches arranged in three tiers [there]. Those on the first tier are well dressed [with] clean, fresh clothes [and olive skin], are very beautiful, with pretty eyes, and full of charm, banter, and coquetry. [Those on] the second tier are of a little lower quality than these. [On] the third tier are the very black, thick-lipped, and dirty slave girls, most of whom are brought to Iran where people like us are

willing to own them. Their price is from thirty to forty tomans to two hundred tomans. Male slaves are cheap. Good eunuchs, young and old, can be obtained there. . . . Thus the wife of 'Ala ol-Molk, who, I heard, had come to Mecca this year bought a young eunuch for two hundred tomans and took [him] back. . . . Transporting them by sea is a source of trouble and dispute.[34]

In a few sentences, Farahani detailed the logistics and attitudes toward the slave trade, intentionally and unintentionally. He discussed the spatiality of the slave market, wherein slaves were divided into three physical divisions per their perceived "beauty and cleanliness," coded words for race, and he offered benchmarks for the costs of the different enslaved men and women.[35]

Farahani's explicitly racist ranking and categorization of enslaved East Africans is echoed not only in British official missives but also in personal travelogues of the government attachés and other publications, including a glossary of relevant vocabulary.[36] Colonel Sheil's wife, Lady Sheil, wrote of the partial abolition of slavery in her travelogue in 1856 and listed the "Bambasees, Nubees, Habeshees" as the three major groups of enslaved Africans in Iran, the former of which she described as "coming from Zanjibar."[37] Thirty years later, in 1886, the same year Farahani wrote his travelogue, Charles James Wills published his own, with similar distinctions between the "Bombassi," "Hubshee," and "Souhali or Somali," definitions that would later inform the *Glossary of Anglo-Indian Colloquial Words and Phrases*.[38] Like Farahani, Wills structured his descriptions from light to dark, attaching a sale price to skin tone and other features associated with places of origin. Other mid-nineteenth-century Persian sources would have used these same geographic markers in slave contracts or other missives denoting the geographical or ethnic identities of the enslaved, such as *Zanzibari, Sudani, Habashi, Bombasi,* and so on.[39]

But instead of using ethnic or geographic markers, Farahani specifically used a racial spectrum, from *sabzeh*, or an olive tone, to *kheyli Siyah*, "very Black," a gradient of Blackness that mapped out their enslavement.[40] By the 1880s, the differences between enslaved East Africans had been collapsed into emergent categories of race, replacing nuanced labels that indicated some knowledge of the enslaved person's origins and background. Enslavement was a *visible* category. Nuanced knowledge of where an individual may have hailed from was given less weight than the individual's physical appearance.[41]

Beyond a dubious and colorist ranking of somewhat Black to very Black, the Persian language also had clear pejorative terms for referring to Black individuals that carried the geographies and violence of enslavement. *Kaka* is one such word. In some ways, it brings together the African and Iranian coasts, as *kaka* is the common word for "brother" both in Swahili and in the dialects of southern Iran, including Shiraz.[42] *Brother* is a term of intimacy and love. But in central parts of Iran, where it is more common to call a brother *dada*, the term *kaka* or, more specifically, *kaka Siyah* took on the form of a racial slur against enslaved Black men, a word that wielded violence in the intimacy of the geographies it references. Despite the term's strong ties to the coastline, its cruelty comes from central Iran. In some contexts, it operated as a crude synonym for *gholam Siyah*, the phrase used in Tehran's 1867 census. Even eunuchs, who were usually given titles of respect such as *agha* or *aqa*, were sometimes referred to as *kaka* as well.[43] The term was used cavalierly by Farahani's contemporaries, including members of the Qajar family and others.[44]

Written in the mid-1880s, Farahani's travelogue also demonstrates the degree to which the Caucasian slave trade had been diminished within Iran's borders. Though Farahani discussed enslaved Circassian girls in the Ottoman court in his travelogue, he made no mention of them being enslaved within Iran. Rather, Farahani expressed some confusion at their enslavement, as Circassians were Muslim and "buying and selling them is inconsistent with the enlightened holy law."[45] By contrast, Farahani referenced laws forbidding the transportation of enslaved Black people via the Persian Gulf as merely obstacles to be circumvented by those with means.

And although the Persian Gulf slave trade had been banned, making it difficult to transport those enslaved by sea, members of the Iranian government still managed to travel outside Iran, purchase an enslaved person, and return to Iran with them.[46] ʿAla ol-Molk was a statesman, governor, and minister of the Qajar court, and Farahani's brief allusion to his wife and the young eunuch indicates a significant barrier to the abolition of the slave trade in Iran: those with the financial and legal means to purchase and import slaves continued to do so even though the slave trade by sea had been banned for decades.[47] In a society where only the elite and wealthy participated in the enslavement of others, how would slavery be abolished if the very members of the government banning the trade traveled to enslave people in their homes?

ARCHITECTURES OF ENSLAVEMENT

In 1778, a 6.1-magnitude earthquake flattened Kashan's urban dwellings. A major city that lay at the intersection of trade routes at the center of the country, Kashan had once been home to caravansaries, castles, bazaars, and homes, all of which crumbled under the sheer force of the rattling earth. Although the local mosque was repaired in the following five to six years, the earthquake's magnitude and regular aftershocks had deterred builders from undertaking sizable developments for decades.[48] As memories of the earthquake faded, well-heeled elites hired architects to build expansive homes for their households, designed to display their wealth and last multiple generations.

Much of the construction took place between 1829 and 1880, coinciding with the Iranian loss of the Caucasian territories and the mounting British pressure to abolish the Persian Gulf slave trade.[49] The wealthiest of these families built their homes with a specific architectural layout that highlighted their status as enslavers. While other prominent urban centers, such as Isfahan or Shiraz, had the spatial confines of preexisting structures to build around, Kashan's earthquake presented its residents with somewhat of a blank canvas for architects and builders alike. These homes offer us a glimpse into a once-imagined future that they would build on ostentation and enslavement.

These new Kashani homes comprised several courtyards and floors with living areas for family members (*andaruni*), space to entertain guests (*biruni*), and a third, separate hall that usually sat alongside the *andaruni* and the *biruni* and would have had access to both.[50] Even though they were constructed at a pivotal moment for abolition efforts, these opulent homes all included separate living quarters for enslaved and free servants of the household. The large slave/servant quarters rivaled other areas of the home and were built to house several people, if not more, to serve the main members of the household in their daily activities.

The owners of these homes designed them in the luxurious design trends of the period. Interiors were covered with mirror-works and plaster reliefs that rivaled the interiors of contemporary palaces.[51] Families such as the Borujerdis had hired Saniʿ ol-Molk, the famed court artist, to paint the walls with flower motifs and other popular designs.[52] The Borujerdi House, for example, raised the standard of home design to such a degree that when their daughter was married into the Tabatabaʾi family, her family required that her in-laws provide her a similar home worthy of her status.[53] Ostad

'Ali Maryam, the architect of the Borujerdi House, was brought in to design the second home.[54] He would later design the Amin od-Dowleh caravansary in the Kashan Bazaar in 1863, commissioned by Mirza Farrokh Khan Ghaffari Amin od-Dowleh, as well as his home. Not only did the construction of these Kashani homes draw on skills and styles from the Qajar court; but they also influenced the tastes of those at the court.

The Kashani mansions reflect a denial among the wealthier classes that the ongoing negotiations and treaties between Persia and the British would result in the abolition of slavery. The inclusion of servants' quarters was not the only sign of their disbelief in abolition: the sheer size of these homes—each measuring in the thousands of square meters—required enslaved labor for their upkeep. This propensity for large homes with dedicated servant quarters was present in nineteenth-century builds in other major cities and was not limited to Kashan.[55] Even Naser ed-Din Shah built a new harem for his wives and their attendants at the Golestan Palace in 1881. The lavish new structure had individualized units for each of his wives, who had increased in number and required more space and accommodations.[56] The expanding of the harem structure as the central node, not only for the wives of the shah but also for the enslaved women and eunuchs, reflects how even the Persian Crown believed in the relative permanence of their reliance on a servant class, even if certain groups of enslaved people were becoming rarer in Iran. As Pamela Karimi has noted, in 1881, the newspaper *Sharaf* published an article on its construction with particular reference to the comforts afforded to the *khoddam*, or servants, of the harem.[57] By 1883, the harem was complete.[58] As with the Kashani mansions, its construction echoed the skepticism about the possibility of abolition: these structures cemented the presence of enslaved people in the very architecture of living spaces.

Although the treaties pertaining to the Persian Gulf stemmed some of the trafficking, Black people remained singularly visible in urban centers in Iran. Their growing rarity yet continued presence rendered them even more valuable as a symbol of social status. Enslaved members of the household were engaged in critical domestic work, such as preparing meals, raising children, and cleaning the home. But the domestic aspects of their work did not mean they were confined to domestic spaces. Those enslaved would have accompanied or escorted their enslavers in the streets, on their errands, or to the bathhouse. Trusted enslaved men and women would have been responsible for procuring valuable goods and groceries from the bazaar. Their numbers may have been limited, but their presence was such that they would have been seen in nearly any public space, a reminder to those who saw them of their enslavers' prestige. The visibility of their physical presence was also wielded in private spaces, where enslavers deliberately dressed the enslaved individuals in particular outfits or clothing.[59] Even as late as 1922, Clara Colliver Rice, a missionary who had traveled through Iran, noted,

> Ladies have often complained to me of the dullness of their own entertainments. . . . There is a great deal of rivalry in their own dress and in that of their servants and slaves, whose clothes they supply. A lady may go to a party wearing a new or rather gorgeous dress or chadar, of which she is evidently proud and conscious. A fellow guest who owes her a grudge will send someone to search the bazar the next day for material of the same kind. Then she will arrange a party, and ask the specially grandly dressed lady to come, and array one of her slave-women in garments of the same material and enjoy the agitation of her guest.[60]

The clothing of the enslaved person was the most intimate form of their visibility within residential spaces, especially as most women would have worn similar chadors in public spaces. But as I discuss in the next chapter, their clothing became increasingly important as enslaved people began to be photographed.

The status and visibility of enslaved Black people had such an influence that less wealthy families tried to mimic enslaving families and would hire women with African ancestry as their personal maids.[61] Of course, many Iranians also employed villagers and others from lower socioeconomic backgrounds in their homes as maids, nurses, or errand boys. But unless they were Black, they would not bring those families the same kind of visible prestige.[62] The visibility of enslaved individuals in cities was a critical component of their enslavement; their Blackness was a visual cue to others that an enslaving household was nearby, a mark of pride and regality. It was this visuality that rendered enslaved Africans so important that they would be counted in a citywide census as *gholam-e Siyah* and *kaniz-e Siyah*—enslaved Black men and women, respectively.[63] Despite the importance of their public presence, some British officials still insisted that there were not many Africans in the central parts of Iran and that they were generally concentrated in the southern provinces, closer to the Persian Gulf. This allowed them to avoid jeopardizing the royal family's enslavement of people and to push for increased patrolling of the gulf.[64]

Although there were laws and regulations to try to thwart them, traders continued to traffic enslaved people through the Persian Gulf. In some cases, the British would board ships to check cabins for smuggled people. In other cases, port officials would pour boiling water over the deck and listen for whether the screams of people would betray their presence.[65] Sometimes they would fire live ammunition and kill those enslaved on board altogether.[66] The British kept files of testimonies and letters discussing the manumission cases at their various residencies throughout the gulf region. British interests were revealed not only in their decision-making but also in the papers that document them. Despite Lady Sheil's assertion that "the negroes of Zanjibar ought to be grateful" to the royal decree and the international pressures behind it, these politics did little to change the daily life of those who, like Khyzran and Walladee, remained enslaved per British approval.[67] Any other questions and details remain unresolved, lost, or distorted by the archival record.

NAMES AND PRIORITIES

Did Khyzran pronounce her own name as two syllables? Or was it pronounced as *Khay-za-rān*, only to be transliterated as "Khyzran" by an English translator at the British Office who was unfamiliar with the vowelization of her name? Regardless of its pronunciation, it was a name likely given to her in enslavement; it meant *bamboo*, a name for a tall and strong woman. Likewise, the letters and missives refer to the young boy as "Walladee." Did his enslaver give him this name, or was it a surname?[68] Walladee is not a typical name; rather, it is Arabic for "my son." Perhaps this was due to a translation error: perhaps Khyzran introduced him as *walladee* as a term of endearment, and the transcriber and translator assumed it was his name. Or is it possible that their ages were listed incorrectly? Maybe Khyzran was not twenty-two years old, or maybe Walladee was not yet thirteen, and maybe Khyzran used *walladee* as a literal relational designation: *He is my son*. If Walladee was enslaved by a sheikh in Larestan, what was he doing in Lengeh? Had Khyzran sent for him, or had she come across him by accident? Or had Walladee also figured out that his enslavement was illegal, leading him to venture out and find a British Office for his freedom? Our questions about the lives of Khyzran and Walladee are endless, and like our questions about the many other testimonies now held in the British archives, they remain unanswered.

The most trying of these questions is whether Khyzran was also sent back to Kamal, her enslaver. And were Khyzran and Walladee ever reunited? The paper trail on them disappears.

Despite these inconsistencies, Khyzran's testimony and the subsequent dealings with Walladee's enslavement reveal the kinds of details the British bureaucracy was interested in. Khyzran's testimony, a little over a page long, is formulaic in its structure and mimics the multitude of similar biographies taken from enslaved people across the Persian Gulf. These testimonies were from those seeking freedom at the British Offices from the 1850s until the 1940s, either in Bushehr in southern Iran, or in other port cities of the gulf, such as Sharjah or Muscat. They begin with the heading "Statement by [name and age]." Sometimes the date is included in the heading; sometimes it is not. The testimony, written as a first-person narrative, begins with the individual's personal and family history, typically referring to details about where they were born, who their parents were, how they were enslaved, who enslaved them, what their treatment was like, and, finally, how they arrived at the agency and their request for a manumission certificate. Many, as Hopper notes, reveal a "precise knowledge of the geography of their homelands."[69] While some scholars have regarded these records as being "in their own voices" (i.e., in the voices of the enslaved), the available archival records are all in English, summarized translations from interviews likely taken in Persian, Arabic, or Swahili.[70] What is lost in these translations, we do not know. Given the uniformity of the testimonies, we can assume that any details not considered germane were excluded from the official transcriptions. Moreover, the testimonies, taken for the bureaucratic machine of the British Offices, lack references to details such as their appearance, their emotional state, their comportment, or their dress. Was Khyzran calm as she advocated for herself and later again for Walladee? Had Walladee cried when he realized he would be re-enslaved?

The motivations behind the abolition of enslavement and the British presence in the Persian Gulf were not necessarily humanitarian; rather, they were political. Hopper has noted that newly freed people were often shipped to other ports, where many were guaranteed to die.[71] Even in cases where freedpeople waited at the British offices for their papers to be produced, they were engaged in cooking, cleaning, washing, and other domestic labor around the offices.[72] In other words, the British had them do the very kind of work they were escaping while withholding paperwork that would have guaranteed their freedom. Yet despite these individual-level decisions that were dangerous and violent to the very people they were claiming to save, the production of "antislavery efforts" became integral to the narrative that the British singularly championed abolition worldwide. Khyzran and Walladee's experience was far from unique. British records show that they were hesitant to interfere in issues of domestic enslavement: though they maintained their power to board ships in the name of freeing the enslaved, they preferred that the enslaved and enslaver compromise with one another, at the expense of the enslaved's freedom.[73] And though we do not know Khyzran's fate, if it were up to the British, she likely never returned home.[74]

The British populace, unaware of their own imperial office's lukewarm takes, still took on the mantle of leading global abolition efforts. In 1873, Naser ed-Din Shah visited England during his European tour, where he was faced with questions about the continued practice of slavery in Iran. The British and Foreign Anti-slavery Society wrote the shah a letter describing the depleted populations from the "vast tracts of the Continent of Africa" in Persia and echoing Sheil's argument that as long as slavery remained legal, there would always be a demand for more enslaved laborers.[75] Naser ed-Din Shah did not leave the letter unanswered, and on July 5, 1873, he had the following letter sent from Buckingham Palace to the society:

> I am commanded by His Majesty the Shah to acknowledge the receipt of your Memorial praying for the abolition of slavery in Persia. His Majesty is glad to be able to inform you that in the year 1851, He entered into a convention with the British government for preventing the importation of African slaves into Persia by sea, and He is now occupied with measures for renewing and confirming the obligations which he then accepted. There are no slave markets in Persia, nor any traffic in slaves entailing misery and cruelty. His Majesty will give you his best attention to the general question of slavery on his return to his country.[76]

The society's pleas with the shah reduced the slave trade in Iran to an African problem, and the shah responded by pointing to treaties and discussions on patrolling the Persian Gulf with the British government. Naser ed-Din Shah left England to continue his travels that same day, eager to visit France and the rest of Europe. His travelogue made no mention of the letter from the Anti-slavery Society or his response. Instead he wrote, "It was evident that the people of England were all sorry and grieved in their hearts at our departure."[77] His travelogue, which was almost immediately translated and published in English the following year (1874), mentioned the servants who accompanied the entourage in passing, listed as simply "attendants" in his rosters for each leg of the trip.[78] And while it is not possible to determine the free or enslaved status of most of these individuals, a person, perhaps a eunuch, by the name of Aqa Baqer seems to have joined their travels.[79] His name is mentioned just once, at the end of a list after a reference to three servants to the grand vizier. Naser ed-Din Shah's attention to responding to claims of slavery while continuing to enslave people at his own court reflected some of the priorities of the Qajar government.

The 1867 census was, in many ways, experimental. Naser ed-Din Shah had undertaken various censuses during his rule, the first of which was in 1853. Depending on the census, different categories were used to distinguish subjects, including home ownership (homeowners vs. renters), age (adult men, adult women, children, or youth), ethnic or city background (Qajar, Tehrani, Isfahani, Azerbaijani, or "other/mixed"), and free or working status (men and wage-earners, male servants, respectable women, servants, children/youth, enslaved Black men, or enslaved Black women).[80] With each subsequent census, the categories shifted to accommodate the different groups the government thought were important to document. But the inclusion of enslaved Black men and women in the Tehran census reflects something about their presence and visibility in Tehran: that it would have been too difficult to overlook them and that they were too distinct to fall into some kind of "other" category. Ricks has noted the discrepancy in the numbers of the census and has argued that the discrepancy of 1,177 people may have been the number of enslaved Caucasians. Surmising what caused the discrepancy, I believe, is futile, as it could have been the result of a calculation error or a myriad of other factors. But the exclusion of enslaved Caucasians from the census reveals a clear understanding that while enslaved Caucasians were expected to disappear, enslaved Black men and women were a distinct and significant category that needed to be maintained separately. In fact, the term *white*, or *sefid*, did not enter parlance to refer to enslaved Caucasians as a noun, nor did it ever take on the connotation of being enslaved. Instead, Iranians would come to identify with the adjective themselves.

Although nominal efforts toward the abolition of the slave trade began in Iran in 1848, it would be another eight decades before Iran's Parliament would vote to free all enslaved people within its borders in 1929. By then, enslavement had already been abolished in Zanzibar and along the Kenyan coast, in 1897 and 1907, respectively.[81] But while the traffic during the late nineteenth century slowed, it did not fully come to a stop. Instead, enslaving families maintained the presence of enslaved Black people through *khanehzad*, children born into enslavement in the homes of their enslavers. The term *khaneh-zad*, "born of the home," states this explicitly. And the indexing of the lives of enslaved people—both adult and child—went beyond the 1867 census or English Agent records. The Qajar and British governments were incomplete in their records on enslaved people, as evidenced both by the inaccuracies of the census data and by the lost paper trail of Khyzran's life. In the years that followed, enslaving families would categorize those they enslaved within their own households with a newfangled device: the camera.

2 LIMITS IN FAMILY AND PHOTOGRAPHY

In 1837, in a handwritten contract only eight lines long, Yaqut Gholam, "Ruby the Slave," lost parental rights to any future children.[1] Instead, he signed the rights to his unborn children off to Mohammad Baqer Selmi in exchange for marriage to an enslaved woman.[2] Enslavers often claimed rights to the children of the men they enslaved, since enslaved status was inherited from one's father. Such an arrangement was not unusual.

But this contract was different. Yaqut Gholam was free. His children would have been—should have been—free.

Despite his name, the contract explicitly identified him as a freedman. His name and title were vestiges of his enslavement. His former status, combined with his Blackness—the contract referred to him as *Siyah-fam*, or "Black-colored"—offered enough proximity to enslavement that six individuals approved of the contract, as their personal stamps testified to its legitimacy along its margins. His newly married wife, here unnamed, was described as a beautiful, sweet, kind, Black-faced Abyssinian woman. The adjectives cushioned the otherwise cruel destiny that Selmi had arranged for her: one without any power in the creation of her own family.

The structure of a family unit changed against the backdrop of the shifting legal status of enslavement in the late nineteenth century. In this chapter, I take on the popular defensive refrain "But they were family!" to interrogate notions of intimacy and belonging in the late stages of legal enslavement in Iran. In recent years, Iranians have often used the phrase to diminish any historic descriptions of enslavement in Iran, as most enslaved individuals worked in domestic spaces as nannies, wet nurses, cooks, or errand boys, and in other roles, performing critical household work around the house.[3] But what does it mean to say that "they" were "family"? By highlighting the domestic realm of this servitude, Iranians often imply there existed a special intimacy that marked it as a benevolent rather than oppressive relationship. I argue that the concept of *khaneva-deh*, or "family," did not carry connotations of intimacy and instead would be better translated as "household." Amy Motlagh and Afsaneh Najmabadi have written on the terms used to describe marriage, families, and the women of the families, highlighting their abstract or negative connotations, none of which convey intimacy.[4] Throughout the nineteenth and early twentieth centuries, the structure of the family followed formulaic patterns that highlighted the forced visibility of enslaved people as part and parcel of their ideal family structure.[5] Piecing together single moments in the lives of both free and enslaved Black men and women in Iran during the late nineteenth and early twentieth centuries, I argue that enslavement remained the dominant social association of visibly Black people in urban centers. The enslaved African domestic served as the face of enslaving families in public spaces. Their visibility was critical to the prestige that enslavement brought these families, and many enslavers took to using photography to preserve the image of those they enslaved. Photographs of the family, or rather, the household, became a key fixture in the homes of enslavers.[6] And while enslavers (and their descendants) may prefer to frame and present these photographs in a particularly rosy light, listening to the photographs allows us to hear the layers of belonging and rejection that remain in the images.[7]

Not only did enslaved individuals symbolize their enslavers' wealth; in some contexts their presence would also have represented the family itself. Both enslaved men and women would have accompanied members of the family as escorts, or they would have independently ventured out of the home to deliver messages or procure items for the enslaving family. Photographing the enslaved members of the household alongside members of the enslaving family operated like a personal index or key, indicating that the presence of this individual represented this particular elite family. The importance of the individual's personality varied from family to family, and as such, the memory of their names is uneven. The inclusion of their faces in these valuable photographs indicates that beyond expressing one's status, their visuality was also being used to identify the public face(s) of the enslaving family. The enslavement of these individuals rested on a forced visibility, and photographs were material manifestations of that enslavement. The forced visibility of enslaved people and the singular association of Blackness to enslavement was dangerous for Black individuals, both free and unfree.[8]

In this chapter I begin with a discussion of marriage as the creation site of an ideal family. I examine the late nineteenth-century court photography of the harem, particularly the wives of Naser ed-Din Shah (r. 1848–96), his children, and those enslaved alongside them, and then I move to photographs of wealthy and elite families who arranged for studio photographers to take their portraits alongside those they had enslaved. These photographs—all posed, positioned, and framed by the enslaving families and the photographers they hired—reveal much about how these families painstakingly depicted themselves as benevolent enslavers, despite evidence of more brutal relationships inside the walls of the home. But as constitutionalism grew in popularity, enslavement proved to be a paradox for enslaving families. Despite the great lengths to which people went to enslave individuals in their homes, the Constitutional Revolution (1906–11) raised questions about the role of the family on a civic level and cast enslaved individuals in domestic spaces as unwanted intrusions on the family unit.

NO CONGRATULATIONS ARE IN ORDER

The contract concerning Yaqut Gholam and the unnamed woman was not a marriage contract. Marriage contracts followed a specific template. They began in the name of God, followed by religious verses and blessings for the bride and groom, and they ended with the mention of the dower, a series of tangible gifts promised from the groom to the bride. Marriage contracts were intended to reflect some beauty. Some had a small floral motif decorating their corners, while others shimmered in undulating waves of gold.[9] The unnamed woman and Yaqut Gholam were promised to each other in those few lines that gifted them nothing and stole their children. There was nothing decorative or beautiful about it.

The marriage contracts of free people—and especially those of the wealthy and elite—served as the main blueprint for creating an ideal family. The dower especially alluded to this. Because the dower had to be paid at the bride's request, dowers had to be specific, concrete, and within the groom's means.[10] A proper dower would guarantee the bride's ability to maintain a proper household. Dowers could be as modest as a single copy of a Qur'an alongside a sugar cube (to represent a righteous and sweet life) to as lofty as deeds to houses or entire villages alongside hundreds of gold coins.[11] The larger the house, the wealthier the home, the more amenities available to the married couple for raising children, the more likely the marriage would be viewed as successful. In some marriages, dowers included enslaved men and women to tend to household responsibilities, including childcare.[12] The domestic roles of enslaved people in Iran made them the ideal dower, as they represented the husband's commitment to his wife's ease in motherhood and domesticity. The ability to buy and gift an enslaved person, however, was a luxury, and enslaved people were included only in dowers that had provided the bride with a wealth of other resources. In turn, brides were expected to provide their husbands with a *jahaz*, which consisted of everyday household items and furnishings. These items might have included rugs, teakettles, blankets, dishes, lamps, sewing tools, and other things needed for their everyday life. Enslaved people were never included in the *jahaz*. Enslaved people were not an everyday commodity; they were foundational to the livelihood of the elite family in the same way a house or a large sum of money would be.

While early nineteenth-century dowers were highly specific in requesting *an enslaved Georgian woman* or *an enslaved Abyssinian man*, the diminishing slave trades around Iran required those drafting the marriage contract to be vaguer in their demands. After all, an unfulfilled dower requested by a wife could render a marriage void. By the late nineteenth century, most marriage contracts requested *an enslaved woman* or *an enslaved man* as part of their dowers, if they mentioned them at all. If a married couple was unable to enslave someone from the beginning of their marriage, they could request to enslave someone later in life, usually using specific language to describe what they wanted: a Black *kaniz*.[13]

WHAT IS A FAMILY PORTRAIT?

The diminishing slave trades in Iran coincided with a major scientific innovation of the nineteenth century: the camera. First invented in 1837, the same year of Yaqut Gholam's marriage, the camera quickly became a favored piece of technology in Iran. Naser ed-Din Mirza, then still a prince, received cameras as gifts from Tsar Nicholas I of Russia and Queen Victoria of Great Britain in 1839, and Nikolai Pavlov took the first daguerreotype in

Iran in 1842.[14] As shah, Naser ed-Din invested in the technology, inviting those skilled and trained in the art of the camera to serve as court photographers, mastering the hobby himself, and even training a few eunuchs as photographers as well.[15] Eventually Naser ed-Din Shah established two separate photography studios at Golestan Palace, one for general photographs, and another specifically for photographs of the harem.[16] The photography of women at this period was a controversial subject, but Naser ed-Din Shah's interest in documenting the harem broke this taboo, creating a new standard for how portraits should be posed and presented, which wealthy families would later adapt in their own homes and local studios beyond the palace walls.[17]

The camera's arrival marked an important moment for the documentation of enslaved individuals. Because of their proximity to centers of power—including to Naser ed-Din Shah himself—enslaved people were among the first generation of people photographed in Iran. While many of the photos remain in private collections, the archival collections at Golestan Palace reveal some of the patterns that structured the depiction of the harem. Most of these photographs were not intended for circulation. The Golestan Palace Photo Archive has reorganized many of the royal albums into loosely thematically oriented binders, and many of the harem photographs are in albums simply labeled "Women." Likely taken in the 1880s, these photographs have since been separated from their original albums, and the only photographs made available to researchers are black-and-white copies of those deemed suitable for the public. The Golestan Palace Photo Archive does not, for example, release photographs that include nudity of any kind. Women in these photographs appear fully clothed, which was not true of all Qajar photography.[18] Similarly, the Harvard-based digital archive *Women's Worlds in Qajar Iran* is another repository with photographs and other paraphernalia that encompasses the lives of the enslaved. In both instances, the domestic worlds of the enslaved are relegated to a women's sphere, regardless of the gender of those enslaved.

Although the photography of the court comprised a broad range of styles and content, a specific genre of photographs would later be mimicked by those emulating the styles of the court. Despite Naser ed-Din Shah's experimentation with various poses and settings, many of the photographs of the harem started to become more formulaic. In these photographs, some people were seated, others were standing, but who was seated and who was standing came to inform what a proper portrait was supposed to look like. And many of these portraits included not only members of the royal family but also enslaved individuals and servants. Their inclusion was critical to the creation of the portraits. For example, in a portrait of Shokuh os-Saltaneh, Naser ed-Din Shah's wife and Mozaffar ed-Din Shah's mother, she was seated, and two eunuchs stood on either side of her (fig. 2.1). Another woman, who was probably enslaved, stands to the back to prevent anyone from interrupting the photograph, although she inadvertently was photographed as well.

In royal photographs, often those whose names were labeled by Naser ed-Din Shah were the ones most likely to be forgotten. While he did sometimes label his wives in his solo portraits of them, they were usually unnamed in large group photographs. Instead, enslaved women or eunuchs were named. The hubris of the court—that their personalities would always be remembered because their power rendered them unforgettable—was critical to his labels.[19] In a series of photographs likely intended for 'Aziz os-Soltan and Hassan Khan,[20] nephews to Naser ed-Din Shah's prominent wife Amineh Aqdas who managed the Imperial Harem Studio,[21] Naser ed-Din Shah labeled an enslaved Black woman "Goli Chehreh" (Flower-face) in several photographs (e.g., fig. 2.2). In one photo, where her face is partially blocked, he labeled her "*Siyah* Goli Chehreh" to avoid any confusion. The additional adjective—*Black*—differentiated her from the free women seated around her.[22] Similarly, an enslaved Circassian girl was labeled *Cherkesi*, simply "Circassian." Without her ethnic label, she may have been mistaken for a woman of the royal family.

One can hardly call the photographs taken at the harem family portraits, but it was these photographs and their norms that came to influence commercial photographers. Many commercial photographers began their careers either at the royal court or in conversation with court photographers. Photographs mainly of women were circulated in photo studios and bazaars, sold to Iranians and tourists alike.[23] The norms of this style of photography became standardized by the early twentieth century, when wealthy families were more commonly able to hire photographers for their own purposes.[24] The enslaving family typically appeared seated, while those enslaved by them usually stood toward the side or even the margins of the photograph.[25] Some members of the enslaving family may have stood, depending on age, gender, and rank within the family. A grandmother, for example, would always be seated in a photograph, but a grandchild might stand. And while there are many exceptions to these rules, certain patterns do emerge from these photographs delineating the enslaver from the enslaved.

2.1 A woman looks on as two eunuchs stand around the mother of the shah. ("Portrait of Shukuh al-Saltanah, mother of Muzaffar al-Din Shah, with two attendants," contributed by Farnaz Behzadi, *Women's Worlds in Qajar Iran* digital archive, record no. 1028A12, http://www.qajarwomen.org/en/items/1028A12.html.)

2.2 Goli Chehreh sits in the front row, third from the left, and Cherkesi sits third from the right. (Album 210: 25, Golestan Palace Photo Archive, Tehran.)

Beyond the studio backdrops, these photographs were taken against a much broader cultural backdrop of abolitionist debates that had erupted among the wealthy and the elite. Many of these debates had been spurred by the Constitutional Revolution (1906–11), which resulted in the creation of the first democratically elected Parliament, the Majles. After Naser ed-Din Shah's assassination in 1896, Mozaffar ed-Din Shah (r. 1896–1907) succumbed to public pressures demanding limits on what they viewed as despotic rule and government transgressions.[26] On August 5, 1906, he agreed to the creation of the Majles. Elections were held that fall, and the shah signed the first Iranian constitution in December of the same year. Less than a week later, Mozaffar ed-Din Shah's death threw the country into more political turmoil that would last several years. Regardless, the political sphere had been opened to the nation. Once simply for those born into royalty and others near them, the world of politics was now accessible to civil society. Young Iranian boys could grow up to be elected to Parliament. Young Iranian girls could grow up to raise boys who might be elected to Parliament. The proper education and upbringing of children was now paramount.[27] The future of the nation rested on it.

The revolution and its aftermath raised pointed questions for Iranians, especially those in elite families accustomed to their assumed proximity to power, which in turn restructured gender roles.[28] Until now the children of the elite and wealthy had largely been raised by enslaved nannies, wet nurses, or other members of a household's domestic staff. As the discourses around the ideal mother and housewife grew more complex, the position of enslaved individuals within the family grew more precarious, a sentiment that was true across the Middle East at this time.[29] Scholars including Afsaneh Najmabadi have discussed the all-engrossing debates surrounding the "daughters of Quchan," women from northeastern Iran who were kidnapped and sold into enslavement by Turkmen raiders.[30] Newspaper articles ran regular coverage on these women, who came to serve as a gendered metaphor for Iran's national integrity. In the following years, Iranians would forget them, quietly concerned with their own family structures and the place of enslaved individuals in their households.

INHERITING BLACKNESS

As East Africans became the last dominant group of enslaved people in Iran, Blackness became so synonymous with enslavement that their visibility made them vulnerable to enslavement even in situations that would have been illegal per Iranian norms. In her memoir, Munes od-Dowleh narrated the story of a prominent merchant who bought a "raisin-colored" woman named Narges for his wife during the Constitutional Revolution. Upon her arrival at their home, Narges begged to be let go.

For three days and nights, she wept, crying, "My mother was a nanny, but my father was a free man, and I am not a slave." After that, she placed a Qur'an in the arms of the haji and his wife, saying, "Don't buy me, I am not a slave girl." The haji's wife, who felt sorry for Narges, said,

> Tomorrow when Omm Ja'far arrives, we will go give you to her and get our eighty toman back. But in the alley, Omm Ja'far will go forward, but you hang back so that you can slip into the women's quarters of the home next to ours, a mullah's home, whose word carries weight. Say, "I have come here to sit *bast*, I am not a nanny, I am free. They want to sell me, but my father was white. Here today and tomorrow on the Day of Judgment, I beg of you—don't let

them sell me like a nanny [*dadeh*]!" Of course, no one can drag you out of that mullah's home, you just stay there and sit *bast*.[31]

Narges listened to the haji's wife, and after her escape, the mullah agreed to provide her safe refuge. Narges could stay in the mullah's home until she was ready to leave. Omm Ja'far realized that she could not force Narges to leave a private home, especially the home of someone with a prominent reputation. She tried to bribe Narges with various presents, insisting that she would never sell her again, but Narges stayed with the mullah and his wife. Omm Ja'far's empty promises, however, did not last long, for she found another buyer, the wife of a parliamentary official. The official's wife agreed to buy Narges, so another eighty toman were exchanged. This time, the official and his wife went to the mullah and asked him to release Narges. He again replied that Narges had to be convinced to leave on her own terms. The official's wife went to Narges, promised her that she was like a daughter to them and that she would be taken care of, and asked if she would please leave with them.

Narges declined.

Eventually, the official's wife convinced the mullah's wife to help ensnare Narges in exchange for a few golden bangles. Even the mullah abandoned his moral position for this new deal and advised the official's wife to ambush Narges en route to the public bathhouse. The ruse worked, and Narges was kidnapped again, for a second time. The official's wife returned home with an enslaved Narges. This arrangement lasted for a few days, until Narges finally escaped to Haji Naneh, a freed Black woman who had served in the shah's harem until Naser ed-Din Shah's assassination. Although the official and his wife reported her missing to the local police force, Haji Naneh's network proved strong. Her home had become a haven for freed slaves, where she protected Narges while seeking her freedom. With Haji Naneh's help, Narges went to the head of Parliament, who deemed the slave trade illegal and granted Narges her free papers.[32]

Despite the democratic aspirations of the Constitutional Revolution, Black women were still viewed as enslavable and vulnerable. While enslaving families insisted that they were generous in their enslavement, that they could achieve a literal picture-perfect "family," Narges saw the situation for what it was. She had seen how her mother had been treated, and she did not want it replicated for herself. The sexual vulnerability of enslaved Black women to the enslavers resulted in free children who inherited their father's status. Despite inheriting their father's freedom, these children still carried the stigma of enslavement and Blackness.[33] As society increasingly equated Blackness to enslavement, her father's free status could not guarantee hers. More than sixty years after Yaqut Gholam's contract dictating that his children would be born into enslavement, Narges nearly faced a similar fate, not because of a contract but because of the brazen attitude of slave traffickers dedicated to maintaining their own livelihood on the lives of others. And although everyone involved in her kidnapping knew her enslavement was wrong, none helped her. It was only when Narges found support from Haji Naneh that she was able to find freedom. Michael Gomez and Eve Troutt Powell have examined how African men and women found community with each other in the US context and in Egypt, respectively.[34] Building on Jessica Marie Johnson's concept of Black femme freedom, Narges's story illustrates this same dynamic in the Iranian context.[35] Even though Narges was born to a free, non-Black Iranian father, which should have granted her freedom by default, the shared experience of being enslaved by virtue of being Black brought Narges and Haji Naneh together. A network of newly freed African women would come to serve as a family for Narges as well.[36]

Others who inherited (and maintained) their freedom still lived with the stigma of enslavement because of their Blackness. Seyyed ʿAbdollah Behbahani served as one of the foremost influential clerics of the Constitutional Revolution. Credited with fostering alliances and supporting the protests that led to the revolution in 1906, Behbahani crafted strategic relationships with members of the court, the British legation, and reform-minded clerics that led the Moderates in Majles. His rise to power was due in part to his father's powerful connections with Naser ed-Din Shah's court, and also to his own ambitions and charismatic character.

Born in 1840, Seyyed ʿAbdollah Behbahani spent the first part of his life in Najaf, where he studied under his father and other local clerics. His father, Seyyed Esmaʿil Behbahani, came from a family of distinguished clerics and carried a notable amount of power within the religious community of Najaf. His mother, Fatemeh, was a *Habashi* woman purchased by his father during a pilgrimage to Mecca. In 1870, during Naser ed-Din Shah's visit to Najaf, his father met with the shah, who recognized his clout and recruited him to serve as a consulting religious authority at the Qajar court. Upon Naser ed-Din Shah's request, Esmaʿil Behbahani moved his family to Tehran and maintained close ties with the seat of power. It was in this milieu that his son, ʿAbdollah Behbahani, became acquainted with the Persian political system and the workings of the capital. When his father died in 1878, ʿAbdollah Behbahani took his father's place as an influential cleric in the Qajar capital.[37]

Behbahani actively participated in the political scene, earning what Abrahamian has called the "unsavory reputation of being pro-British" for publicly smoking tobacco in support of the shah and the British during the Tobacco Protest in 1891.[38] By the early twentieth century, however, Behbahani was an active constitutionalist, advocating for limits on monarchical power. In 1906, Behbahani allied with another *mojtahed*, Mohammad Tabatabaʾi, and led the pivotal Qom protests of clerics clamoring for a constitution.[39] After the establishment of the Majles, he participated in parliamentary debates in support of moderate candidates, though he was not actually an elected representative.[40] In the unrest of 1908–9, when Ahmad Shah Qajar bombarded Parliament, the shah identified Behbahani as a key constitutionalist and placed him under house arrest.[41] Finally, with the reopening of the Majles in 1909, Behbahani was selected alongside Tabatabaʾi as the mojtahed leaders of the Moderates Party, the main rival to the more secular Democratic Party, led by Hassan Taqizadeh.

Behbahani is said to have garnered so much power that he often held official meetings in the convenience of his own home, excluding those who disagreed with him. These power moves, coupled with his egotistical reputation, led his opponents to call him Shah ʿAbdollah, or, more commonly, Shah Siyah, "the Black King." While at first glance this may seem like a complimentary epithet, it was not.

Combining the title *shah* with the blackness of his skin, his detractors attempted to label him as an unfit despot. "The Black King" constituted a direct reference to his skin and his autocratic, and at times, authoritarian decisions that his opponents viewed as unfair or undemocratic.[42] The title labeled Behbahani a hypocrite, who, despite claiming to want limits on the shah's power, was not opposed to cultivating a cultish following for himself. The inclusion of *Siyah*, however, is unmistakable. By highlighting Behbahani's skin color, they insulted him for inheriting his enslaved mother's Blackness. Behbahani's participation in the political sphere was cut short on July 14, 1909, when followers of his main rival attacked and assassinated him.[43] Although political assassinations were becoming increasingly common during this period, to his detractors, his life was seen as beyond the limitations Blackness *should* have placed on him, just as

Narges's life was viewed fitting for an enslaved girl and nothing more. Their status in Islamic law—free, as inherited from their father—was tempered by Iranian society's now strengthening association between being *Black* and *enslaved*.

The desirability of an enslaved nanny or other domestics, however, was fiercely debated during this period. Newspapers such as *Danesh* took the question of domestics and their intrusion on the family very seriously when it began printing in 1910.[44] Written by and for elite women, *Danesh* published articles geared toward educating mothers on the care of their children and toward the evils of allowing nannies to take on these responsibilities. The inclusion of non–family members in a household threatened the very education of the children. While many of the wealthier families enslaved African women as their children's nannies, other families also employed poorer local women to fulfill the role. Regardless of the specifics, *Danesh* was clear: Do not bring nannies into your homes. If you must hire a nanny, hire a beautiful and educated woman.[45] Enslaved women were typically viewed as neither.

Even women who claimed a deep love for their nannies called for their removal from the household. Taj os-Saltaneh, the daughter of Naser ed-Din Shah, wrote about her close relationship with her African nanny, whom she referred to as "dearest nanny," "my nanny," or "Lady Nanny," but never by name.[46] A princess, Taj os-Saltaneh was raised in the royal court, her mother always nearby but almost never present in her upbringing. In her memoir, written in 1914, Taj os-Saltaneh recalled her deep attachment to her nanny, whom she loved "despite her horrifying looks": "But if only I could have had all of this love that I had for my nanny and have described here for my venerable mother instead. Instead of [telling you about] an unworthy black, I could have told you stories about my mother instead."[47]

The attachment to wet nurses was an intimate one that persisted beyond childhood. Some remembered their nurses in their wills and testaments, either providing for them financially with a monthly stipend, or asking that others pray for their nurse who had passed on before them.[48] The inclusion of nannies in wills highlights their unique status in the household—not quite family but also not quite the strangers that *Danesh* had cast them as.[49] Taj os-Saltaneh viewed these relationships as unnatural, and an impediment on her own relationship with her mother. Wet nurses should not, and could not, take the place of one's own mother.

But portraits orchestrated by enslaving families suggest that the best families were those that had enslaved individuals, including nannies, in

2.3 The sewing machine is a farce. (Private family collection, Kerman, Iran.)

their midst. In one photograph of an enslaving matriarch Shazdeh Galin, an enslaved woman, and their children visually insinuated that the presence of an enslaved woman would allow the enslaving mother to better embody maternal femininity. The alternating arrangement of enslavers and enslaved in the photograph presented their racial harmony as a family unit. As Krauthamer and Willis pointed out, "Such images create a visual narrative of the romantic myth of mutual obligation and affection, captured in that rhetorical image favored by slaveholders of the 'family, white and black.'"[50] Contrary to the suggestion that nannies and wet nurses might ruin children or ruin their relationships with their mothers, the portrait (fig. 2.3) contended that children raised under the loving arm of their nanny, here an enslaved Black woman, are just as beautiful and genteel as any other children. The eldest daughter of the enslaving family, here photographed in the center, wore a floral hat, a chic sweater, and brightly patterned tights, emphasizing a new societal understanding of sophistication, all while sitting next to her nanny. Her refinement, as attested to by the photograph, was also a guarantee that her baby sibling would also grow up to be similarly "refined" and "genteel," as was suitable for their family reputation. And while the enslaved woman, the nanny, embraced the young baby, the enslaving matriarch was shown as tending to important motherly and feminine activities, such as sewing, ironing, even smoking a hookah. The posing of the photo was, of course, a farce, as the several layers of fabric render the sewing machine inoperable.

But what about the nanny's daughter? A young *khanehzad*, a child born to domestics in the home they serve, she appeared almost defiant, her arms crossed and her lips pressed together. Wet nurses were often mothers to their own children in the same age range as the children they nursed, and many of these children were photographed in family portraits. The photograph suggested that the young enslaved girl may learn to be genteel from the enslaving family, just as her mother has matured to be graceful and maternal. In this way, it insinuated that with enslavement, both families could benefit and reach an ideal femininity that would be otherwise impossible without enslavement.

PHOTO TEMPLATES

Two portraits from two different families reflect the patterns of family portraits that had crystallized by the late nineteenth and early twentieth centuries. In both photographs, an enslaved Black man stood behind a row of seated children. Both photographs were taken in front of an illustrated backdrop of a European-style home.[51] The children of the enslaving family appeared in their finest clothes, the enslaved men in a standard uniform for their status—rounded hat, buttoned-up overcoat. The portraits differed in the details, as one portrait included five children sitting on a bench, while the other only had three children. But both speak to the same sort of language of photography and enslavement. This was not a family portrait; it was a portrait of the children of the enslaving family chaperoned by an enslaved attendant (fig. 2.4). The enslaved man's presence here did not necessarily indicate love; rather, it gestured to whoever would have seen the photograph that these children were well cared for.

On the back of figure 2.5, an inscription provides another layer of context: "Dedicating this photograph of the children to you, an invitation for you to come to Tehran. ʿAli Naqi Khan, Badiʿ oz-Zaman, Sayf od-Din Khan. But Sayf od-Din is much better than his photo, his face looks very black because of a shadow."[52] Sent as a memento to entice someone to visit, the inscription, perhaps written by a parent, clarified that Sayf od-Din, the young boy on the right, was not nearly as black as his photo suggests, lest

2.4 "Family portrait" of enslaving children and a man whose name they can't remember. ("Family portrait," Farnaz Behzadi, *Women's Worlds in Qajar Iran* digital archive, record no. 13100A14, http://www.qajarwomen.org/en/items/13100A14.)

2.5 Portrait from a family who clarified that their child's face was not as Black as that of the enslaved man behind him. ("Group portrait," Iran Khanum and Amirdokht Ghaffari, *Women's Worlds in Qajar Iran* digital archive, record no. 16178A30, http://www.qajarwomen.org/en/items/16178A30.html.)

the viewer confuse the child of the enslaving family with the Black man standing right behind him.

And who was that man? Another inscription on the back named him as Abo'l Qasem. The archival caption describes him as a *khanehzad*. His parents were enslaved and he was born enslaved, likely in the same home. And their Blackness was critical to their enslavement, hence the need to differentiate Sayf od-Din. No, Sayf od-Din was not Black; of course not, that was just a shadow. Sayf od-Din was the enslaver, not the enslaved. Nothing was mentioned about Abo'l Qasem's Blackness—nothing more needed to be said.

As British patrols in the Persian Gulf worked to diminish the trafficking of enslaved people into Iran, wealthy Iranian families began to keep

2.6 A framed photograph of children: the enslaved and his enslavers. ("Group portrait," Yasaman Kalantari ʿAmiri, *Women's Worlds in Qajar Iran* digital archive, record no. 16193A38, http://www.qajarwomen.org/en/items/16193A38.html.)

their enslaved domestics for longer, postponing or denying their freedom and eventually raising their children as enslaved within their homes. *Khanehzad* were not new in Iran, but they were now represented in a new way: through photography. These children were often photographed alongside the children of the enslaving family.

These young enslaved children are not limited to one or two photographs; they appear in portrait after portrait, their lives limited to the small frame that captured them without much additional information. Sometimes these photos were framed so that the family could put their ideal household on display. Those who inherited these photographs from their enslaving ancestors often have little to add, only insisting that their families were very kind to the enslaved children.[53] But in these portraits, they were always distinguished from the children of the enslaving family, whether by position, as in figure 2.6, where the children of the enslaving family are all seated, either on chairs or on the floor, while the young enslaved boy was the only one forced to stand.[54] His expression—he was clearly angry—makes us wonder what else he was forced to do. His expression was part of the photograph, a contrast to the sons of the enslaving family, who merely looked blank or even a little smug. There was also a contrast in clothing, as in figure 2.7, where the young enslaved girl was the only girl of her age and height not wearing a scarf. With the exception of two much younger children, she was the only girl with her hair showing, tightly pulled into two braids behind her head. As I mentioned in the introduction, this is one of two photographs contributed to the *Women's Worlds in Qajar Iran* archive by the same individual. This archival record names her Suski, a diminutive of *susk* (cockroach), a racist reference to her being small, young, and Black.[55] Her unkempt appearance—wrinkled clothing, unbuttoned collar—was a choice made by her enslavers, who wanted her presence to be distinct from the other children in prim white scarves and to justify the unclean claims of her name.[56] At first glance, one might see a family portrait, but the details mark those pictured as within or beyond the frames of the family.

A later photograph of the same household (fig. 2.8) shows the little girl—as well as the other children in the photograph—as slightly older, wearing a chador with stylized bangs, more similar to the dresses of the other young girls of the household.[57] While many of the same individuals are pictured in both portraits, only the little girl's appearance is dramatically different, a visual testament to her maturity over the years. Viewed in tandem, the photographs show how the enslaving family commissioned

2.7 Who braided her hair? ("Amir Hishmat family," Bahman Bayani, *Women's Worlds in Qajar Iran* digital archive, record no. 31e137, http://www.qajarwomen.org/en/items/31e137.html.)

2.8 All around an oil painting. ("Children of Yamin al-Saltana," *Women's Worlds in Qajar Iran* digital archive, record no. 31e141, http://www.qajarwomen.org/en/items/31e141.html; also in *Asnad-i Banuvan dar durih-yi Mashrutiyyat*, published by the Majles Library. Text from *Women's Worlds in Qajar Iran*.)

these portraits not only to demonstrate their prestige but also to make an argument for the civilizing mission of slavery—a disheveled young girl became a genteel young woman. At first glance, one might see the photographs of the little girl as different people in each of the photographs. And while it is possible that the enslaving household had enslaved multiple little Black girls in their service and uncreatively called them the same racist name, it is more likely that the household intended for the little girl to look radically different in each photograph, to project the idea that enslavement could have a radically beneficial impact on the people they enslaved. At a time when enslavement was visibly on the decline, photography could demonstrate a family's status and the supposed benefits of enslavement. As Krauthamer and Willis have noted, "Photographers and slaveholders produced images that aimed to present slavery as an appropriate, beneficial, and benign institution based on natural racial hierarchy."[58]

Newspapers established during the Constitutional period, like *Danesh*, would have targeted the matriarchs of these families as their intended audience. But these portraits reflect a rejection of abolitionist rhetoric. Contrary to the articles that clamored for enslavers to not allow the enslaved to care for the family, these photographs presented the enslaving family as caretakers of the enslaved, signaling that their enslavement of them was a noble effort. The legacies of these portraits and the memorialization of those they featured is as uneven as the power dynamics that structured the photographs themselves. In figure 2.9, the differences between the two boys—one enslaver, one enslaved—is made even more stark by what they hold in their hands.

The enslaving child, named Aqa Shazdeh, held a pen and paper while sitting upright in figure 2.9, as if about to jot down some notes, while the young enslaved child stood next to him, holding up a pen case. As Wexler has shown, the sentimentality of the portrait was for the benefit of the enslaver, not the enslaved.[59] The enslaved child, whose side of the photograph is completely ripped while the other side is almost entirely intact, was left as an afterthought and yet was a completely integral character to the completion of the photograph. Not only was the enslaving boy educated, as evidenced by his writing on paper; the enslaved boy also propped up a pen case as a dutiful servant. The photographer and enslaving family posed the young boy as a source of support for his enslaver's edification, perhaps an effort that could result in his own education as well. When the descendants of the enslaving boy showed me this photo, they proudly

2.9 Pen, paper, and pen case. (Private family collection, Kerman, Iran.)

2.10 Body language. ("Group portrait," Yasaman Kalantari 'Amiri, *Women's Worlds in Qajar Iran* digital archive, record no. 16193A6, http://www.qajarwomen.org/en /items/16193A6.html.)

shared that their great-grandfather was the first medical doctor in their family. They swore that their great-grandfather was very kind to the en-slaved child. But they could not recall what happened to him.[60]

———

What became of Yaqut Gholam, his unnamed wife who was said to be sweet and beautiful, and their children who were promised to Moham-mad Baqer Selmi? What happened to those children, who were born into enslavement despite all norms dictating otherwise?

Though family portraits that included the *khanehzad* and other en-slaved members of the household began to fall out of favor in the 1920s and '30s, they did not disappear entirely. In a household photograph (fig. 2.10), we see the same pattern again. A grandmother sat at the center, surrounded by her children and grandchildren. The women wore fash-ionable dresses with drop waists and scalloped edges, the man a double-breasted suit with wide lapels. Only the grandmother covered her hair; the other women appeared with their perfectly coiffed hair, an indication of their progressive values. The women wore heels so new they shined.

While the members of the family all appeared calm, comfortable, and confident, a young Black woman to the left exuded discomfort. Her arms were wrapped around her as though she felt exposed, her eyes narrow as she looked into the camera. Is it possible that she was a *khanehzad*, born and raised in enslavement by this family? One wonders whether she, like the grandmother, would have preferred to be covered in a scarf and chador but the family forced her to wear a dress and heels to highlight their own refinement. The photograph is undated, which raises another series of questions. When was the photo taken? Either the photo was from the 1920s, to show how advanced the family was in their values, or it was taken in the 1930s, after the emancipation of all enslaved people in 1929. If this woman was no longer enslaved, perhaps she was made to pose with the family as a "servant" despite reenacting the same position and status visually foisted on enslaved people prior to their emancipation.

This photograph, like others before it, was not unique. The photograph served to catalog the memory of the enslaved for the enslaver, for their benefit. But at the Qajar court, the photographs of eunuchs took on a life of their own. Although Naser ed-Din Shah commissioned the photographs and indices of the royal eunuchs to memorialize their presence as the last generations of enslaved eunuchs in Iran, their photographs inspired something very different. Their lives and afterlives are the subject of chapter 3.

3 PORTRAITS OF EUNUCHS AND THEIR AFTERLIVES

Naser ed-Din Shah took photographs of Agha Jowhar, Bashir Khan, and others all on the same day. He sat them on the same carved wooden chair, in front of the same fabric backdrop, under the same lighting. He saved their photos in the same arched album opening; he wrote their names at the top of each photo. After some time, he would return to the album to add another inscription, *marhum*, to the side of the frames: "Receiver of God's Mercy."

They had died, and Naser ed-Din Shah had recorded their deaths, one by one next to their photos. *Marhum* Agha Jowhar. *Marhum* Bashir Khan. *Marhum*. Who would remember the eunuchs? Who could forget them? Haji Firuz, Haji Bidel, Haji Sorur, Aqa Soleyman, Aqa Salim, Aqa Mehrab, Haji ʿAli Gholam, and Bashir Khan were all eunuchs at the court of Naser ed-Din Shah. They were everywhere yet nowhere.

Enslaved eunuchs, castrated men who were prized for their bodies, seem to have been present in every corner of everyday elite life. But their memories have been largely left at the mercy of private journals, memoirs, and photographs belonging to their enslavers. Often they are quiet in these sources, mentioned in passing and or simply acknowledged for their presence. Who would remember them? ʿAzod od-Dowleh asked himself this question in 1886 when writing about his childhood at court. The forty-ninth son of Fath ʿAli Shah (r. 1797–1834), he created an index of the eunuchs he remembered, especially those who were not as famous, so they would not remain completely obscure, since they had no means of leaving behind descendants for their names and deeds to be remembered.

If a little more time passes, they will have been completely forgotten.[1]

——————

The Qajar dynasty began its rule with a complicated relationship with eunuchs: its founder, Agha Mohammad Khan Qajar, was castrated.[2] An act of retribution and revenge, his castration was intended to prevent him from ever challenging the Zand dynasty.[3] In 1779, Agha Mohammad Khan led an insurrection against the ruling power. By 1789, he had established his dominion over Iran. Despite his castration, Agha Mohammad Khan (r. 1789–97) still followed common royal protocol and maintained a small harem of his wives and adopted children. Although eunuchs traditionally served as liaisons between harem and king, the eunuchs of the nascent Qajar court had a diminished presence outside the harem to avoid upsetting Agha Mohammad Khan.[4] His nephew and heir Fath ʿAli Shah (r. 1797–1834), however, ruled by virtue of his sexual virility. With over one thousand wives and hundreds of children, Fath ʿAli Shah established his kingship through marriages and alliances with powerful groups and tribes across Iran, a clear contrast to his uncle's rule.[5] Fath ʿAli Shah's expanded harem required extensive staffing, and so eunuchs became entrenched in their roles as key managers of the royal court and harem.

As gatekeepers of the harem, eunuchs worked in close contact with women without raising suspicions of sexual intrigue. Their castration rendered them the ultimate symbols of pomp and prestige. Valued for their desexualized and emasculated presence, eunuchs crossed boundaries between the private and more public zones of the court. But the royal enslaved eunuch, I argue, was not simply a status symbol; rather, the eunuch's presence was a visual metaphor for the Iranian Crown. Anyone entering the Qajar palace would first meet with the chief eunuch. Their very presence indicated that a royal was nearby.

Yet the memories of these eunuchs were fragile. Their castration precluded them from the foremost means of preserving their identities—the ability to have children to inherit their name and maintain their legacies. While the mutilation of the body and castration is expressly forbidden in Islam, eunuchs had served royal families in Iran and elsewhere in the Muslim world for centuries, and their decreasing numbers signaled a change.[6] As eunuchs became more difficult to traffic into Iran, their presence became increasingly equated with the wealth and pomp of the Qajar court. Most significantly, however, their deaths marked the end of an era, not only the gradual end of enslavement but also the end of a particular lifestyle, gendered spaces, and gendered categories that operated along a spectrum rather than as a binary.

The forced visibility of royal eunuchs indicated a healthy palace operation, one where the shah had a lavish harem, his wives numerous and heirs plenty. The eunuchs, then, became a visual symbol for the health and the virility of the court, as their presence indicated the presence of sexually active women of childbearing age. The gendered spaces of the court meant that many who visited—nobility, ambassadors, and other heads of state—would not have seen the women who resided there, including wives, children, and enslaved individuals. Eunuchs, however, would have indicated their presence instead.[7] Their looming deaths threatened the health of the court, the ability to maintain a harem, and the ability to visually project the health and future of the dynasty to others. Their gradual extinction ultimately brought their enslavement as a forced visibility into sharper focus, leading to their memorialization in photography.

In this chapter, I focus on the literary and visual representations of eunuchs where they symbolized the Qajar court. Together, I demonstrate how the visibility of eunuchs served as a shorthand for prestigious enslavement, and how this was wielded by the Qajar court as a sign of their pomp and circumstance, and by their detractors as an image of their vile backwardness. Finally, I highlight how the photographs of eunuchs, which had been taken as a sort of memorialization of their presence, ultimately led to a very different type of legacy—one of blackface and minstrelsy. Because of their proximity to power, eunuchs were among the first people to be photographed and to photograph, as Naser ed-Din Shah trained a few of them as assistants in this regard.[8] The camera's recent arrival in Iran allowed photographers to document and memorialize the last generations of royal eunuchs, who despite their castrations had come to represent the fertility and virility of a functioning court.

Eunuchs represented a liminal, "in-between" space that, once eliminated, left a void in a gendered spectrum that remained unfilled. The fluidity of gender and sexuality in modern Iran has remained a central topic of analysis, and scholars including Afsaneh Najmabadi and Staci Gem Schweiller have attributed changing categories of gender to European influence or the advent of photography.[9] I argue that while both of these may be true, the extinction of eunuchs as a common category of gender within Iran also contributed to the normative idea of a gender binary where male and female genders were viewed as distinctly oppositional to each other during the early twentieth century.[10] The disappearing presence of eunuchs made gender appear less like a continuum and more like a clear duality in Iranian society.

In the case of Qajar Iran, eunuchs represented a link between men and women on the gender continuum. They dressed in clothes meant for men and were typically given masculine names, but their place at court largely revolved around the harem and women's spaces. While scholarly arguments about the gendered status of men and women during the Qajar period have rested on their sexual abilities, the gendered status of eunuchs was distinct, representing a category that existed independently of their sexual abilities. This is because the severity and extent of their castrations varied: some eunuchs still maintained sexual lives and took on marital partners, while others did not participate in sexual activities.[11] Regardless, some eunuchs have been described as symbols of sexual attraction, which I discuss below. In her historical novel *In the Palace of Flowers*, Victoria Princewill has imagined what kinds of sexual relations may have existed, coerced or consenting, between eunuchs and their enslavers, men or women.[12]

Eunuchs were often referred to with honorifics, their first names always accompanied with a title such as *agha*, *aqa*, *haji*, or *khan*. Three of these terms are definitively masculine. *Agha*, however, was a title used primarily for women and for eunuchs. *Agha* did not sound quite so different than *Aqa*, and it involved slight inflection to indicate one's castrated status rather than to ascribe a feminine identity to them entirely. When used in the title of a eunuch, however, I translate it here as *Mr.* to capture the respect of the term, although *Mr.* does not express the gendered connotations. Despite these expressions of respect, however, their legacy was hamstrung by their inability to leave behind biological heirs, leaving their memory vulnerable to the whims of their enslavers.

A STORY TO JUSTIFY CASTRATION

The presence of eunuchs at court rested on the sexual anxieties of noblemen and the possibility of enslaved men intermingling with their wives.[13] This anxiety is perhaps best summarized in the frame story of *A Thousand*

and One Nights. An amalgamation of stories from across Asia and North Africa, *A Thousand and One Nights* has been told and retold for centuries.[14] Though *A Thousand and One Nights* is famously remembered for its extravagant stories of hidden treasures and wish-granting jinn, the frame of the story revolves around a pair of royal brothers whose wives betrayed them by having affairs with enslaved men.[15] The story struck a chord with Naser ed-Din Shah. As a young prince in 1846, Naser ed-Din Mirza visited Tabriz, where 'Abd ol-Latif Tasuji's 1845 Persian translation of the Arabic version was read out loud to him.[16] Within two years, Naser ed-Din Shah ascended the throne and commissioned an illuminated manuscript of the piece with no expenses spared. Sani' ol-Molk oversaw forty-two artists working on the project until its completion in 1855.[17] Although the original frame story was set in the Sassanian era, Sani' ol-Molk reimagined it through the lens of the Qajar court and drew on contemporary motifs to depict the clothes, furnishings, and even architectural details.[18] Despite these realistic details, the story was just a fantasy, not only for its inclusion of monsters or talking fish but also because the only enslaved men in the presence of the Qajar harem were castrated and the shah did not have to fear betrayal.

A Thousand and One Nights begins with Shah Zaman, who prepares to leave his kingdom to visit his brother Shahrbaz. Shah Zaman leaves his palace but returns abruptly at the last minute, only to find his wife in the arms of a lover, an enslaved Black man. In the manuscript's illustrations, his fully erect penis is in the hand of Shah Zaman's wife, his nose and lips are exaggerated in shape and size, and a golden earring hangs from his ear, caricaturizing his Blackness and signaling his enslaved status. The manuscript included an illustration of the following scene as well: Shah Zaman kills his wife next to her murdered lover, his eyes rolled back, his mouth gaped open, and his penis flaccid.

Shah Zaman arrives at his brother's palace, morose and depressed. He declines his brother's invitations to go out for a hunt, only to witness his brother's wife in the arms of her lover, another enslaved Black man, amid a garden orgy of enslaved men and women. Sani' ol-Molk's illustration depicts him as fully erect as well. While Shah Zaman finds relief in witnessing this betrayal of his brother, Shahrbaz deals with his anger and contempt violently, marrying a new virgin woman every night and executing her the next morning until he marries Shaherzad, who narrates riveting tales with cliffhangers every night, causing the king to postpone her execution until he realizes his love for her.

Although eunuchs did appear throughout the story of *A Thousand and One Nights*, the frame story was only possible because of their absence, where women were intermingling with other men whenever they thought the princes had left. Had eunuchs been present guarding the harem, they would have protected the princes' honor, preventing men from entering the gendered space and engaging in sexual liaisons. A healthy court—one that appeared orderly, where the wives appeared devoted to the shah—relied on these enslaved and castrated men.

PHOTOGRAPHING JEWELS

In a seated portrait likely taken in 1872 (fig 3.1), Agha Jowhar sits upright with impeccable posture. His eyes were closed; his lips pursed. His face was long, his fingers elegantly extended, and his height barely contained by the wooden chair from India, said to have been one of Mahd ʿOlya's favorite chairs.[19] His name, Agha Jowhar—"Mr. Jewel"—reflected the kinds of typical names given to enslaved men, equating their presence to a string of bright gems meant to reflect its owner's wealth.

Agha Jowhar's portrait was one of a series which included the photographs of many of the shah's eunuchs, including Bashir Khan (fig 3.2). He was clearly the oldest of the group, face gaunt, eyes narrowed, hunched over. Who was Bashir Khan? Was he the same Bashir Khan who had raised the shah and served as the chief eunuch of the harem until his execution in 1859? During the summer of 1859, in clear defiance of the shah's orders to not follow him into camp, Bashir Khan declared that he had changed the shah's diapers enough to not have to listen to him. Upon learning of his arrival, Naser ed-Din Shah cruelly had him executed there. His body was left unburied in the desert, a final act of forced visibility.[20] Because scholars have dated these photographs to either 1865 or 1872, we can assume this individual photographed was another Agha Bashir, another eunuch given the same name as the former—now murdered—chief eunuch.[21] His name was a popular one for eunuchs; it meant "bearer of good news," as they were often responsible for delivering messages and missives to the shah.[22] After 1859, that chief eunuch was replaced by another named Agha Javaher, "Mr. Jewels."

The similarity and duplicity of the names given to Agha Javaher, Agha Jowhar, or Agha Bashir underscores the imagined interchangeability of the eunuchs, even if they had been granted what seemed like a singular

3.1 Agha Jowhar Khan, Mr. Jewel. (Album 362, no. 34-1, Golestan Palace Photo Archive, Tehran.)

3.2 Bashir Khan, Mr. Bearer of Good News. (Album 362, no. 38-2, Golestan Palace Photo Archive, Tehran.)

status. These names replaced their own names, but whether they were old enough to remember their birth names is another detail we cannot know. Yet Agha Javaher had a lengthy history at the Qajar court. Born in 1800, Agha Javaher was brought as a young castrated child to the court of Fath ʿAli Shah, who gifted him to his son, Kamran Mirza, until the latter succumbed to cholera in 1821. He was then sold to the wife of the head of the treasury, whom he served until he received his manumission papers sometime around 1867. He worked for Galin Khanum, the wife of Naser ed-Din Shah, for a few years before Bashir Khan's murder, at which point, Agha Javaher received the title *khwajeh-bashi* and continued to work in the harem as the chief eunuch.

E ʿtemad os-Saltaneh, the court historian and translator, noted his life and death on Saturday, the seventeenth of Rabiʿ al-Awwal 1305, or December 3, 1887, when Agha Javaher had passed away before sunset. E ʿtemad os-Saltaneh's entry is brief. He began with the weather; it had rained heavily, and ended with Naser ed-Din Shah's hunt. The shah had killed two wild boars. Agha Javaher, Eʿtemad os-Saltaneh writes, was a kind, calm, and good person.[23] He also wrote that he was *maʿqul. Maʿqul* here is a strange word, and I struggled with translating it. Did Eʿtemad os-Saltaneh mean "intelligible," as opposed to the other eunuchs, many of whom spoke pidgin Persian? Or did he mean understandable or sensible in terms of his actions managing the court? Or perhaps he meant it as a synonym for the active term *ʿaqel* (wise) but used the passive tense to both acknowledge and temper his praise of the Black eunuch. Agha Javaher would be buried at the Shah ʿAbd ol-ʿAzim Shrine the next day, the same shrine that would be Naser ed-Din Shah's resting place after his assassination in 1896. They respected him enough to bury him at the local shrine, but not enough to heed his wishes about his preferred place of interment—Najaf, the burial place of ʿAli ibn Abu Talib, the first Shiʾi imam and cousin of the Prophet.[24] Agha Javaher, who for so long outlived his enslavers, was finally laid to rest, a stark contrast to his predecessor's end.

Agha Javaher left behind sixty thousand toman as well as land and villages. The villages were given to ʿAziz os-Soltan, Naser ed-Din Shah's favorite nephew, but it is unclear what happened to the money. Had Agha Javaher set up a charitable endowment in his name? Or was the money dissolved by the government, gifted to other princes of the court? Eunuchs typically had no direct inheritors.[25] Their inheritances either went to charities or were funneled back into the hands of the royal family. While scholars have often pointed out that royal eunuchs were distinct from other enslaved classes because they amassed power and wealth, that power and wealth disappeared almost immediately after their deaths, their money rerouted, their names even given to a new eunuch in their stead.[26]

Marhum.

BEYOND DEATH

Death haunted eunuchs. Castrations were not easy surgeries, and many children did not survive them.[27] These operations were not uniform: some removed the testicles or penis, others removed both.[28] All were dangerous surgeries that risked their lives, made them vulnerable to infections and blood loss, and, if they survived, permanently scarred and mutilated the individual for royal or elite servitude.[29] Reports on castrations within Iran are few, though it likely did occur to meet demands for castrated

3.3 Eunuchs were often made to pose with the princes they served. (Album 302, no. 9, Golestan Palace Photo Archive, Tehran.)

boys.[30] Most castrations seem to have been conducted shortly after the trafficking of young boys from their homelands. These violent operations were merely stops in a larger Middle Passage that structured their enslavement. By the time they arrived at the royal court, they had already survived several severe traumas, and now their inability to bring life into the world served as a critical factor in the roles they would play.

If they survived the castration, however, they were expected to live long lives. Agha Javaher lived for eighty-eight years, passed between several people in ownership and servitude. Before their deaths, eunuchs were a major part of everyday life at the harem, so much so that their presence came to represent the harem and the royal court itself. Their deaths touched the court entirely, creating some disruption until they were replaced by another enslaved, castrated man, perhaps given a similar name.

Years after Naser ed-Din Shah's rash execution of Bashir Khan, he could no longer afford to murder his eunuchs. And although their lives may have been spared, violence against them was still tolerated. These instances are often mentioned as an aside, like where Taj os-Saltaneh mentioned 'Aziz os-Soltan firing a gun and permanently injuring an-other eunuch, 'Abdollah, in the leg, causing a limp for the rest of his life.[31] Or the photograph of another eunuch that shows Agha Davud propping himself on a crutch, the caption explaining that he had become injured after wrestling with an enslaved woman forty days prior.[32] Or when another eunuch, Agha Sa'id Khwajeh, delivered an aggressive letter on behalf of a vizier to Zell os-Soltan, the eunuch deflected the grave situation to avoid punishment as best as he could with humor.[33] These were all everyday forms of violence that the eunuchs had to navigate, even as their lives became rarer and more valuable with time.

With the diminishing avenues of enslavement and castration, the deaths of eunuchs represented a looming extinction of their roles and the maintenance of royal rule. Their omnipresence at court resulted in their regular inclusion in court photography, but their pending deaths seemed to color the photographs differently. Their inclusion in photographs, especially in staged portraits with children (as in figs. 2.2 and 3.3), would have preserved the contours of rapidly changing court life for these young royals, who had enslaved rows of eunuchs for their comforts. Naser ed-Din Shah's cataloging of eunuchs and other enslaved people hinged on the political and social moment. His government was, after all, legally responsible for the abolition of the slave trade, even if halfheartedly enforced.

When the last Caucasian eunuch at the Qajar harem passed away in the mid-nineteenth century, his death created a visible absence after the centuries of white eunuchs at the royal court.[34] But despite the halted traffic of enslaved Caucasians into Iran during the earlier half of the nineteenth century, Naser ed-Din Shah managed to enslave a few more white eunuchs until the last years of his reign. They were photographed and mentioned in several places, a temporary reassurance that this royal tradition of enslaving castrated boys and men to serve the harem was still a reality.

Photographs of royals surrounded by eunuchs and attendants were not limited to children; they included the shah and others as well, as a way of visually reinscribing the functioning virility of the court through those visibly infertile. The presence of eunuchs indicated that the shah, unlike the princes of A Thousand of One Nights, had control of his court, even if the viewer did not have access to the harems directly. These photographs, paired with the brief references made to them in memoirs and daily journals, indicate more than just the virility of the court. They also point to a racial dichotomy between the Caucasian and Abyssinian eunuchs, wherein the Caucasian eunuchs are identified as white, and the Abyssinian eu-

3.4 A lack of facial hair distinguishes the eunuchs from the others. ("Group Portrait: Naser ed-Din Shah and His Eunuchs," photographed by Antoin Sevruguin. Myron Bement Smith Collection [FSA A.4], Freer Gallery of Art and Arthur M. Sackler Gallery Archives, Gift of Myron Bement Smith, Antoin Sevruguin, FSA A.4 2.12.GN.51.02.)

nuchs as Black. Within this racial gradient, Iranians occupied a nonracialized zone from which they could use *white* and *Black* as racial labels that identified an enslavable other.

In a photograph of Naser ed-Din Shah and his attendants (fig. 3.4), a few white eunuchs appear in the crowd of nearly twenty attendants standing around the shah. Their presence is marked by their pale skin and lack of facial hair, a distinct contrast to those with stylized mustaches and the few Abyssinian eunuchs present. The second person from the left, ʿAziz Khan Khwajeh,[35] was noted for his beauty, a trope that seems to have framed the presence of white eunuchs at the Qajar court.[36] Jean-Baptiste Feuvrier, who served as a court physician from 1889 to 1892, described ʿAziz Khan's noted beauty in his memoir: "Tall, slender, with fine features, a pale white face, a soft beardless face, which give him the appearance of a young girl in spite of having thirty years. How many I have seen, especially in Russia, giving attentions to him normally reserved for the fair sex, which was very awkward for the shy Aziz Khan. He was thus often taken for a woman in man's clothes, whereas in reality he is only a eunuch of the royal *andarun*, lent by his mistress to Emin es Sultan."[37] 'Aziz Khan's feminine appearance made him the object of desire to men on multiple occasions. While Najmabadi's research has demonstrated that young men were often attractive to older men, only outgrowing their attractiveness with the emergence of their full facial hair, the description of 'Aziz Khan's beauty indicates a different kind of attractiveness which the eunuch could not grow out of—they simply existed in it.[38]

Foreigners like Feuvrier were not the only ones who described Caucasian eunuchs in complimentary terms; 'Azod od-Dowleh also remembered the Caucasian eunuchs of his childhood similarly. In his memoir written in 1886, where he provided the names of the eunuchs he remembered so that future generations could remember them as well, he only provided details on the lives of the Caucasian eunuchs. He described one as a "Yusuf of the court," and another as the "partner of the court."[39] The only Caucasian eunuch described in less generous terms was a certain Khosrow Khan, who openly resented his enslavement and reminded the court of his noble origins.[40]

Abyssinian eunuchs, however, were not described in terms of beauty and attraction, and their pasts were seldom acknowledged. Black eunuchs were often described by Iranians and non-Iranians alike as extremely tall and overbearing. In that same portrait of Naser ed-Din Shah and his attendants (see fig. 3.4), Haji Sarvar Khan stands to the back, nearly a head taller than the next tallest person in the photograph. As the chief eunuch, Haji Sarvar Khan was also given the title *E'temad ol-Haram*, or "the Reliance of the Harem," a position he held from 1887 until Naser ed-Din Shah's assassination in 1896.[41] Like Agha Javaher, Haji Sarvar Khan had also moved between enslavers, first serving Dust 'Ali Khan Mo'ayyer ol-Mamalek 'Nezam od-Doleh' and later Naser ed-Din Shah.[42] His responsibilities would have ranged from greeting ambassadors or beating those who failed to greet royalty appropriately with a wooden cane.[43] Feuvrier wrote about him as well, calling the head eunuch "a great Abyssinian, more than two meters tall, with legs and arms like those I have seen on other eunuchs, that have developed beyond measure."[44] The power entrusted to him and other eunuchs determined the day-to-day happenings of the royal harem. Here Taj os-Saltaneh describes Agha Nuri, assistant to the harem custodian:

> It behooves me to describe this chief eunuch to you. About forty years of age, he was sallow-complexioned, ugly and repulsive, and

had a strident voice. When he announced the *qoroq*, especially, his voice could be heard from a great distance. He wore a white sash around his perpetually dirty blue frock from which hung an enormous bunch of keys, and he carried a sturdy cane in his hands. Exceptionally cruel and fearless, he treated everyone with cold reserve. He had special charge of the entrance to the *andarun* and jealously watched all the comings and goings. No one entered or left the seraglio without his permission. Even His Majesty the Sultan's wives, after obtaining their husband's leave, needed to be dismissed by Agha Nuri Khan. If he saw fit, he could deny them permission. The thirty or forty eunuchs who served in the harem had all been committed to his charge by the harem custodian. He took his job very seriously and was far more attentive and exacting than his master. The care of all the ladies had been entrusted to him.[45]

The princess described Agha Nuri Khan in much harsher terms, not at all like Feuvrier's description of 'Aziz Khan. His "strident voice" could be attributed to his castration, which Hathaway notes rendered older eunuchs' voices like that of a "shrieking woman."[46] His "dirty frock" too could have resulted from his castration, as eunuchs were known to soil themselves due to their incontinence.[47] 'Aziz Khan was simply noted for his fine, soft features and his shyness around unwanted sexual attention. By contrast, Agha Nuri was deemed ugly.

The power of eunuchs limited how people viewed them. In his memoir of life at Naser ed-Din Shah's court, his grandson Dust 'Ali Khan described Agha Bahram, another commanding eunuch of the harem, as having "a formidable appearance: large, red eyes, strong cheekbones, and large protruding lips. When he laughed, one could see his boar-like teeth shine through."[48] Dust 'Ali Khan's description blends reality with a dark, racist fantasy. Agha Bahram did not have red eyes. Nor did he have boar-like teeth. These descriptions only make sense in the context of a warped view of Blackness, a twisted perspective that gave enslaved Black eunuchs special nonhuman characteristics. Dust 'Ali Khan further notes that Agha Bahram was respected by all at court—by the shah, his viziers, noblemen—and that he could solve all important problems. His portrait (fig. 3.5) was not unlike those of Agha Jowhar and Bashir Khan, and it incorporated the same key elements: eunuch, chair, studio backdrop.

But Agha Bahram's portrait was different. It exuded a sense of strength. Labeled with his name and title—"Agha Bahram, Amin-i Aqdasi's

3.5 Agha Bahram, whose album frame stifled his pose. (Album 330, no. 9, Golestan Palace Photo Archive.)

آغا بهرام خواجه باشی اندرون

eunuch"—the portrait conveyed the image of a healthy eunuch with steady composure. His upright posture and strong gaze evoked a sense of control in the photograph, as if he was about to stand and leave to sort out the problems of the harem as soon as his portrait was taken. Even the tightly cropped photograph barely fit into the oval album slot, reinforcing the impression of his domineering presence.

In a photograph of Naser ed-Din Shah and his eunuchs (see fig. 3.4), however, Naser ed-Din Shah himself appears aged, holding a cane with one hand and resting the other hand on the head of Agha Moham-mad Khan, a namesake of the Qajar dynasty's founder. Contrary to the stereotypes of eunuchs as tall and lanky, Agha Mohammad Khan seems to have had dwarfism. He was photographed often. When he was pho-tographed next to children, only his wrinkles distinguished him as an adult.[49] Photographers even went as far as seating him on a chair atop a couch to photograph him at their preferred height.[50] And while research-ers have described Agha Mohammad Khan as a favorite of the court, it is easy to see that his presence was often viewed as a sort of entertainment.[51] His enslavers would call him Faqir ol-Qaʿemeh—"Poor of Height"—and make him assume all sorts of different poses and positions, to both highlight and humiliate him as a little eunuch.[52]

The diminishing numbers of eunuchs paired with the growing objectification of their bodies meant that individuals like Agha Mohammad Khan were under increased scrutiny. For centuries, eunuchs had been replaceable with similar names and roles passed down to each other. Now, in the late nineteenth century, the entire institution of eunuchs guarding harems was threatened, and their presence was viewed perhaps not as abnormal but certainly no longer as normal or replicable. Court photographers took their portraits in order to remember not only the pomp and wealth they represented but also their very existence. They had to be photographed before their deaths, which would threaten the routines they were enslaved to maintain. With these photographs, royals hoped to keep their memories of their lavish lifestyle alive.

In life and in death, these photos were always for the enslavers, not the enslaved.[53]

CARICATURING POWER

Beyond photography, eunuchs came to symbolize the monarchy and power in ways they perhaps did not expect. While the Qajar court had posed its eunuchs to visually represent the harem, others seized the same imagery to skewer the ruling class for their excesses. Fictional works such as those of Mirza Fath ʿAli Akhundzadeh highlight the racism that framed the lives of eunuchs. For Akhundzadeh, the presence of eunuchs had less to do with the virility of the court and more to do with the cruelty of enslavement.

Akhundzadeh—also known by his Russian name, Akhundov—was an Azeri writer who worked as a translator in the Russian bureaucracy. He lampooned elites and highlighted social injustices in his short stories. He often focused his social critiques on Iranian society,[54] which were either written in Persian or translated by a close correspondent during his lifetime.[55] Critiques of human relationships were central to Akhundzadeh's writing. He set his stories against the backdrop of Persianate nobility and included the enslavement of eunuchs to critique the politics of governing elites.[56] In "Vazir Khan-e Lankaran," Akhundzadeh highlights the racist abuse that enslaved eunuchs endured in the homes of elites. While the story follows the family of a powerful vizier and his two wives, the eunuch, Agha Mas'ud-e Siyah, or "the Black Agha Mas'ud," plays a minor role in the story. He first appears to hand his enslaver, the vizier, a cup of coffee that he had requested. The vizier turns to receive the coffee, but instead hits the cup and spills it on Agha Mas'ud's head. "Get lost, you half-burned jackass, I have no patience for this. What kind of place is this for drinking coffee?" the vizier yells at Agha Mas'ud. Here Akhundzadeh has combined a generic insult, *jackass*, with a racial slur, *half-burned*, which acts as a double entendre for the burning coffee as well as his skin tone.

In another story, "Yusuf Shah," an astrologer predicts misfortune and calamity for Shah 'Abbas, which his viziers decide to avoid by deposing the shah for two weeks until the stars move into a more fortuitous alignment. In the interim, a random man, Yusuf, is placed on the throne and chaos ensues. Yusuf, who has no idea why he has been enthroned, turns to the shah's eunuch Agha Mobarak and asks for clarification: "From your color, I can see that you must be a good person. . . . You have always been in Shah 'Abbas' andarun, so it would be impossible for you not to know of the matter."

In these stories, Akhundzadeh was not concerned with the eunuchs themselves; they are minor characters who stand to the side and fade into the margins of the storyline. But he clearly used the eunuch characters as representative—not of the nobility and elite's virility or wealth but, rather, of their immoral characters and personalities. Yusuf, who was not part of the nobility, addresses the eunuch with some respect, highlighting his color as a sign of his good character. The vizier, on the other hand, yells at the eunuch for his own mistake—a scalding mistake that the eunuch has to pay for both verbally and physically. Akhundzadeh demonstrated how eunuchs were the most knowledgeable about the affairs of court and yet were denied any respect by those who enslaved them. Through his writings, Akhundzadeh associated the Persian ruling class with eunuchs and enslavement more generally. Perhaps this is because of his own family history: Akhundzadeh had an African ancestor who had served at Nader Shah's court.[57]

Others, regardless of their personal associations, would also associate the royal family with their eunuchs. Although the Qajars had propped up eunuchs to represent them when greeting foreign emissaries or other international guests as a sign of their refinement and status, foreigners had come to view the enslavement of eunuchs as depraved and represen-

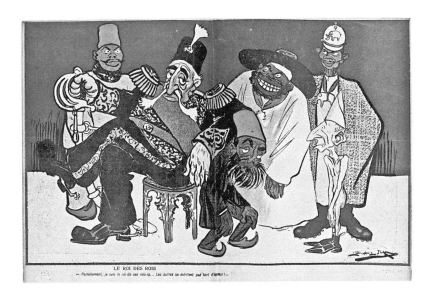

3.6 "The King of Kings." (*L'assiette au beurre*, July 22, 1905, 264–65. https://gallica
.bnf.fr/ark:/12148/bpt6k1048198t/f2.item.)

tative of the excesses of the Crown. After the assassination of Naser ed-
Din Shah in 1896, Mozaffar ed-Din Shah inherited the crown and with
it, the overindulgences of the harem.[58] Although he had a much smaller
harem than his father's, he still enslaved eunuchs to maintain not just the
court's gender boundaries but also its reputation. By the early twentieth
century, the Qajars' reliance on eunuchs was well known in Europe and
the United States, and eunuchs had come to represent a particular image
of the Qajar court: one of incompetence.

On the eve of his arrival in France during his 1905 European tour, the
entire issue of *L'assiette au beurre* lampooned Mozaffar ed-Din Shah, depicting him entering the red-light district out of nostalgia for the harem
or doing a ritual ablution to purify himself from shaking hands with
the French president Emile Loubet. In other pages of the magazine, the
magazine's cartoonist lampooned Europe itself as a blackface caricature
of "civilization."[59] The racist imagery of the magazine also built on knowledge of Mozaffar ed-Din Shah's retinue of eunuchs. In an image labeled
"The King of Kings" (fig. 3.6), the magazine mocked the royal Crown for
its self-aggrandizing title, picturing Mozaffar ed-Din Shah as seated on a
stool, surrounded by Black caricatures portraying several heads of state,
including the sultan of Zanzibar, Ali bin Hamud, who stands to the left,

and the Ethiopian king Menelik II, who grins menacingly to the right. The Ottoman sultan Abdulhamit II appears as a Black man and props up Mozaffar ed-din Shah's arm.[60] The caption, in Mozaffar ed-Din's voice, reads, "Excellent, I am the king of these kings, no one else has received such honor," while Menelik II bends forward, as the Ethiopian Crown also referred to itself as "the king of kings."

The fashioning of the caricature resembles Qajar court photography of the royal sitting, flanked by Black eunuchs standing around him. In this case, though, these men were not eunuchs but heads of state; L'assiette's commentary was a racist mockery of the excesses of royalty. This imagery demonstrates the extent that the Qajar court had come to be associated with not only their eunuchs but also the photographs of them.[61] Their physical appearances also speak to the caricatures of Africans that had been developed in European periodicals, now applied to a vision of the Qajar king and his entourage.[62]

PLAYING BLACK

But one did not have to look abroad, to France or elsewhere, to find examples of racist comedies that mocked enslaved eunuchs. Despite the elevated status of eunuchs, they were still enslaved and thus subject to mockery at the Qajar court as well. Court jesters, like Karim Shireh-yi and others who followed him, set the stage for clown performances to delineate the contours of a new genre of comedy, siyah-bazi—literally, "playing Black"—that drew directly from the stereotypes of eunuchs.

Known by his clown title, "Intoxicated Karim," Karim Shireh-yi's reputation at Naser ed-Din Shah's court is widely known, and references to him and his troupe continue to circulate in Iranian popular culture, where he is remembered as the father of Iranian comedy.[63] Born in Isfahan, Karim left his hometown and arrived in Tehran sometime around the mid- to late nineteenth century, where he charmed Naser ed-Din Shah and served as chief court jester. In the name of humor, Naser ed-Din Shah gave Karim Shireh-yi carte blanche to say whatever he wanted, whenever, without fear of retribution. Although some admired his gall for critiquing powerful free members of the court, his style gave rise to later troupes that focused their attention on the enslaved as well. With a free rein, Karim, along with his all-male troupe and others after them, engaged with a cavalier mimicry of Blackness. Although the specific individuals involved with his troupe alternated, they were referred to as *jama'at-e moqaleddin*, or "a gathering of imitators." Their imitated accents and mannerisms of specific people were often set in the same places where they performed.[64] The humor of these performances relied on the audience's knowledge of the people they imitated. The more ridiculous their imitation, the more energized their audience's response.

Photography, then a novel and exciting piece of technology, encapsulated its own genre of mockery. Consider, for example, this photograph of a sleeping lion in chains with a few tamers kneeling around her (fig. 3.7), taken by the famed court and commercial photographer Antoin Sevruguin sometime in the 1880s.[65] Sevruguin's photograph entered the tourist market, and several versions of it were printed, including one where Sevruguin had whitewashed the background to emphasize the men and the lion more sharply.[66] The photograph made for the perfect souvenir for tourists who wanted proof of Orientalist fantasies that Persians could tame animals. Another photograph of men (clowns) taken during Mozaffar ed-Din Shah's court makes light of the photograph. A few "hunters" stood and knelt around the "hunted" man; one propped up his leg, while another held a snake protruding from his pants, a stand-in for his penis (fig. 3.8). Their facial expressions were as serious as in Sevruguin's portrait, as if they were in the presence of a very large and dangerous animal, which underscores the vulgar humor peddled in the photograph. The machismo of mocking the hunted's oversized penis underscored the overt sexual humor employed in the troupe's portrayal of eunuchs. Their castration served as the reason they were not only enslaved but also featured in comedy shows at their expense.

Jesters mocked photographs of eunuchs. In figure 3.9, a clown dressed as a eunuch stared back at the camera. The eerily painted eyes on his papier-mâché mask made him like he was looking straight ahead. Aside from the whites of the eyes, the mask was painted entirely in the same dark hue, with no differentiation between the lips, eyebrows, or skin tone. This not only added to the creepiness of the mask but also allowed it to obscure its mistakes for including facial hair—a mustache and small beard—for a eunuch. The framing of the clown's photograph is unmistakably like those taken by Naser ed-Din Shah, where the eunuchs appear seated against a plain background, wearing their typical rounded hats and overcoats.

3.7 Hunters with the Hunted, part 1. (Stephen Arpee Collection of Sevruguin Photographs [FSA A2011.03], Freer Gallery of Art and Arthur M. Sackler Gallery Archives, Gift of Stephen Arpee, 2011, Antoin Sevruguin, FSA A2011.03 A.01a.)

3.8 Hunters with the Hunted, part 2. (Glass plate no. 1869, Golestan Palace Photo Archive.)

The similarities between the photographs of Naser ed-Din Shah's eunuchs and the masked minstrel were not coincidental. Photographs of the minstrels (figs. 3.8–10) were taken by Mirza Ebrahim Khan, a court photographer during Mozaffar ed-Din Shah's rule (1896–1906). His father, Mirza Ahmad 'Akkas, had served as a court photographer during Naser ed-Din Shah's rule (1848–96) and was privy to his taste in photography. Mirza Ahmad had trained his son himself, and Mirza Ebrahim had grown up accompanying his father on his projects.[67] This shared visual lexicon, however, diverges from the original intentions. Unlike the photographs of eunuchs that memorialized their existence, the photograph of the clown eunuch mocks them on two levels: first, to taunt their memories; and second, to ridicule the very act of photographing a eunuch. The photograph of the minstrel suggests that eunuchs were not only abnormal or grotesque in their physiques but also undeserving of the special attention they received.[68]

While later minstrels would grease their faces with a black ointment, the clown in figure 3.9 wore a mask, making his costume easily assembled. The deep wrinkles and impressions of the papier-mâché, paired with the inclusion of facial hair, indicate that the mask was intended not to create a realistic or lifelike resemblance but, rather, to surprise or horrify the viewer. Eric Lott describes the black mask in US minstrelsy shows as offering "a way to play with collective fears of a degraded and threatening—and male—*other* while at the same time maintaining some symbolic control over them."[69] The mask could be removed or manipulated, a metaphor for the eunuchs' servility and ultimate exclusion from society.

Photographs of the clown "eunuchs" in group settings reveal more about the role of race in the humor. In one photograph (fig. 3.10), three men sit on a bench, each playing specific characters: a Black eunuch, a Black king, and a white eunuch. The Black "eunuch" did not wear a mask. The jester's own Blackness sufficed to play the role. Instead, he held a wide-eyed expression that conjures similar imagery from American minstrelsy performances. His expression, coupled with his plain uniform, made his role as a eunuch recognizable and clear. The white eunuch, however, is wearing a papier-mâché mask similar to the one discussed in figure 3.9. His long, thin nose and wide, droopy eyes all represent a caricaturized Caucasian eunuch. A light-skinned individual wore this mask, the color of which resembled his exposed hands, resting on his legs. Although the discourse of Aryanism was steadily gaining traction in Iran, these performers viewed themselves as both racially different from and

3.9 Court jester in papier-mâché mask. (Glass plate no. 1475, Golestan Palace Photo Archive.)

3.10 Court jesters imitating a king and his eunuchs. (Glass plate no. 288, Golestan Palace Photo Archive.)

visibly too similar to the Caucasians.[70] An Iranian could not simply perform the role of a white eunuch by manipulating his facial expressions into a wide-eyed look or a blank expression. Because it was difficult to distinguish Caucasians and Iranians in court photographs, the clown needed to visually claim his role as an enslaved Caucasian eunuch and prevent being taken for a "regular Iranian." An Iranian clown playing the role of an enslaved Caucasian required the use of a mask. The strange, elongated mask evokes an intellectually deficient personality rather than a demure one.

Between the two "eunuchs" was another Black man, smiling underneath a bejeweled crown and embroidered robe. He, like other Black men in circus and comedic troupes, was likely a freedman who had joined in search of economic opportunity.[71] The inversion of race—a Black king flanked by a white and Black eunuch—indicates the malleable representation of race in these early minstrel shows. The elasticity of the roles remained, as Saidiya Hartman has noted, "within the confines of the tolerable."[72] In this case, a Black king might have seemed to challenge the perceived racial order, but if the show presented his role as ironic, it would have remained within the confines of the tolerable. In the following years, when Seyyed ʿAbdollah Behbahani was called Shah Siyah—"the Black king"—as a slur during the Constitutional Revolution, one imagines that those using the slur were also conjuring the same imagery that delegitimized Black power in minstrel shows.[73]

Light-skinned Iranian clowns required masks in roles for the enslaved, white or Black, to prevent people from mistaking them for a different kind of character, as though to signal that their own enslavement was impossible. Black clowns, however, appeared regularly without masks, as their skin tone *was* the humor. Although clowns and jesters were typically non-Black Iranians, the few Black men who joined occupied a particular space. Unlike the others, they did not need masks to imitate eunuchs or other Black men. As freedmen, they were imitating past forms of themselves, only without the mutilation.[74]

These clowns and their shows also identified the changing boundaries of what was normal within Iranian society. The same clown who played the king was photographed again several years later, still performing at the Qajar court. Dressed in nothing but a loincloth, the Black clown was joined by two others, one little, one fat.[75] The photograph and their performance confirmed that their bodies were strange and of interest to viewers.[76] But fatness was common at the Qajar court, as was the presence of Black

3.11 Haji Firuz. (Album 362, no. 42-1, Golestan Palace Photo Archive.)

people, and a little person, Agha Mohammad Khan, served as a eunuch at Naser ed-Din Shah's court. So why present their bodies as abnormal? Social norms were in flux, and what had once been considered normal or beautiful was now foreign or repulsive.

Minstrels did not limit their ridicule to enslaved Black people and their bodies. Other photographs show clowns standing on stilts, their faces covered with bearded masks wearing turbans and *thobe*s to evoke a stereotype of Arab men.[77] E'temad os-Saltaneh's memoir shows that even an Austrian military routine taught to the Iranian army was subject to exaggerated imitations at these court jester performances.[78] Caucasian eunuchs, little people, and fat people were all mocked alongside Black people, creating new boundaries of abnormality.

These troupes harnessed the crudest of stereotypes, creating a new series of memories attached to Black eunuchs, their bodies, and those early photographs of them. These norms would shift again with the 1929 Manumission Law. As freedmen left the troupes, the genre would solidify into the form that continues today. These performances would be canonized as a genre unto itself, "playing Black" or *siyah-bazi*.

——————

The loudest legacy of enslaved Black eunuchs, their memory, and how they continue to be connected to blackface is probably best conveyed in the story of Haji Firuz, which I discuss further in chapter 5. Throughout his lifetime, Naser ed-Din Shah enslaved many eunuchs at court, some of whom he watched enter old age and pass away. One of these eunuchs was Haji Firuz, who had served in the harem until Naser ed-Din Shah appointed him to a camp.[79] The move garnered pushback from the harem, and reports of women crying over his leave reached the shah.[80] Alongside Bashir Khan and Agha Jowhar, Naser ed-Din Shah also photographed Haji Firuz (fig. 3.11), placing his portrait alongside the others in his album. Eventually Haji Firuz passed away, and Naser ed-Din Shah returned to the album to write *marhum* to the side. Within a generation, photographs of eunuchs like Haji Firuz went from representing the Qajar court to becoming the center of vulgar comedies.

Would Haji Firuz be forgotten? Haji Firuz, "the Victorious Haji," shared his name with others across Iran, other enslaved Black men.[81] Soon he would share his name with a holiday caricature in blackface. Many did forget him.

PART II
ERASURE

Many date Iran's modernity with the rise of Reza Shah and his reforms, including the Westernization of people's dress, the creation of European-styled urban centers, and other changes in the outer appearance of Iranian society. In the southern port city of Daylam, however, some remember him for a particularly specific encounter. During his centralization campaign of Arabistan in 1924, Reza Shah arrived in Daylam, where he stayed for one night.[1] Throughout his trip, hosting families would sacrifice an animal—usually a goat or a sheep—for the royal's health and success.[2] Upon the shah's arrival to Daylam, however, a family allegedly insisted on sacrificing "a member of their household"—a Black man named Karbalayi Hassan Behbahani.[3]

As the story goes, only the shah himself was able to stop the family from executing their plans. The ability to offer an enslaved human for sacrifice emphasizes the family's wealth while also demonstrating their callous behavior toward human life out of purported respect for the shah. The story continues to be told and retold by some Daylami families, though Reza Shah never mentioned it in his travelogue.[4] He did, however, mention an equally rattling story of an Iranian spice merchant in Karbala who, upon the shah's arrival to the shrine city, tried to sacrifice his own children for him.[5]

Was this the same traumatizing story that is told and retold in Daylam for its shock value? Did the families in Daylam change the sacrifice from children to an enslaved man? Perhaps Karbalayi Hassan Behbahani was not the name of the enslaved Black man but, rather, the name of the spice merchant living in Karbala. Or is it possible that Reza Shah or his editor changed the story from an enslaved Black man to children? Maybe the sacrifice of an enslaved person was too at odds with his imagined modern nation, whereas the sacrifice of a citizen's own children represented how much Iranians loved him and the nation. The shift between the stories demonstrates how narratives get twisted, rewritten, erased, and manipulated.

Five years later, Reza Shah's government would pass the law rendering all slaves free. On a Thursday afternoon right before the Iranian weekend, Majles met to consider a rush bill. It read as follows: "In the country of Iran, no one will be known as a slave [*bardeh*], and any slave who enters Iranian soil or the coastal waters of Iran will be hitherto recognized as free. Whoever buys and sells humans as slaves or treats another human in a proprietary manner or is involved in the trafficking of slaves will be disciplinarily imprisoned for one to three years."[6] Parliamentary members debated the bill briefly; one member voiced his opposition. They voted, and it passed. Iran abolished slavery on February 7, 1929.

Reza Shah never mentioned his encounter in Daylam, and he is not commonly remembered for the Manumission Law. Most people do not remember that enslavement remained legal in Iran until 1929. This is due in part to his own government's erasure of any reminders of enslavement. He wanted them to forget.

4 HISTORIES OF A COUNTRY THAT NEVER ENSLAVED

In 1977, Queen Farah Diba sponsored the *Introduction to the Art of Black Africa* exhibition in Tehran (fig. 4.1). The exhibition featured artifacts borrowed from major African museums in fourteen countries: Mali, Senegal, Guinea, Sierra Leone, Liberia, Côte d'Ivoire, Upper Volta, Ghana, Togo, Benin, Nigeria, Cameroon, Gabon, and Zaire. Objects like hair combs, statues, staffs, swords, and wooden masks were on display for six weeks from November 1 to December 16 and were open to the public mornings and afternoons. The exhibition and its catalog placed importance on a key misconception—that the connections between Iran and Africa were new and ripe for exploration.

> In recent years relations between Iran and the countries of the Black Continent have greatly expanded. Iranian embassies have been opened in many of those countries, and ambassadors and important political figures have come to Tehran from Africa. . . . We are greatly pleased to see our capital has become the meeting place of the strong, flourishing, and living culture of Black Africa with Iran's own rich culture. . . . It is hoped that the efforts . . . [of] "An Introduction to the Art of Black Africa" have constructed a bridge for the passage of all aspects of relations between countries that have been made distant from one another by deserts and seas.[1]

The catalog's introduction continues with a brief history of the continent, including a few paragraphs about colonialism and the Atlantic slave trade.[2] The closest acknowledgment of Iran's history of enslavement was a single sentence that did not actually reference Iran at all: "On the east coast of Africa, too, Zanzibar and other places exported slaves to the markets of Arabia."[3] Passive tense and geographic markers excused Iranians from any responsibility.

Even more galling, the exhibition was held in Bagh-e Ferdows, a renovated nineteenth-century palace once staffed by the Qajars' many attendants, including enslaved East Africans.

The Manumission Law of 1929 began the process of abolition in Iran as one of erasure. Contrary to how it would be framed, the Manumission Law was not merely a formality or a public relations campaign. Those who were still enslaved typically did receive their freedom, but the scope of that freedom was imbalanced. In the simplest of cases, the freedperson might have been elevated to the status of a paid servant, receiving a small allowance while still maintaining the same role. For other freedpeople, their enslaving family would resettle them in a nearby village, asking them to return to perform household chores or serve guests at larger parties or gatherings.[4] A younger freedwoman was sometimes married to her enslaver, changing her status from an enslaved woman to a wife, which allowed him to maintain his sexual access to her within a new legal status.[5] In other situations, the freedperson married a distant relative. It is difficult to locate consent in any of these arrangements, and we can imagine that most were done out of convenience for the enslaving family. Of course, we can assume that not all enslaved people learned of their freedom at once. Some families chose to keep the news of the law from the people they enslaved, instead hiding them from the public and the public from them, a stark contrast to the forced visibility that once defined their enslavement.[6] In any of these situations, the power dynamic—the power imbalance—remained static, even if the formerly enslaved and their descendants were compensated for their labor. Nor did freedpeople ever receive compensation or reparations for their stolen lives. But the trajectory of their lives after abolition has remained unwritten, largely because they were disappeared from urban centers.

In cities where enslaved people—especially those of East African ancestry—had once been visible in public spaces, these shifts dramatically diminished the numbers of Black people. They were either shuttled to nearby villages or kept within the confines of their homes, away from

4.1 Poster for *An Introduction to the Art of Black Africa*. (Author's collection, digital copy held at archive.ajammc.com; photographed by Iylana Nassiri.)

the public eye. Enslaved peoples had once embodied their enslavers' wealth and status. The public nature of enslavement had ensured that anyone would have encountered enslaved people in streets and bazaars as a perpetual reminder of their own status. The manumission of enslaved people ended this practice, and people were less likely to encounter enslaved people and, in turn, people of African ancestry in urban areas. The exception here was in the South, where Black people have been part of the social fabric for centuries. Their presence was often independent of an enslaved ancestry, though not always.

Regardless of their ancestry, all individuals living within Iran received citizenship almost immediately after the 1929 abolition. In the 1930s, the name and citizenship laws legally rendered freedpeople Iranian citizens and equal to other Iranians, including their former enslavers. All Iranians, including freedpeople, received birth certificates and other national documents after 1930 and 1932, when Reza Shah's government made it a requirement for every citizen to have identification documents and standardized family names.[7] The new citizenship of freedpeople, however, was sometimes marred by racial slurs disguised as family names. For most Iranians, receiving birth certificates with official surnames was an opportunity to define their identities, and many chose lofty last names with grand meanings such as "dignified," "intelligent," "respectable." Others chose names that were related to their geographic, ethnic, or regional origins, and some chose names related to their professions. Some families of African ancestry received legal names that directly reflected their African ancestry or former enslaved status, including Zangoi or Zangbari, "of Zanzibar"; Azadi, "free"; and Gholam, "a male slave," while others received Kakai, an intimate racial insult.[8] As with any bureaucratic procedure, the level of consent here was questionable, and while most families chose their own names, a government official could have readily provided a newly freed person with a less desirable name such as a slur.

Unlike other abolition laws around the world, the 1929 Manumission Law did not make freedpeople or Black Iranians into a separate legally recognized class or minority. Instead, they were recognized as fully Iranian, even if their everyday experiences said otherwise. The lack of ethnic or racial designations in any census records or other government documents created its own archival silence, making it more difficult to track down these racist realities.[9] Other silences came from the freedpeople themselves. After 1929, the stigma of enslavement was one that many wanted to forget and avoid in favor of asserting a local Iranian identity, even if their ancestries continued to be discussed in private spaces. Together, these elements have contributed to a collective erasure that makes it difficult to answer questions about those who were once enslaved, their descendants, and whether they were ever able to find freedom.

Abolition as erasure made it possible for non-Black Iranians to deny any history of enslavement within their borders and to "introduce" Black histories into Iran, as though Iran did not itself have a Black history. This chapter focuses on the factors that enabled and cemented these erasures in a matter of decades. It begins with the Manumission Law of 1929, then moves through the textual, architectural, and visual changes that restructured Iranian society to accommodate a new vision of modernity that erased the presence of enslaved or formerly enslaved people entirely. Intellectuals and politicians, as well as urban planners and architects, tacitly rewrote Iran's recent past and complicity in enslaving people, unraveling the institution that had marked high status for centuries. This form of abolition drove freedpeople and their pasts into a forced invisibility on a national scale. In this way, their lives have been redacted from the national discourse.[10] This redaction moves beyond the neglect of Black histories and existence; it encompasses a complete forced disappearance from the national record. This history continues to be denied by many throughout Iran: "We did not have slaves" (*Ma bardeh nadashtim*). The "we" assumes a voice for all Iranians.[11] How did it become so commonly accepted that no Iranians engaged in enslavement? The answer lies at the intersection of a process of erasure, a revisionist narrative, and the peripheralization of Black Iranians.

After the Manumission Law took effect, Reza Shah and his cabinet did little to benefit the freedpeople even as they were granted citizenship in the years to come. Instead, changes erased any footprints of enslavement, and references to the enslaved were destroyed or left unwritten. While Reza Shah erased narratives of Iranian slavery, his son Mohammad Reza Shah introduced revisionist narratives of race and enslavement that would dramatically change worldviews in Iran. Dictionaries, textbooks, and other sources of knowledge left out references to an Iranian history of slavery. *Bardeh-dari* took on an entirely US-oriented connotation, where it now referred to the chattel enslavement of people on cotton plantations in the Americas. The very term that was used to manumit all enslaved people in Iran was now relegated to a foreign and distant place. In the decades that followed the Manumission Law of 1929, narratives about enslavement and race—particularly about Black Americans—supplanted Iranian examples in the national imagination. The promotion of the Aryan myth, coupled with a mangled translation of the Cyrus Cylinder that led to the common refrain "Cyrus the Great freed all the slaves," thoroughly displaced histories of enslavement on a national scale.

A MERE FORMALITY

Almost immediately after his coronation in 1925, Reza Shah prioritized abolition as the first step in Iran's modernity and compatibility with Western values. In 1926, the Iranian diplomat Prince ʿArfa signed onto the Slavery Convention in Geneva and declared that slavery had been long abolished in Iran. He argued that, given Iranian commitment to antislavery efforts, the British need not continue their ongoing naval searches of Iranian boats in the Persian Gulf.[12] One year later, in 1927, the Ministry of Interior publicly affirmed its commitment to international agreements banning the slave trade.[13] In 1929, the minister of justice, ʿAli Akbar Davar, went to Majles with two pieces of legislation: a budgetary bill, and a rush bill on the abolition of enslavement.[14]

Davar introduced the bill as a mere formality, framing the law as one geared toward foreigners unaware of Iran's international obligations to the eradication of enslavement, since Iranians had allegedly abandoned the practice years prior.[15] Davar emphasized the urgency of the bill and asked if anyone was opposed. One representative, Seyyed Reza Firuzabadi, immediately denounced the bill, decrying it as unnecessary. According to Firuzabadi, slavery had already been essentially abolished in Iran. Just two years prior, he shared, he had tried to purchase an enslaved person with the intention of freeing them, but there were none to be found. Firuzabadi described enslavement in Iran as a benevolent institution, one where *vahshi* (wild) and *jangali* (of the jungle) people could assimilate into a civilized, Iranian Muslim culture. Other parliamentary representatives were noted to have agreed with him in the minutes, though their names were exempted from the record. Another representative named Dashti echoed Davar's point that the traffickers of people to Iran's coastline in the Persian Gulf were generally foreigners, again deflecting any Iranian responsibility for the trade or ongoing enslavement. In sum, Davar, Firuzabadi, and other representatives all agreed that enslavement was no longer an issue in Iran; they differed only on whether it merited parliamentary attention if a de facto abolition had already occurred. The brief debate ended with a vote, and by the end of the assembly, Majles declared the bill law.

The text of the Manumission Law was short, but in those few lines, it quietly redefined enslavement as it abolished it. The law was printed on the last page of the minutes, which sold for a single *qeran* later that day.

HEADLINE NEWS

The Persian language has a broad and nuanced range of vocabulary for describing enslaved people, from terms that define their enslavement per gender, birth status, the type of forced labor, and more. The Manumission Law used *bardeh*, a catch-all term for all slaves irrespective of gender or status. The decision to use *bardeh* seems innocuous, except that the term had typically not appeared in legally binding or socially relevant documents prior to the legislation. Other terms were far more ubiquitous— *kaniz, gholam, zar kharid, khadameh, khanehzad*. Even Firuzabadi and others referred to *kaniz* and *gholam*—enslaved women and men—in their parliamentary discussion of the legislation. Perhaps the text used *bardeh* for the sake of clarity, since *kaniz* and *gholam* could technically also refer to servants. *Kaniz* and *gholam* were not so vague—they had, up until abolition, been the prime terms for describing the enslaved in a myriad of legal documents.[16] But *bardeh* and *bardeh-forushi* had been used in international legal writings with Europeans—for example, the 1882 treaty with the British and the 1890 Brussels Conference—perhaps because they were more easily translated into English as "slave" and "slave trade."[17]

Like the English term *slave*, *bardeh* served as a catch-all term that referred to all enslaved persons and did not distinguish based on status or gender.[18] Further, *bardeh* neatly corresponded with *bardeh-dari* (the holding of slaves), the closest word to *slavery* in Persian, and *bardeh-forushi* (the selling of slaves) to *slave trade*. *Kaniz* and *gholam* did not fit neatly into similarly all-encompassing terms.[19] There was no such corresponding term to describe the overarching system in which they existed. Instead, their presence was a foregone conclusion in the society they were enslaved in. The implementation of *bardeh* and *bardeh-dari* on a state level reflected the adoption of a new vision of enslavement and abolition, where the presence of enslaved people was not integral to society but, rather, a subsystem of society that could be added or removed through legal action. The use of *bardeh* publicly redefined the Iranian understanding of enslavement in 1929.

"No one will be known as a *bardeh*" may have seemed like a strange announcement, since Persian speakers did not usually call the individuals they had enslaved as *bardeh* in the first place. But that was the first line of the Manumission Law. And *Ettela'at*, Iran's major daily newspaper in Persian, also reported the ratification of the new law with the same language later that afternoon.[20] The first column on the newspaper's front page announced the new law with the headline "Bardeh-forushi," or "The Slave Trade." The article repeated the same framework that the parliamentary minutes had described—that slavery had been "abandoned" for quite a while now and this law was merely passed as a formality. One wonders why a rush bill and a column on the front page of a popular newspaper would be devoted to an institution that both claimed was already gone from the Iranian landscape. After all, Parliament had also voted on another law pertaining to taxes on butchered meat, the implementation of which would have been more immediately relevant to the population.[21] But the newspaper did not feature the new meat taxes on its front page. Instead, it reported on the Manumission Law.

Why devote so much energy to dismantling an institution that allegedly had not existed for years? For starters, one could argue that it was because enslavement still had a real presence in Iran. But *Ettela'at*'s article highlighted a different point: "Our government has been in support of [abolition] and was not interested in the slightest possibility that in any corner of the world, someone could say that slaves were still being sold in Iran."[22] The law was out of concern for Iran's reputation, not any concern for those living under enslavement. The idea that Iranians did not and had not engaged in enslaving other people became paramount to the Manumission Law.

The minister of justice, the parliamentary representatives, the very text of the Manumission Law, and even the *Ettela'at* news article all echoed the same reasoning: *Iranians were not the ones enslaving people; it was those foreigners, people who didn't understand Iran's international obligation to abolition.* All emphasized that the law targeted foreigners, as though the idea of Iranians enslaving or smuggling people into Iran was preposterous. "Foreigners in the Persian Gulf" conjured imagery of Arab traffickers. International media outlets seemed to think similarly as well. In the days and months that followed, newspapers around the world reported on Iran's Manumission Law. The *New York Times* described Iran's move to abolish slavery as one that may "influence other Oriental countries to do away with slavery" and framed Iran as a leading country in abolition efforts in the region.[23] A few years later, in 1931, the *Times* of London published a similar article on Iranian history and geography with a section on the slave trade, which detailed the efforts to halt the trafficking, including British involvement.[24]

Although the public discourse seemed to praise Iranians for their newly asserted abolitionist ideology, privately the geopolitical considerations concerned the British, as they still patrolled the Persian Gulf under the guise of abolishing slavery. Since Iran's 1848 government decree, the manumission documents had been granted unevenly, usually involving the escape of an enslaved person either to local government offices or to the British Residency, and even then, freedom was not guaranteed.[25] The British had long used nineteenth-century treaties aimed at abolishing enslavement to search Iranian ships in the Gulf. Iran's new law, however, declared enslavement illegal and freed all enslaved people, thus negating the need for the British to oversee this process. For months after the Manumission Law, the British struggled to articulate a reason internally to justify their presence, with messages such as "I agree that Persia cannot be given right of search on the High Seas" or that the passage of the law would "weaken our position internally."[26] The ability to board ships was a key extension of their power in the Persian Gulf, and the British were especially concerned about whether the new law undermined the 1882 treaty that had given them the ability to board vessels under the pretense of abolition. As the British debated how to maintain their post in the Persian Gulf, they continued to receive those who had escaped from enslavement seeking their help.[27] The British Residency and consulate general in Bushehr had dealt with individuals seeking freedom for decades prior to 1929. After the Manumission Law, the British maintained their operations in the Residency, continuing to intervene in cases where enslaved people had been denied their freedom. As the number of cases involving enslaved East Africans had been reduced, the British turned their focus to enslaved Baluchis.[28] Because of the famine in Baluchistan during the 1920s, the British questioned whether those seeking help were actually in need of freedom papers or were just using them for food. In return for their room and board, the British officials had them work around the consulate.[29] In other words, the British replicated some of the patterns of domestic enslavement in the name of freedom. The British referred to the "powerlessness of the [Iranian] government" repeatedly throughout their documents, perhaps to assure themselves of their own purpose, but as former slaves no longer required manumission papers to prove their freedom, the British role in abolition had been significantly reduced.[30]

Iranian newspapers told a different story. As the traffic of East Africans came to an end, internal populations—especially the Baluch, continued to be vulnerable to enslavement in the Persian Gulf.[31] In November 1929, the newspaper *Shafaq-e Sorkh* printed a short article about the continued trafficking of people along the Makran coast. The article, titled "For the Prevention of Smuggling," was based on a report given to the Ministry of Finance. The article raised questions about the efficacy of the Manumission Law in the Persian Gulf, where traffickers used loads of tobacco to smuggle enslaved men and women in Rudbar, Bashakard, and Baluchistan. The report, like discussions around the Manumission Law, explicitly blamed Arab traders for the ongoing traffic.[32] If the government does nothing to prevent the expansion of the trade, the article continued, it will have grave consequences for all—especially for Iran's reputation. The leak and publication of a confidential report put the Ministry of Finance on high alert as they sent missives to other agencies demanding to know, "Where did the newspaper receive this information from?" The ministry went so far as to ask the newspaper to retract the article, and in turn the newspaper petitioned other agencies, including the police, to prevent this act of censorship.[33]

REBUILDING TO FORGET

Reza Shah did not just want to abolish enslavement. He wanted people to forget it ever existed. Early urban revitalization projects, including initiatives from the Ministry of Interior and Parliament, promised to revamp the urban aesthetic with wide promenades and new government buildings.[34] The Ministry of Finance, for example, was one such structure, built to reflect the government's new and modern perspective on the economy.

Before the Ministry of Finance could be built, Reza Shah began construction on the Golestan Palace in the 1920s. By the 1930s, three-fourths of the structure had been destroyed, including the harem building and other living spaces of the court.[35] The harem building once housed the many individuals enslaved at the Qajar court, women taken as temporary wives, others enslaved as domestics, and the eunuchs charged with guarding them. Royal spaces that accommodated enslavement—or, to put it more strongly, required and relied on enslavement—served as reminders of the government's participation in the slave trade. Although the harem building was also associated with the polygamous tradition of Iranian kings, its destruction was not necessarily a condemnation of polygamy. Reza Shah himself had several wives as queen consort, and the Marriage Law of 1931, often misremembered as an antipolygamy law, only encouraged monogamous marriages and required their registration in state registries.[36] Instead, the destruction of the harem demolished footprints of the government's complicity in enslavement.

The demolition of these physical reminders distinguished the Pahlavis from the Qajar kings and their enslaved entourages. In place of the harem structures, the government erected the Ministry of Finance, a nod to the reorganization of the economy after the abolition of enslavement.[37] The Ministry of Finance building continues to tower over the rest of the Golestan Palace, a visual conquest comparing the strength of the two competing dynasties in their spatial representations. Contrary to the Qajars, the strength of the Pahlavis was determined not by the number of enslaved people in its harem but by its unabashed modernity. Through the destruction of these buildings, especially the harem, the history of enslavement was physically removed from Iran's official history. By 1977, the Iranian government had listed Golestan Palace as a state museum, which was admitted as a UNESCO World Heritage Site in 2013.[38]

Golestan Palace was not unique in its trajectory of becoming a museum. Bagh-e Ferdows was a nineteenth-century palatial structure converted into a twentieth-century museum. Home to the *Introduction to the Art of Black Africa* exhibition in 1977, Bagh-e Ferdows needed no introduction to Africa. It had passed through the hands of various princes and princesses, all of whom undoubtedly brought enslaved East Africans into the space. Originally built by Mohammad Shah Qajar in the early nineteenth century, the building was passed down to Naser ed-Din Shah, who then gifted it to his daughter Esmat od-Dowleh and her husband, Amir Dust Mohammad Khan Moʿayyer ol-Mamalek, to commemorate their marriage. Esmat od-Dowleh and Moʿayyer ol-Mamalek's wedding was held at Bagh-e Ferdows, an event so ostentatious that it was described as the most expensive wedding in Iran at the time.[39] One wonders how many enslaved Africans worked at the wedding, and how many more arrived attending to their enslavers, the guests.

Bagh-e Ferdows, like other elite residencies from the nineteenth century, had numerous rooms to house the various members of the household, including the enslaved. Its upkeep required enslaved labor. In the absence of enslavement, these structures were too unwieldy for their owners to maintain them. After the 1929 Manumission Law, most of these homes were abandoned or converted into other structures. By the 1970s many had become museums. In 1977 it was the backdrop to the *Introduction to the Art of Black Africa* exhibition. Today Bagh-e Ferdows is home to Tehran's Cinema Museum.

The abandoning of large sprawling compounds was not limited to properties belonging to the royal family. Houses changed with abolition. Iranian architects had long designed elite homes with separate gendered spaces. These homes were not just where enslaved individuals had lived alongside those who enslaved them. They had served as the sites of enslavement as well. Most urban spaces in Iran did not have a market dedicated to the enslavement or trade of people. Enslavers traded, sold, or bought enslaved people from the convenience of their own homes. They served as markets, their price and worth negotiated in the same spaces where they would have spent their days eating, sleeping, and working. The homes doubled as prisons, limiting the mobility of enslaved people. The Manumission Law rendered these spaces redundant.

Families could no longer house their enslaved domestics with them or rely on them for nursing their babies and raising their children. Changes in social norms that made family life more public meant that wealthy and elite families no longer required eunuchs or other enslaved people representing them as a sign of their wealth. The idea of the ideal *khanevadeh*—once understood as a patriarch with his wives, extended families, children, and as many enslaved domestics and servants as possible—was turned on its head. The ideal family narrowed to just the nuclear family. Even Taj os-Saltaneh complained that attendants prevented marriages from being romantic, that their intrusions on the family disrupted the natural love that was meant to flow between spouses.[40] And now, with the manumission of enslaved people, elite and wealthy families regarded love marriages and intimate family relationships as aspirational ideals. Enslaved people were no longer key to ensuring a healthy marriage; their presence was no longer required to legitimize a marriage contract. For so long, enslaved domestics and eunuchs were arbiters of gender boundaries, slipping between spaces free men and women could not enter. The homes that once housed them were unwieldy and out of touch with the new direction of society. Instead, single-family units served as the new standard of modernity, where the nuclear family could raise healthy children as future citizens.

Iranian architects in urban centers adopted residential floorplans that were more Western, replacing the gendered women's and men's quarters (*andaruni* and *biruni*) with European-style living rooms, bedrooms, and entertaining areas (*mehmankhaneh*).[41] With the removal of enslaved people, intimate strangers in the home, strict gender boundaries were no longer practical between members of the nuclear family. With time, Iranian homes began to include innovations that eventually replaced roles formerly played by the enslaved, such as electricity and regular delivery of drinking water.[42] The legacy of enslavement was erased not only spatially but also functionally.

The abandoned homes, much like the Golestan Palace or Bagh-e Ferdows, have since been converted to museums or tourist attractions. In Kashan, investors and the city tourism council bought the structures, renovating them as boutique hotels and house museums.[43] In these instances, the enslaved/servant quarters were either closed to the public or completely renovated into administrative centers or in-house restaurants, welcoming both locals and tourists to a sanitized history devoid of references to enslavement.[44] In Bushehr, the nineteenth-century homes of enslavers had a similar fate. One such home is the location of the Iranian Studies Association in Bushehr. The enslaved/servant quarters serve as its administrative office today. These visual and spatial choices deny the history of enslavement without ever mentioning it.

SLAVERY AND RACISM WERE AMERICAN

In the 1930s, 'Ali Akbar Dehkhoda embarked on a new project: compiling the first and most comprehensive modern dictionary of Persian, the *Loghat-nameh*.[45] The *Loghat-nameh* remains a useful reference, and it pairs dictionary definitions with quotes, lines of poetry, and other textual examples of each word's application. Dehkhoda passed away before this gargantuan task was complete.

In 1958, two years after Dehkhoda's death, his partner, Mohammad Mo'in, released a new edition of the dictionary with a detailed definition of *bardegi*, the catch-all term for "slavery" (the state of being enslaved) in Persian. Although the entries in the *Loghat-nameh* often included historical examples of the term's usage, the definition of *bardegi* is uniquely extensive, amounting to hundreds of words that detail the history of enslavement from its beginnings in Mesopotamia to the US Civil War. The definition ends by saying that the 1926 Geneva Convention on Slavery ended enslavement worldwide, with an oblique reference to Asia and Africa. The definition, which is cited as taken from *The Persian Encyclopedia*

(*Da'irat al-Ma'arif*), makes no mention of Iran nor the Manumission Law of 1929. In the single most authoritative source on the Persian language, enslavement was defined as a global phenomenon that existed nearly everywhere except Iran. Instead, it heavily emphasized slavery in nearly every other region, especially the Americas.[46]

Although the dictionary cited *The Persian Encyclopedia*, that work had copied its definition from another source: the 1953 edition of *The Columbia Viking Desk Encyclopedia*, published by the Iranian Government Press. *The Persian Encyclopedia*'s editor refrained from adding or implicating Iran in the definition, even though the government had used the same term for "slave," *bardeh*, in its 1929 Manumission Law.

The dictionary definition reflected a cognitive dissonance that Iranians would come to buy into: that enslavement was not an Iranian problem. Soon the term *bardeh* was turned on its head—it stopped referring to domestic enslavement and instead referred exclusively to chattel forms of enslavement, especially US plantation slavery.

Throughout the 1960s, Iranians further associated histories and legacies of enslavement with US forms of anti-Blackness and Black resistance through their exposure to regular reports on the civil rights movement, the Black Power movement, Malcolm X's assassination, and Muhammad Ali's rise to fame. The visuality and extended focus on US civil rights and Black Power movements in the 1960s and '70s cemented this erasure. Iranians were already familiar with US society through their school curricula, travel, American films, music, and poetry, and high school history textbooks that contained chapters on basic American history.[47] In many ways, the dictionary echoed what many Iranians would come to believe: that "true slavery" was what they had seen and read in *Gone with the Wind* and *Uncle Tom's Cabin*.[48]

Events in the United States provided Iranians with a racial lexicon that would replace Iran's recent history of enslavement and provide them with an image of a Black individual, mostly men, who endured suffering and oppression at the hands of white oppressors. Newspapers regularly discussed the inherent racism of US internal politics and social structures. By 1965, numerous articles reported on the widespread violence against Black Americans and the protests in response to institutionalized white supremacy and segregation in America.[49]

Iranian newspapers used Malcolm X's assassination on February 21, 1965, to educate Iranian audiences about the plight of Black Americans and the unfolding of violent events in the United States. *Ettela'at*, the most widely circulated Persian-language newspaper based in Tehran, reported on the murder and its significance.[50] The newspaper provided regular updates on his death, even printing a striking photograph of Malcolm's open casket, an uncommon visual for Muslim Iranians, who traditionally bury their dead in shrouds.[51] In the week following the assassination, the newspaper announced that his death called attention to the history of Black Americans at large:

> The murder of Malcolm in the last week has, once again, captured the attention of the world to the problems of America's Black people, especially to the association of Black Muslims. Everyone wants to know, what is this organization like? What role did Malcolm play in it? Why did he split from it? The *Autobiography*, the translation of which we will begin studying, answers these questions and others. Malcolm had finished this autobiography a few days before his murder, and it is interesting to note that he predicted his death in them. It will be translated based on publications from the famous weekly the *Observer*, published in London.[52]

Following the *Observer*'s lead, *Ettelaʿat* announced its plan to publish serialized tracts from Malcolm's *Autobiography*, cowritten with Alex Haley, to answer these questions.[53] The *Observer* published two longer tracts from the manuscript under the title "Malcolm X/My Story" on February 21 and March 7, 1965, each time dedicating almost a full page of the newspaper to the pieces.[54] Extensively abridged from the full-length autobiography, *Ettelaʿat* broke up the larger tracts into shorter installments and published them in fourteen installations between March 1 and 16. Sometimes the tracts included parenthetical asides, contextualizing bits of American history or summarizing years of Malcolm's life to highlight the more dramatic turns of the autobiography.[55] Iranians connected the ongoing racism to the US history of plantation slavery and the aftermath of the Civil War.

Photographs of Malcolm filled *Ettelaʿat*, establishing his dynamic persona as an orator, leader, and family man. Each installment included the same photograph of Malcolm in midspeech. A later serial segment of his *Autobiography* about reading the Honorable Elijah Muhammad's teachings in prison was accompanied by a photograph of Malcolm giving a speech next to Elijah Muhammad. The newspapers, however, often referred to the Nation of Islam's leader as "the Honorable Muhammad," eliding his first name or transliterating it as ʿAli jah Muhammad, "Like Ali in Dignity, Muhammad." Although the Arabic/Persian equivalent of Elijah is Ilyas, the translators did not recognize Elijah as a religious name and either removed it to make "Muhammad" more prominent or provided a transliteration with a legible meaning. Instead, Elijah Muhammad's traditional skullcap emphasized a recognizable Muslim identity to *Ettela ʿat*'s audience.[56] Another issue paired headlines about Malcolm with photographs of Elijah Muhammad and Martin Luther King Jr. as the remaining leaders for Black Americans.[57] Although the rifts between Malcolm's and King's approaches to Black rights were well known in the United States, the Iranian press elided these differences to highlight their similar roles for the Black American public.[58] Other photographs of Malcolm X's sister Ella Mae Collins, wife Betty Shabazz, and daughter Ilyasah were published in separate articles. This provided further context for seeing Malcolm as a devoted family man, something that the *Ettela ʿat* editors believed American newspapers failed to do.[59] While some of these photos were republished from the *Observer* and other wires, *Ettela ʿat* did not republish images that would have placed Malcolm in a negative light for their audience. Photographs from Malcolm's arrest for dealing drugs, for example, were excluded from the translations taken from the *Observer*.[60] In short, the Iranian newspaper presented Malcolm as a righteous Muslim and ideal revolutionary. His photograph was a constant fixture in the papers for months after his assassination.[61]

Malcolm's autobiography has been translated and retranslated multiple times under radically different titles, including *Malcolm X: Gangesteri keh Rahbar-e Mosalmanan-e Amrika Shod*, or *Malcolm X: The Gangster Who Became the Leader of American Muslims*, currently in its eighth edition.[62] The press had adapted its title from the description on the cover of the 1966 Grove Press edition: "He rose from hoodlum, thief, dope peddler, pimp . . . to become the most dynamic leader of the Black Revolution. He said he would be murdered before this book appeared."[63] Despite the variable (and questionable) titles, Malcolm's legend endured in the Iranian collective memory long after assassination reports in newspapers. Malcolm's popularity and his death spurred interest in and translations of other African American writers and thinkers as well. For example, in 1967, the popular literary magazine *Khusheh* announced Mahmud Kiyanush's translation of a compilation of African American poetry, *Az klasik ta modern (From the Classical to the Modern)*.[64] A few years later in 1973, Ahmad Shamlu would publish his collection of world poetry, including fifty-three poems by Langston Hughes.[65] While the diversification of literature was well received, the *Autobiography* remained overwhelmingly popular.

After Malcolm's death, the language the press used in describing the developments in the United States grew more racialized. Three years later, when first reporting King's murder, *Ettelaʿat* ran the headline "Racists Killed Luther King" and described the escalating protests after his assassination as "a Civil War in America."[66] The Civil Rights Act of 1968, however, presented a "victory for Black Americans," and articles asked how the gap "between Black and white" could be bridged in America.[67] The following day, the newspaper introduced the Black Panthers' Stokely Carmichael as the rising Black leader in the United States: "Carmichael: The Black Man Who Wants to Set America on Fire."[68] Carmichael's descriptor was not metaphorical. The Iranian press had reported that the *New York Times* building had been bombed after Malcolm X's assassination and that areas of Harlem burned down after King's.[69] Although the United States had attempted to counter these images by sending Duke Ellington on tour in Iran in 1963, the cultural power and continuity of Black American uprisings eclipsed the limited positive associations of jazz.[70] Iranians became intimately familiar with representations of Black Americans harassed by white people in positions of authority.

Muhammad Ali's conversion and resistance to the Vietnam War was also closely followed in Iran. In 1969, *Ettelaʿat* also serialized translations of Jack Olsen's *Black Is Best: The Riddle of Cassius Clay*, retitled *Man yek ghahreman-e Siyah hastam*, or *I Am a Black Champion*. Following *Ettelaʿat*'s lead, Eskandari Press published it as an autobiography in book form. At the request of the Ministry of Cultural Affairs, the manuscript was submitted to the National Library to preserve the translation.[71] Muhammad Ali's public conversion, name change, success, and resistance to fighting in the war made his autobiography an exciting one for the Muslim-majority audience with growing grievances against the US government, then a close ally.[72] Alex Haley's *Roots: The Saga of an American Family* was also translated into Persian upon its release in 1976.

As the 1979 revolution drew closer, Iranian revolutionaries marshaled a specific image of Black Americans: seekers of salvation through Islam. Of the various Black Americans whose stories had been translated into Persian, Malcolm X's life resonated with these revolutionaries the most—some regarded Malcolm X as a modern-day version of Bilal ibn Rabah, the enslaved Abyssinian freed by the Prophet Muhammad.

Years later, after the revolution, the newly established Islamic Republic issued Malcolm X postage stamps for the "Universal Day of Struggle against Race Discrimination" in 1984.[73] Recognized by the United Nations, the day was originally intended as a response to a peaceful 1960 antiapartheid demonstration and its violent end in South Africa.[74] The Iranian government, eager to take a public stand against racial injustice, produced a stamp that reoriented the focus from South Africa to the United States.[75] The stamp framed an illustration of Malcolm X with his hand to his ear, the common stance for performing the Muslim call to prayer, with the Prophet's Mosque in Medina in the background. Red, yellow, and white silhouettes represent Malcolm's message of equality between all races. The stamp calls on the memory of Bilal, the first and best-known muezzin in the history of Islam. By integrating the images of the two most recognizable Black Muslim legends to promote an ideal of Islamic racial justice, the stamp evokes Malcolm's transcendental presence almost twenty years after his assassination. Ironically, Black Iranians, the overwhelming majority of whom were Muslim, were never described in similar terms.

But the stamp rests on the recognizability of Malcolm X for Iranian audiences. In fact, his name does not appear on the stamp, as Iranians would have easily recognized the leader even twenty years after his death.[76] His distinctive glasses, facial hair, and, most important, his Blackness in an Islamic context were sufficient to locate his identity. His outfit, however, was not the iconic suit and tie Malcolm was widely photographed in. Instead, the artist replaced his Western clothes with a plain white *thobe* with a high neck and flared sleeves, an exact replica of Bilal's outfit in the international 1976 film *The Message*.[77] Widely watched in Iran, the film served as the major source of visualizing the life of the Prophet, Bilal, and other companions for many Iranians. The stamp, in turn, visualizes Malcolm X as Bilal, in stance, dress, and role as a Muslim. Issued on March 21, 1984, the stamp's release date on "World Racial Day" corresponded with the Iranian New Year.[78] The stamp cemented how Iranian revolutionaries melded together Malcolm X and Bilal's images to serve as a shorthand for an idealized Blackness only available to non-Iranian Black individuals, as Black Iranians were never acknowledged. Although Iran's postal service had featured other ethnic minorities native to Iran, such as Kurds, they have, to my knowledge, never issued a stamp featuring a Black or Afro-Iranian.

Enslavement and its racist legacies were understood as an American phenomenon, an American problem, and an American history.[79] Pahlavi-era textbooks never referenced Iranian slavery and never described Iran's complicity or participation in the transnational slave trade. Malcolm X came to take on the image of an ideal Black man in Iran. And events like

An Introduction to the Art of Black Africa could frame the history of African enslavement as an entirely foreign history, either American, Atlantic, or Arab, but absolutely not Iranian.

BLACK AFRICA, WHITE IRAN

As enslavement was erased from the historical record and repackaged as a foreign concept, Blackness too was removed from the public sphere, and by extension it was removed from the collective memory. During the twentieth century, Iranians embraced the nationalist Aryan myth, the idea that they were true inheritors of an Aryan past.[80] Iranians did not begin to view themselves as "white" until after the enslavement of those considered "white" had dwindled completely. The remaining presence of enslaved East Africans, now easily recognized as "Black," created a binary that Iranians were able to buy into. The ideologies of Aryanism and whiteness further built on the binary, embedding Iranians in a global worldview that connected them with Europeans and placed them at the top of a racial pyramid. Although the contours of the myth were formed during the nineteenth century, the Pahlavis, especially Reza Shah's successor, Mohammad Reza Shah (r. 1941–79), embraced and encouraged any connections, however flimsy, back to an imagined ancient, white Iran.[81] In fact, the title of the exhibition, *An Introduction to the Art of Black Africa*, not only highlighted the art's Blackness but also tacitly reminded the viewer of the stark contrast between *Black* Africa and *white* Iran.[82]

Mohammad Reza Shah attempted to connect his rule to ancient Iran through the legacy of Cyrus the Great (r. 559–30 BCE), which played a very specific role in revisionist Iranian histories of enslavement. In 1971, Iran gifted a replica of the Cyrus Cylinder to the United Nations along with a translation. Although scholars have long recognized the cylinder as a generic edict issued after conquering a new region, Mohammad Reza Shah declared in 1968 that the artifact was the first human rights charter of mankind, arguing that the imperial conqueror was actually pro–democratic rule and that he had introduced twentieth-century standards of human rights in the sixth century BCE.[83] The translation presented to the United Nations by Princess Ashraf, Mohammad Reza Shah's sister, is truncated, only highlighting the lines that may be interpreted as human rights. One line says, "I freed the citizens of Babylon from the yoke of servitude."[84] Somehow this has been misconstrued to suggest that Cyrus

II freed *all* enslaved people from forced labor—a dramatically incorrect idea, as Babylonia was expected to send a tribute of five hundred enslaved boys to the Achaemenid king every year.[85] Other translations of the Cyrus Cylinder that circulated drifted further and further from the original text, including one with the line "I hereby abolish slavery; my governors are ordered to prohibit the exchanging of men and women as slaves within their ruling domains. Such a tradition should be exterminated the world over."[86] The recent history of enslavement, which had just been abolished decades earlier, was erased.

Instead, it was entirely replaced with the idea that Iranians had never enslaved people within their borders and had even championed abolishing enslavement 2,500 years ago.

▬

Kashan's 'Abbasi House, much like Bagh-e Ferdows, is now a tourist attraction and museum. A large, framed photo of a woman posing with a vacuum and dressed in Qajar fashion hangs outside the restaurant. The caption reads, "Taking a souvenir photograph of the arrival of an electric vacuum to Tehran."[87] Indeed, this would have been a noteworthy moment if the photograph did not come from Shadi Ghadirian's *Qajar Series* (1998), a set of thirty-three stylized photographs commenting on the state of women's rights in Iran.[88] The inclusion of this photograph at the Abbasi House, where the servants' quarters have since been renovated into a *sonnati*-style restaurant, further obscures the history of enslavement. In homes such as this one, the matriarch would not have vacuumed her home with the convenience of an electric household appliance. Not only did the technology not yet exist, but even if it had, she would have relied instead on the forced labor of an enslaved person.

But what is enslavement in the Iranian context? If we had to rely on museums, dictionaries, encyclopedias, and edicts sent to the United Nations, it would be near impossible to find out. Despite this erasure, the legacy of enslavement remains tangible in popular culture.

5 ORIGINS OF BLACKFACE IN THE ABSENCE OF BLACK PEOPLE

Remember Haji Firuz, the eunuch at Naser ed-Din Shah's court who shared his name with so many others? Many remember his name only to forget him.

———

Perhaps the most visually grotesque and vehemently defended legacy of enslavement in Iran is *siyah-bazi*.[1]

Siyah-bazi, or "playing Black," is a genre of minstrelsy theater that has effectively been canonized as a type of Iranian folk theater. Although the performances have morphed in structure and content, all *siyah-bazi* shows feature a main character, the *siyah* (Black) who in service of a king or upper-class merchant routinely misunderstands or miscommunicates his tasks. The plot hinges on the *siyah* and the trials that befall him as he pursues his enslaver's orders. Sometimes there is a romantic interest, and the *siyah* appears as a lustful, unacceptable partner to a young woman. The *siyah* speaks in a high-pitched voice in pidgin Persian, wears simple clothes, uses exaggerated mannerisms, and appears with a blackened face. These tropes draw directly from stereotypes about enslaved eunuchs during the last stage of enslavement in Iran, when its overwhelmingly Black population of enslaved people were forced into visibility. Because enslaved Black women outnumbered enslaved Black men and eunuchs throughout the nineteenth century, one might have expected caricatures of enslaved women to have been more common in Iran.[2] But it was the rarity of eunuchs and the new abnormality of their bodies that made them victims of this mockery. The racialization and forced visibility of enslaved eunuchs led to their caricaturization as a means of not only presenting a crude comedy performance but also demarcating the new boundaries of what was normal versus abnormal.

Despite the direct influence of enslaved people on the contours of minstrel shows, blackface caricatures—both acted and drawn—actively erased their Black muses. Some blackface actors insist that their use of blackface is not intentionally reminiscent of Black men; rather, it serves as a visual cue for the audience to follow the funniest character onstage.[3] Satirical magazines also framed caricatures of Black men as stand-ins for a neutral party or an outside observer in their political critiques. The erasure of enslavement after 1929 created a deep cognitive dissonance among most non-Black Iranians: even the most obvious remnants of enslavement and the memories of the enslaved were viewed as anything but. I argue that the basic contours of these performances relied extensively on the changing boundaries of racial stereotypes and emerged as a fixed genre only after the 1929 Manumission Law, when abolition erased the subjects of imitation and the jokes lived on even as audiences forgot who they were.

Blackface, or *siyah-bazi*, is not limited to the theatrical stage; it is a public affair during Nowruz, the start of the new year that coincides with the spring equinox. Haji Firuz is the name of a holiday minstrel, the herald of Nowruz and harbinger of spring's arrival. Haji Firuz was also the name of a eunuch at Naser ed-Din Shah's court (fig. 5.1). There are a few records that refer to him: lines in memoirs here and there, a photograph in that same series discussed in chapter 2, and other documents, including a letter that indicated there was a mass uproar in the harem when Haji Firuz was sent away to a military camp.[4] The people of the harem didn't want him to leave. They cared for him. They cried for him to come back; they wanted him close by, to cater to their whims and needs. But none of that stopped his name—a name that enslaved him—from becoming associated with a dancing, tambourine-waving character. Haji Firuz himself, the person, along with the other eunuchs of the court, were erased in favor of a minstrel show.

But after 1929, when all elements related to enslavement, including buildings, language, and even the freedpeople themselves, were pushed into a forced invisibility, how did *siyah-bazi* with its direct and obvious references to enslaved eunuchs come to be so popular and commonplace?

5.1 Photograph of Haji Firuz, a eunuch at the Qajar court, taken by Naser ed-Din Shah. (Album 362, no. 42-1, Golestan Palace Photo Archive.)

For non-Iranians and others familiar with other traditions of blackface minstrelsy, in the United States or elsewhere, the connection between enslaved Black men and their caricatures is obvious.[5] But within the Iranian academy and the broader community, the denial of any relevance of race or racism in the construction of these theatrical and visual caricatures is often hostile and continues to this day in Iran and the Iranian diaspora. Like other members of the African diaspora, however, Black- and Afro-Iranians have maintained that the practice is derogatory toward Black people, castigating them as caricatures beyond Iranian-ness and furthering racist stereotypes. Defenders of blackface in Iran shield themselves from criticism by arguing that they are laughing with, not at, the blackface character; that the practice is old, ancient, unrelated to enslavement or Black people; and that it demands to be preserved in the name of national tradition. But *siyah-bazi* in its current form remains inextricably connected to late nineteenth-century dynamics of enslavement, even if its defenders say otherwise. And the continued perpetuation is insulting to Black Iranians and society at large.

An examination of blackface in Iran reveals much about each stage of enslavement and erasure. Although early performances relied on papier-mâché masks to mock a range of people, Black freedmen sometimes joined circus troupes and played the role of a Black eunuch without the aid of a mask, merely manipulating their facial expressions to create a similar effect.[6] A central theme in *siyah-bazi* is the hypersexualization and desexualization of the main character, similar to the sexual tensions that defined eunuchs as men who required castration to interact freely with court women without suspicion. As enslaved Caucasians disappeared from court and from Iranian collective memory, "white" collapsed as an enslavable category, and Iranians came to see themselves as "white" against the Blackness of the enslaved. By the 1929 Manumission Law, several actors had built their reputations directly on mocking enslaved Black eunuchs, and the Caucasian eunuch character disappeared from these shows.[7] Freedmen left the troupes, and the genre would solidify in the form that continues today, with non-Black Iranian clowns leading the way. With time, other examples of blackface proliferated in the market as magazine caricatures or holiday characters that further normalized its prevalence in Iran.

Although scholars and practitioners like William Beeman and Bahram Bayzai agree that these *taqlid* or "imitation" performances grew out of the nineteenth century and were especially influenced by Karim Shireh-yi's tenure at the Qajar court, they have been discussed in a vacuum as a static folk genre that reflects some of this cognitive dissonance. Bayzai, for example, has attempted to construct as many different lineages as possible for the *siyah* character, pointing toward Black individuals in Safavid-era miniatures as examples of minstrelsy.[8] But the presence of Black people in Iranian art does not amount to evidence that they were engaged in blackface, nor does it justify it. Bayzai's defense of *siyah-bazi* as a form of Iranian theater with African influence has been confusing for some, as he wrote and directed the acclaimed film *Bashu: The Little Stranger*, which has been hailed for its championing of Iranian diversity and its antiracist message.[9] Bayzai's ability to produce such a film critiquing casual racism in Iran while also producing blackface theater demonstrates the level to which many Iranians have avoided confronting the racism of blackface theater. And while Beeman has suggested that "black makeup preceded the African designation,"[10] he has provided no evidence for such a claim, and it seems likely that the black makeup was popularized as enslaved Black men and freedmen disappeared from the urban centers of Iran.[11]

This chapter explicitly connects these histories and demonstrates how the later caricatures cemented the erasure of Black people and their enslavement in Iran. From the 1950s onward, the black visages of characters in blackface films, plays, and print were often used and described as visual markers of a special *other*—a knowing yet naive individual whose presence was used to point out political and social discrepancies and hypocrisies. This chapter is not concerned with the specifics of plotlines. Rather, it examines the framing of blackface characters as part of a timeless Iranian tradition that purports a color-blind approach to Iranian society while resting on the assumption that a blackened face can distinguish a character from non-Black Iranians.

IMITATION AS SIYAH-BAZI

In his memoir, Saʿdi Afshar's history of *siyah-bazi* connected the modern theater to the mocking of enslaved Black people:[12]

> If you want to know about the history of *siyah-bazi* in Iran, then I have to tell you that *siyah-bazi* in Iran has a three-hundred-year-old history. . . . But with the arrival of Zabihollah Maheri, the trajectory of *siyah-bazi* changed [from court jesters] and in reality, became more full and complete. From that point on, the *siyah*

became a pivotal role. The Late Maheri, who was known as "Maheri the Goldsmith," had connections with the Qajar court and would come and go there regularly. He was extremely smart and excitable and would commit everything he saw to memory.

He was witness to the mannerisms of the Black servants who worked there. In a distant past, they used to bring African and Abyssinian Blacks as servants at the royal court. . . . After some time, these servants would learn Persian, but they couldn't pronounce the words correctly and would sometimes stutter. So for example, they would say *sandali* as *safdari* or *bademjan* as *bamanjan*. Whatever Zabih saw at the Qajar court, he would describe for the Mu'ayad brothers Hosayn Aqa and Ahmad Aqa, both of whom were actors and directors. . . . Hosayn Aqa and Ahmad Aqa Mo'ayad, along with Zabihollah came to set the framework for *siyah-bazi* in Iran.[13]

Afshar was born in 1934, just a few years after the Manumission Law that freed all enslaved people within Iran. By the time he was a teenager, *siyah-bazi* had solidified to a specific genre of theater, where an individual played the role of a *siyah*, "a Black," by applying a black ointment to their face, cracking jokes, and exaggerating their mannerisms all while speaking a pidgin Persian in a high-pitched voice. And thirteen-year-old Sa'di Afshar knew this, which is why he smeared his light-skinned face with soot from the heater pipes to entertain guests at a holiday party in 1947. It was his first time playing a *siyah*.

Although Karim Shireh-yi is remembered as the father of Iranian comedy, Afshar credited Zabihollah Maheri as the father of *siyah-bazi* in his memoir. Though the mocking of Black eunuchs and other enslaved people likely predated Maheri's visits to the court, Afshar attributed the methods to him because of his role in transforming the show from a niche court performance for royals and their courtiers to one that would be seen throughout Tehran and beyond. "Playing Black" was rooted in the enslavement and mockery of Africans, but Afshar's reference to its origins was unemotional. For Afshar, this was merely a fact, not a condemnation. If anything, it was positive.

Afshar identified Maheri as the person who not only snuck into the royal court to study the mannerisms of the last Black eunuchs in Iran but also as the individual responsible for training the next generation of actors who would appear onstage in blackface.[14] *Siyah-bazi* moved away from Karim Shireh-yi's *taqlid* theater, which involved the mockery of individuals whom both the actors and audience would have been familiar with. Maheri began to train actors who had never interacted with enslaved eunuchs, and he continued to train them after the Manumission Law. He identified young actors with potential, like Mahdi Mesri, and would arrange for them to learn how to play a *siyah*.[15] By the time Sa'di Afshar first greased his face at the holiday party in 1947, Mahdi Mesri had risen to fame and appeared regularly in blackface at Shahin Theater, where Afshar would try to see him perform.[16]

Non-Black Iranians greased their faces with a black ointment to play the role of a *siyah* typically named Mobarak, a common name given to enslaved Black men during the Qajar era. In these plays, the *siyah* was a servant to a wealthy merchant or a king. In addition to the visual and audio cues distinguishing the *siyah*, the character continually misunderstands basic statements, resulting in nonsensical interactions and resolutions. These situational comedies would critique class and power, punching up at the elites, while further entrenching themselves deep in a racism rooted in patterns of enslavement. Although enslavement was rendered illegal, these plays continued its cultural legacy, creating comedy performances based on racial stereotypes dating from the last fifty years of legal enslavement in Iran. Racism could live on in the performances.

The canonization of *siyah-bazi* as a clear genre of theater stripped it of the ad-libbing that would have guided many of the performances at the Qajar court. Masks (like those discussed in chapter 3) were abandoned, and actors blackened their faces instead so they could contort their facial muscles into odd and exaggerated expressions. As the name indicates, *siyah-bazi* shows revolved entirely around the *siyah*, "the black," the character in blackface whose presence was informed by stereotypes about Black eunuchs. The fake high-pitched voices of the *siyah*, for example, were meant to mimic the voices of castrated men whose voices never deepened with puberty, mixing up the syllables of Persian words on their tongues.[17] *Siyah-bazi* shows came to embrace a racial binary instead of the spectrum that had faded away during the late nineteenth century. The enduring presence of the *siyah* confirmed the final racialization of East African eunuchs as generally Black without the specificity of terms like *Habashi*.

As references to enslavement were erased during the Pahlavi era, *siyah-bazi* shows came to be defined by different myths with alternate genealogies for the blackened face of the *siyah*. Even though the *siyah* always played the role of a servant, that role was gradually distanced from direct references to enslavement. The actor's blackened face was explained away as a visual cue for the main character rather than a racial device.[18] Yet caricatures of Black men would only grow across media in the twentieth century. While different elements would fade from the overall performance, they all hinged on a visibly blackened face with exaggerated expressions.

DOLLS, MAGAZINES, AND MORE

Blackface caricatures relied on more than just visual references for their minstrelsy. Many of their names were derived from common names for enslaved Black men during the nineteenth century. To be clear, these caricatures relied on names that were forcibly given to enslaved men, names that replaced their independent identities to reduce them to a lesser status. These caricatures, whether found in men busking in the streets, as dolls, or as printed cartoons, all relied on a mix of language and visuality to perform their minstrelsy to the fullest.

Haji Firuz wears a red outfit and a rounded hat while playing a tambourine and singing in a high-pitched voice, mispronouncing a short, partially nonsensical rhyme: *My master, hello, my master, hold your head up high, my master, sugar goats, my master, why don't you laugh!*

He also appears in blackface.

Haji Firuz, the new year's herald, developed out of *siyah-bazi* sometime in the twentieth century. In 1951, Mahdi Akhavan-Sales wrote a footnote to a Nowruz poem in which he described his hatred of the Haji Firuz practice that had emerged out of Tehran for its ridiculing of enslaved Black men.[19] Earlier references to the Haji Firuz character are scarce, and illustrations depicting him began to commonly appear from the 1950s onward in newspapers and print magazines published in Tehran. By the 1960s, the inclusion of Haji Firuz in print magazines was unexceptional and even expected.[20] References to a Haji Firuz during the nineteenth century, however, are limited to the court eunuchs or other enslaved men from around the Persian Gulf.

Like the *siyah*, men playing the role of Haji Firuz contort their bodies and exaggerate their movements, dance to nonsensical songs, and greet people with *sonboli-alaykom* (hyacinth upon you) instead of *salaamu alaykom* (peace be upon you), swapping a common greeting for a coded phallic reference. From the mid-twentieth century onward, men from lower socioeconomic backgrounds dressed in red outfits and blackened their faces around Nowruz to busk on sidewalks and at traffic lights to earn some money from the Nowruz holiday cheer. At the same time, material representations of Haji Firuz grew more common as well, further embedding his visuality into Nowruz traditions. Haji Firuz dolls and greeting cards signal that by the 1960s and '70s the character had expanded beyond simple street performances or newspaper comics.[21] Since then, Haji Firuz has been consistently portrayed with a red outfit, a rounded hat, and a blackened face.[22] All material renderings rely on a blackened face to visually indicate *This object is a Haji Firuz*.[23] Haji Firuz, in its many iterations, strayed away from its initial muse but kept the elements that mocked him the most. Other media, such as satirical magazines, did the same with their blackface caricatures, some of which had even more directly racist contours.

Take, for example, *Towfiq* magazine. *Towfiq* was considered a groundbreaking publication. The first humor magazine in Persian, it sold around 30,000 copies on regular weeks and up to 100,000 for special issues at the height of its fifty-year run, from 1923 to 1971.[24] Issues were filled with articles and columns about current affairs, domestic and international news, and amusing stories. Its print history is usually divided into three phases. The first phase (1923–40) is marked by the founder Hosayn Towfiq's imprisonment and subsequent death after his release in 1940. The second phase (1940–53) is dated to the burning of the periodical's offices and family home in 1953.[25] Its most significant period is the third phase (1958–71), when the periodical hit peak circulation. This is also when it introduced its titular protagonist and logo: Kaka Towfiq.

From the midcentury onward, *Towfiq*'s titular character appeared regularly throughout the pages of the satirical magazine. He was a smiling caricature of a Black man with an oversized nose, large ears, and wide eyes. He often appeared wearing patched-up clothing indicative of low social standing and was used as a tool for the illustrators to make political commentary without referring to any particular person.

"Kaka Towfiq" is not a name. As mentioned earlier, *kaka*, a colloquial term in the Shirazi dialect, is most closely translated as "brother" or "bro" when used between individuals of equal social standing.[26] It was also a slur for enslaved Black men across Iran. *Kaka*, paired with the enslaved's first name, asserted one's intimate access to and power over them.[27] The name *Towfiq* is derived from the surname of its founder, Hosayn Towfiq, and relatives who took control of the periodical after his death in 1940. Following a brief period of cessation after the attack on their offices, his nephews revived the weekly and were responsible for the introduction of the blackface caricature in 1958.[28] Together, then, this slur linked the enslaved caricature to the magazine and, by extension, the entire Towfiq family in a proprietary manner. He served them and the reader. He offered them political and social commentaries packaged in quick one-liners about completing their household chores, and he served the weekly by becoming the face of its satirical and racist humor.

Tellingly, the titular character was first introduced to audiences on the cover of the Nowruz issue in 1958, where he was dressed up as a Haji Firuz, banging his tambourine while dancing in the same manner as those who busked in Tehran's streets for the holiday season. As Abbas Towfigh noted in his book, the caricature was first illustrated as a young man, and the figure aged over time.[29] In the first issue, he didn't have his signature white beard. Instead, he had large, thick lips. As the titular character became an older man, his lips were covered by his beard, which had gradually become stragglier.

On the magazine covers, it is important to note, the titular character is not presented as enslaved. Instead, he was beholden to the audience, the viewers who bought issue after issue to read his retorts and laugh at his shenanigans as he revealed problems and hypocrisies in Iranian society. The reference to enslavement is hidden in plain sight. Although defenders of *siyah-bazi* and blackface caricatures more generally claim that the blackening of the face is just a visual device to highlight a joke's punchline, *Towfiq*'s covers highlight that the blackface character was built on anti-Black stereotypes from Iran's history of enslavement or incorporated from racist Darwinist ideas. In figure 5.2, the editors had decided against their usual covers that satirize political or social events and instead turned the focus on the titular character's inappropriate libido. In the illustration, he beckons his wife or lover—absurdly named Gishniz (Cilantro)—from behind the stage curtain, and she asks him, "*Kaka*, dear, what is going on behind the curtain?"[30] He answers, "Come and I'll show you!"—a coy invitation to sex in a public space.

His sexual incompetence—a trait inherited from jokes about eunuchs—reveals itself in another racist stereotype, a son shown in figure 5.3: a monkey named Mamuli. The titular character refers to him as his *bandeh-zad*, which colloquially means "descendant of me." *Bandeh* is not a neutral term here: it is another word for "slave." In conversational Persian, it is used to humbly refer to yourself as the slave of the person you are speaking to, as a sign of respect or deference, even among peers.

When the titular character uses this language, however, the term *bandeh* verbally reinscribes him as an enslaved person for the viewer. The clear dehumanization of a child presented as a monkey—or for lack of a better term, a half-breed—reflects how European eugenics had been incorporated into an Iranian paradigm of race in the twentieth century.[31] Although later writings by Abbas Towfigh have described Mamuli as the titular character's "friend," the affiliation remains vividly vulgar.[32] The magazine tweaked the trope of the sexually incompetent blackface character to demonstrate that his fertility is only good for producing an anthropomorphized animal.[33] In a later issue, the cover features the titular character with another child, also presented as a blackface caricature. He is introduced as Mobarak, that same name once given to enslaved Black men and the most common name for a *siyah* in *siyah-bazi* shows.[34]

Towfiq's success was built on anti-Blackness. The more successful the weekly became, the more it put the titular character's image on the magazine. Indeed, the titular character did not appear in the weekly regularly until the 1960s, and by the end of the decade his semblance appeared on nearly every single page. *Towfiq*'s pages were filled with crass humor that targeted all sorts of different groups: Armenians, conservative Muslims, people from a lower socioeconomic class, and others. But the magazine's success was based on its clear anti-Black racism. In 1971, after *Towfiq* had run for nearly fifty years, the Pahlavi government shut it down—not for its racism but for its unflattering comics poking fun at major officials and criticizing the general state of affairs.[35]

Following *Towfiq*'s shutdown, the editors regrouped and did what they did best: they created another satirical magazine that used a blackface caricature as its mascot, this one named Yaqut (fig. 5.4).[36] This character also used a once-common name for enslaved Black men.[37] Launched on the eve of the 1979 Revolution, the magazine *Yaqut* echoed much of what *Towfiq* had done, lampooning politicians and highlighting social hypocrisies or ironies. *Yaqut* had a similar style to *Towfiq*, complete with an eponymous blackface caricature that was both mascot and active commentator on the Iranian revolution and its aftermath. The editors illustrated Yaqut like their former titular character, as a Black man with exaggerated features reflecting anti-Black stereotypes. Both characters appeared on the covers of their respective magazines, guided the reader through different columns, and appeared in comics satirizing the latest political developments of the week. Unlike its predecessor, however, *Yaqut* would be short-lived, and it only printed for a few years.

5.2 and 5.3 Covers of
Towfiq magazine from
the 1960s. (*Towfiq* magazine, Firestone Library,
Princeton University.)

سال اول شمارهٔ نهم دوم اسفندماه ۵۸ قیمت ۳۵ ریال
نگاهی سیاسی، اجتماعی

در چند نقطه به مجاهدین خلق حمله شد

قابل مصرف هم در عزا و هم در عروسی !

5.4 Yaqut. (Cover of *Yaqut* magazine, author's collection. Many thanks to Hushidar Mortezaie for sharing this with me.)

Yaqut's character sometimes appeared as a Black man and sometimes as a man in blackface. The inclusion of both versions reflects the slipperiness of these memories in late twentieth-century Iran, where the history of enslavement had been so effectively erased from the public sphere that even those participating in its vulgar and racist visual legacy had lost track of who or what exactly they were referencing. Like its predecessor, the magazine was popular for its political commentary and offensive caricatures, and *Yaqut* served the reader.

Once again, for a brief period, there were many Yaquts in Iran.

AN ANCIENT TRADITION

These shows and performances did more than erase the individual personalities and identities of those enslaved in favor of flat, one-dimensional characters that lacked dignity. As the memory of enslavement faded in Iran, the justifications for these shows reduced references to the history of enslavement as well. In some ways, this was a glaringly difficult task. The stereotype of a Black man played by a person in blackface feels like an overly direct reference; to many who watched these shows at face value, it was an obvious and direct connection. Even major actors and playwrights have openly discussed the connection between *siyah-bazi* and enslaved Africans at the Qajar court.[38] Yet scholars and other consumers have vehemently defended Haji Firuz and other *siyah-bazi* characters as divorced from any reference to enslavement or Blackness, even though these performances require, at the bare minimum, a man in blackface singing and dancing for a "master."

While the presence of Haji Firuz was more or less accepted during the Pahlavi era, the push to defend Haji Firuz as an ancient tradition came to the fore after the 1979 revolution.[39] While some had denounced Haji Firuz during the Pahlavi era, none threatened the existence of Haji Firuz until the Islamic Republic exerted more control over popular culture in Iran. Some of the narratives that developed during the Pahlavi era became more formalized and virulent in response to the new government. In the case of the Dutch holiday blackface character Zwarte Piet / Black Pete, Gloria Wekker has drawn on Stuart Hall's notion of "ritualized degradation" to highlight "a representation that is so natural that it requires no explanation or justification."[40] Until the 1979 revolution, that was very much true about Haji Firuz as well. Part of Ayatollah Khomeini's support was drawn from his ability to indict the United States—and by extension its allies, including the shah—as the peak example of injustice and racism.[41] *Siyah-bazi* jeopardized the Islamic Republic's asserted reputation as a leader of antiracist and anti-imperialist movements in the Global South, as most non-Iranians would have easily recognized it as blackface. The issue, then, was not merely that Haji Firuz was racist but that it made Iran *look* racist, if anyone were to come across it.

In the early years of the Islamic Republic, government officials cracked down on *siyah-bazi* as they did other forms of entertainment, including popular music and dancing. Some *siyah-bazi* theater actors continued with their shows but were instructed to not paint their faces. Haji Firuzes were generally discouraged—as their performance often involved song and dance—and were sometimes arrested. Because the Islamic Republic had broad censors and bans across all forms of entertainment, many viewed these new policies as "antihappiness," instigating campaigns to preserve Haji Firuz in the face of an oppressive state.[42] Because of his association with Nowruz, which is remembered as a pre-Islamic Iranian holiday, the defense of Haji Firuz became especially important to many who felt antagonized by the Islamic Republic.

In light of these new policies, those defending him developed facile explanations that link the minstrel to older Iranian culture. Some attributed his blackface to soot from the Chaharshanbe Suri fires that Iranians jump over on the last Tuesday night of the year, while others suggested that Haji Firuz was actually a Zoroastrian priest whose face was blackened from tending to a sacred fire. Neither of these explanations holds much weight: jumping over a fire does not make anyone black in the face, and the Zoroastrian emphasis on purity makes it nearly impossible for a mobad's face to be blackened from any of their rituals. These explanations took symbols that are popularly regarded as native or ancient to Iran despite the logical leaps necessary to connect them to Haji Firuz in the name of a shared cultural heritage.

Some complex explanations evolved as well, where some tried to link Haji Firuz to literature of national importance. In 1983, Mehrdad Bahar described Haji Firuz as a reincarnation of Siavash, a character in Ferdowsi's *Shahnameh*. The *Shahnameh*, a tenth-century epic, gained significance among nationalists in the twentieth century who viewed it as a preservation of a pure pre-Islamic "Persian" past and culture. The *Shahnameh* presents Siavash as a chivalrous and dignified prince. His name, originally *Sia-vakhsh*, referred to his black horse.[43] Over time, *Siavash* became more common, and defenders of Haji Firuz in the twentieth century in-terpreted *Sia-vash* as "black in appearance" to fit their explanations.[44] This interpretation diverges from premodern etymologies of the name, and nothing in the *Shahnameh* suggests that Siavash was Black or a jester.[45] Regardless, Bahar linked Haji Firuz to Siavash, arisen from the dead, his blackened face an ashy return to the living world.[46] Bahar's treatment ig-nored any of the direct links between Haji Firuz's persona and the cari-catures of African slaves at the Qajar court, including his pidgin Persian, high-pitched voice, and expressions of servitude. Instead, Bahar echoed narratives that had emerged in the Pahlavi era that worked to erase refer-ences to enslavement or Blackness. This narrative justified Haji Firuz's presence in Nowruz festivities and turned his person into a cultural cause that must be preserved for the sake of history. These methods of connect-ing Haji Firuz to elements of an imagined pre-Islamic Iran framed the threats to the caricature's existence as an attack on an Iranian cultural identity by a hardline religious government.

Sa'di Afshar's death in 2013 triggered another wave of revisionist his-tories of *siyah-bazi* theater. Sa'di Afshar's admirers took to writing eulogies not only for him but also for *siyah-bazi*. These memorializations called him "the last *siyah-bazi* actor, the last pillar of *siyah-bazi* theater" and lamented that this allegedly age-old craft would die with him.[47] Even before his death, Sa'di Afshar himself had emphasized the importance of teaching the craft to the next generation of actors, suggesting that there were not enough people teaching or learning how to "play black."[48] Afshar mentioned that he had heard of professors teaching "playing black" at the university, but only to one or two students a year. In interviews and in his own memoir, he stressed the difficulty of playing the role. Unless another generation seri-ously took on the mantle of *siyah-bazi*, the genre would soon be extinct.

But *siyah-bazi* shows and actors continue their work in Tehran and other major cities of Iran. While some people within the industry, like playwright Mohammad Hosayn Naserbakht and Sa'di Afshar, have ac-knowledged the links between the enslavement of Black men and their portrayal in "playing Black" theater, many deny any connection, as a matter both of self-preservation in the industry and of a refusal to con-sider its racist implications.[49] The erasure of enslavement and the en-slaved works on two levels here. Those who do acknowledge the history of enslavement do not believe the theater is problematic, as they assume that the end of enslavement meant the end of Black people in Iran and that the mockery is thus bereft of any harm. Those who do not acknowledge a history of enslavement argue that it cannot be harmful at all, as there is no harmful history to connect it to.

But Haji Firuz, Mobarak, *Towfiq*'s titular character, and Yaqut are all entangled and intertwined with the same stereotypes of enslaved Black men, the ones who would have been called *kaka* as a racial slur. The term *kaka* connected these different forms of blackface—a holiday minstrel, a genre of film and theater, and a print caricature. In the magazine, his name "Kaka Towfiq" defines the character as a whole; he is even referred to as simply *Kaka jun*, or "*Kaka* dear." Some *siyah-bazi* films, too, deployed "Kaka" as a name, as in Mas'ud Kimiyai's *Dash Akol*, where the antagonist Kaka Rostam appears in a blackened face.[50] While *Dash Akol*'s characters speak in a specific Tehrani accent associated with historic films, most *siyah-bazi* characters speak in a specific pidgin Persian, swapping syllables or mispronouncing words to create another layer of humor mocking the character's intelligence. Pidgin Persian is a critical element of *siyah-bazi*, aurally identifying Haji Firuz minstrels and the *siyah* character in blackface plays. One book dedicated to preserving Sa'di Afshar's craft for future generations of *siyah-bazi* actors includes an entire glossary to canonize these words with their "correct" mispronunciations. The section is titled "*Loghatnameh-ye zaban-i kakai*," or "Glossary of the *Kaka* Language."[51]

———

In March 2021, the Tehran Municipality announced that it was temporarily suspending blackface in its Nowruz performances because they had learned of scholarship that had connected blackface to a history of enslavement.[52] The deputy mayor of Tehran, Mohammad Reza Javadi Yeganeh, explained the city's decision by retweeting links from the Collective for Black Iranians and sharing links to recent scholarship.[53] The Iranian social media landscape immediately weighed in with much debate as to the validity of the claims of racism. Many accused the Tehran Municipality of extending the Islamic Republic's chokehold on people's annual traditions and happiness.[54] Others applauded the decision, saying it was high time that Iranians let go of Haji Firuz. Others still acknowledged that Haji Firuz was a strange tradition and decried it for its impropriety, but not because they believed it was linked to racism or the mockery of any specific group. For the entirety of the Nowruz period—the first thirteen days of the Iranian calendar—debates over whether or not Haji Firuz was racist swarmed the internet. After the thirteenth day, however, the discussions went silent almost immediately. In many Iranian celebrations, both in Iran and in the diaspora, Haji Firuz remained a critical element of the holiday.[55] His presence has remained largely unchallenged. Even the Tehran Municipality's decision to suspend blackface did not challenge Haji Firuz as a character and permitted the rest of the racist charade to continue during their investigation. As of this writing, no updates on the Tehran Municipality's temporary suspension have been announced, nor have any conclusions of the investigation as to whether Haji Firuz is actually racist have been shared.

6 MEMORIES AND A GENRE OF DISTORTION

Memory is slippery. It is fickle. And as memories become complicated, some will bend them to suit their interests. An enslaver's memories of those they enslaved, for example, might have changed throughout the twentieth century. The same family might have been proud to share or present those they enslaved in social gatherings, always sending them on errands or keeping them by their side, ready to open doors, greet guests, and more. But after abolition, those memories might have been erased or rearranged. Because it was no longer in vogue, respectable, or even acceptable to have kept enslaved people in one's service, many enslavers and their descendants reframed their descriptions of the people their family had enslaved, sometimes describing them as their "right-hand man" or as a "second grandmother"—and often, most crucially, as not enslaved at all.

These descriptions rely on globalized understandings of enslavement that said that *bardeh-dari* referred only to US plantation slavery or chattel slavery. This flawed and self-serving logic allowed enslavers to reimagine the people they enslaved in their homes as members of the family, as though their status as *kaniz* or *gholam* merely involved semantic titles, not terms that indicated a hierarchy or power discrepancy in the household. Take, for example, the host and live translator of a film screening and interview with Farhad Varahram and his film *Siyahan-e Jonub-e Iran*, or *The Black People of the South of Iran*. The host refused to translate *bardeh* as "slave" and instead used "laborer," defending her decision by saying that Iran had never had slavery, only a type of feudalism.[1] She knew this, she shared, because her great-grandfather had fallen in love with a *kaniz* and married her. She did not mention whether the *kaniz* had also fallen in love with her great-grandfather, or whether she had any say about marrying him.

Like the host of the film screening, descendants of enslaving families repeated claims that there was no power differential. "After all," one person in Kerman told me, "they ate whatever was left over from meals. Other Iranians could not afford to live like the slaves. If that wasn't enough, they could pick fruit from our trees." Plus, she added—unknowingly parroting the same defenses of slavery given on the parliamentary floor in 1929—they learned to be civilized.[2] The ability to pick fruit from trees does not negate the looming reality that they were enslaved and denied the dignity of living life on their own terms. But these people would tell you otherwise. One individual did share with me that some enslaving families were particularly cruel and violent to the people they enslaved, even going so far as to sewing a person's mouth shut if they spoke back to them.[3] This same person, however, was very clear: *Our family was not like that.*

While these narratives rest on norms and stereotypes surrounding enslavement prior to 1929, they erase the taint of enslaving people from these family histories in recent decades. Even their defenses reveal much about how their families viewed those they had enslaved: that they were not civilized, that they could just scavenge for food, that they loved them as members of the family. This chapter examines the memories and narratives that persist and perpetuate the ongoing process of erasure today, a genre of distortion unto itself. Drawing on Trouillot's four stages of historical erasures (the making of sources, the making of archives, the making of narratives, and finally the making of history), this chapter focuses on the third stage, the making of narratives.[4] The narratives of the enslaving families are particularly critical. Because of their power—and their dominance over each of these stages of history-making—the narratives of enslavement in Iran have typically framed enslavers as generous, benevolent, and typically good people who just happened to have enslaved other people. To be clear, some sources and narratives do come from enslaved people and their descendants. But in the official spaces that create histories—institutional archives, academic forums, and so forth—those sources have not been privileged or shared and remain the minority among other more dominant narratives.[5] I am optimistic that this is changing and that future writings will introduce different sources that challenge these narratives. Until then, an examination of these histories requires closer consideration.

This chapter focuses on narrative-building as its own genre because it reflects the extent to which histories that rely on the oppressor tend to invoke a similar tone and even language. Trouillot's four phases are particularly resonant in the case of Iranian history-making, where (1) many extant written and visual sources concerning enslavement were documented by enslavers; (2) almost all sources pertaining to the history of enslavement held in archives were donated or contributed by the enslaving family; (3) the narratives all take on a similar benevolent tone; and (4) historians take these narratives and sources at face value, and the dominant historical writing about Iran's history of enslavement insists that it was a mutually beneficial relationship. Our focus here is the third phase of history-making, where the language of personal histories of enslavement in one's family takes a euphemistic turn. This is true both in family settings and in public dialogues. This chapter focuses on these narratives and describes them as a genre of distortion, involving narratives from enslaving families and their descendants written in English for a diasporic and/or non-Iranian audience. This is not because these narratives do not exist in Persian; rather, it is to demonstrate their longevity and long-distance nature. By examining four narratives of various lengths—an academic article, two books, and an Instagram post—we can identify five elements that distort a history of enslavement:

1. An emphasis on the shared love between the enslaver and the enslaved, especially highlighting how much the enslaved was devoted to their enslaver.
2. Referring to the enslaved as a member of their family, with only a cursory mention of their birth family (if at all).
3. Explanations that the enslaved was not "really" enslaved, *or* explanations of why the enslaving family had no choice but to enslave someone in their home.
4. The assertion that because of their intertwined family history with enslaved Black people, they and their families understand race and racism better than others who did not enslave people in their homes.
5. The element especially unique to these Iranian-based narratives: the urge to educate their audience about what enslavement may or may not have looked like in Iran. Because of the deep erasure of enslavement, these individuals wield their intimate knowledge to shape what may or may not count as enslavement, absolve their ancestors of blame, and present themselves as an authority on a matter that many in their audience might be learning about for the first time.

The greatest distortion, however, is that narratives from the enslaved and their descendants are conspicuously absent. If abolition was a process of erasure, it certainly erased their perspectives from larger national platforms. This silence is multilayered—descendants of the enslaved were discouraged from speaking their truth both directly and indirectly, after experiencing intimidation from their enslavers' families or in an attempt to avoid or minimize the stigma of enslavement as much as possible. As such, the dominant narratives that remain in published form or in archival institutions are usually from the hands of an enslaving family and their descendants. The silences and the vacuum of voices have allowed enslavers and their descendants to claim this space, distort these memories, and give an increasingly rosy view on their past, attributing a kind of prophetic infallibility to their enslaving ancestors. It is in this way that the experiences of the enslaved are, again, forcibly invisibilized or ignored, their presence rendered palatable to a (formerly) enslaving class, and ultimately described as not enslaved at all.

BLURRING MEMORIES

One need not have enslavers in one's ancestry to uphold enslavers' myths. At a talk at a large R-1 institution, one established professor scoffed at my lecture, saying, "Sure, they were slaves, but it's not like we had separate water fountains for them!" Others have said similar things along the lines of *Well, we did not whip our slaves!*, or other direct acts of violence typically associated with chattel slavery. Most often, people told me, *We never had slavery!* referring to ahistorical narratives about Cyrus the Great.[6] I heard similar statements at dinner parties and in other casual conversations.

In all three of these statements, the individuals—non-Black Iranians in Iran and in the diaspora—used the word *we* to describe the actions of enslavers a century ago, if not more. In other words, they identified with the enslaving class, even though none of them lived during the period of legal enslavement, and none predicated their assumptions or claims on their own personal family histories.[7] In the same way that descendants of enslavers have generally assumed the prophetic infallibility of their ancestors, these individuals ascribed a prophetic infallibility to all Iranians—and perhaps Iran itself. One might note that many Iranians are quick to critique Iran in other arenas, both currently and historically, depending on their political beliefs and ideologies. But something about the topic of enslavement causes a knee-jerk reaction.

Others react differently. *Ah yes, slaves*, they say, *my family had slaves growing up. One served as our driver.* You might press this person to say more, and you learn that they are referring to someone who might have worked with their family for a few months or years in the 1950s or '60s—someone who arrived from a nearby village looking for work, who agreed to work in exchange for room and board, and who left for another job on their own volition.[8] These individuals, usually young men but sometimes women as well, did various chores—cooking, cleaning, or, like the example above, chauffeuring—until they could get on their feet in a new city. Their voluntary entry into such a role and the ability to leave and access to mobility definitively means these are not examples of enslavement. But because of the lack of a cash salary, the domestic nature of these roles, and vagueness of vocabulary describing servants after the 1929 Manumission Law, some have compared it to enslavement. This is a superficial assessment that reflects how muddled these terms have become and how they allow Iranians to deny a history of enslavement altogether.[9]

Some take it a step further, making a false acknowledgment cloaked in a denial of enslavement as a unique category. *Yes, yes, a history of slavery*, they say, *much like how all Iranians were slaves to the shah before the revolution, were they not?* These metaphorical comparisons cheapen the violence of enslavement and its racial traumas. Erasures of enslavement make room for these claims, like all Iranians having been "slaves" to the shah, that do not distinguish between life under a despot versus a life enslaved.

But more and more, I have come to realize that the erasures around Iran's history of enslavement are incomplete and are rather more like whispers that sometimes erupt into loud outbursts. This makes sense, after all, as abolition only took place not too long ago, in 1929. Usually those from enslaving families have remained quiet, referring to their family's history as asides in hushed tones. This tendency to remain quiet plays a large role in academia and particularly in Iranian Studies, a field overwhelmingly shaped by scholars of Iranian heritage, most of whom grew up in Iran or hail from royal or wealthy elite families. This generation of scholars did not research Iran's history of enslavement.[10] It remained only in the footnotes of their books or in passing references that diminished the role of the enslaved in Iranian history.

Once in a while, this past and its memories come to the fore. At the 2016 Association for Iranian Studies conference in Vienna, a descendant of the Qajar royal family responded to a panel on Iran's history of race and enslavement with this comment: "I grew up with slaves. And let me tell you, the Black ones were the fun ones. And they weren't slaves—they took care of the babies and shopping. Sometimes we even left them alone with kids." She added that they also let them go to the movie theaters.[11] The claims here, and others like them, are strange. The princess in question was born over a decade after the 1929 Manumission Law, in 1940. The math here does not add up and only begs more questions, although the most likely scenario is that her family kept their formerly enslaved domestics as servants after 1929, a status that was often more of a semantic change than anything else.

Although this anecdote may seem silly at first glance—a Qajar princess who did not grow up at court inserted herself in a conversation about Iranian enslavement by recalling her memory of servants—it is important for other reasons as well. This princess is a major benefactor of the academy: she sponsors conferences and other forums and serves on the boards of several different academy-oriented organizations. Her comment that day began with an admonition that she is sorry to see that so many people in Iranian Studies no longer know what they are talking about. This is because, she continued, they have taken to studying things they have not lived through. Aside from the rejection of the entire discipline of history, she inadvertently negated her own opinion as well, as she had not lived through the period of legal enslavement in Iran either. Perhaps the only other remaining interpretation of her comments, then, is not that they were servants but that her family kept them enslaved after they were legally freed.

The princess is far from unique. Similar claims and examples abound. Baroness Haleh Afshar's peer-reviewed article in *Ethnic and Racial Studies* is a prime example of this genre of distortion. Afshar wrote about Sonbol Baji, her family's nanny, who was enslaved at the Qajar court as a toddler, just two years old, and was later expelled once Ahmad Shah disbanded the harem. As Amy Motlagh has written, although Afshar wrote about Sonbol Baji's memories as an example of a different kind of feminism, Afshar did not grapple with any of the troubling aspects of their family dynamic.[12] Instead of acknowledging the kinds of pain that Sonbol Baji may have experienced, Afshar doubled down and emphasized that Sonbol Baji's younger years enslaved at the harem were the best years of her life.[13] Most blatantly,

Afshar impressed upon her reader that Sonbol Baji was enslaved in a different way, not what you would think of when you think of the word *slave*:

> Sonbol Baji's experience is very distinct and different from those of "black" American slave women working on plantations or in households. . . . Hers was an urban, urbane, and leisured life. She was neither sex object nor a domestic worker; she had the allure of the exotic, a beautiful child who had been a playmate of the royal children. . . . In the harem she was a friend and confident [*sic*] of the princesses. Looking back she recalled gaiety, laughter, singing and a joyful life where the leisurely pursuit of amusement, health, and beauty were the main concerns.[14]

Within a few sentences, Afshar rejected the audience's expectation of what it meant to be enslaved. For Afshar, because those enslaved at the harem were first and foremost status symbols and signs of wealth and power, she did not believe such a position could be a difficult one for anyone to hold. Similarly, she did not seem to realize that her own relationship with Sonbol Baji involved a power imbalance, or that Sonbol Baji may have had her reasons for not complaining about her life to Afshar.

Afshar switched between the active and the passive tense to give Sonbol Baji as much agency as possible, while emphasizing that her family did not intend to enslave her. For example, Sonbol Baji "arrived in the harem" at the age of two and "stayed" until the disbanding of the harem.[15] But when she mentions the Qajar court or her grandfather's enslavement of Sonbol Baji, the verbs tend to be passive: "she was brought," or "she was taken in by my grandfather." Afshar did, however, note that Mozaffar ed-Din Shah wanted an exotic child in his entourage.[16] Sonbol Baji was likely "taken in" by Afshar's grandfather after he paid a sum for her. And although Afshar maintains that she was neither "a sex object nor a domestic worker," these seem to be what her fate held for her: after arriving at Afshar's house, she was married to a relative and bore him a son. Like so many enslaved and formerly enslaved women before her, it is unclear whether she had a say in the marriage. After the unexpected death of her husband, Sonbol Baji took on the task of raising Afshar's mother from infancy and "moved in with her" (again, the active voice) when Afshar's mother married and left her childhood home. Despite this, Afshar insisted that Sonbol Baji was not servile but was, rather, "in charge."[17] While Afshar shared each of these turns of Sonbol Baji's life as examples of her agency, it is unclear whether Sonbol Baji had chosen to do any of these things or whether Afshar only imagined her power.

While Afshar did argue for a non-US-centric definition of enslavement, she advocated for a definition that required a suspension of logic, where, in Afshar's imagination, the enslaved enjoys their enslavement, finding it as luxurious as the life of those who enslaved her. This genre of distortion tends to also rely on photographs to prove the point of the enslaver—that is, their inclusion in a "family photograph" must mean they are "family"—as though having photographs of family members with enslaved domestics is somehow either unique or altogether negates their enslavement.[18] But Motlagh has noted that in a photograph of Sonbol Baji, Afshar, and her brother, Sonbol Baji appears forlorn and sad, a far cry from Afshar's persistent suggestions that Sonbol Baji loved being enslaved and felt like a member of her family.[19] Indeed, the photograph betrays its prime function: this photograph of Sonbol Baji, like others taken during the late nineteenth and early twentieth centuries, was meant for the enslaving family, for their self-aggrandizement. These photographs were not for those they enslaved, and certainly not to present them as members of a family. People like Afshar, who were the young children in the photographs, would grow up to use them again as adults to prove their family's grandness and generosity.

Even the shortest of these narratives—an Instagram post from 2020—echoes these sentiments in abbreviated form. Shared at the height of the #BlackLivesMatter protests in the aftermath of George Floyd's murder, the post includes old color photographs of a Black woman, her hair covered by a scarf in an Iranian home, sitting in front of a birthday cake. The caption manages to squeeze the elements of a genre of distortion into a limited word count. The author of the Instagram account, an Iranian British woman, shared a slightly different narrative while still maintaining the same core aspects of a genre of distortion. The post, which was intended to show solidarity with Black people at a time of historic uprising, stated clearly that she understands racial tensions in a way that other Iranians have been blind to, not only because she has been treated as Black in London (a statement she emphasizes with the parenthetical aside "yes, really") but also, and primarily, because she has memories of "Masoumeh, the help and my bonus grandma." While the author referred to Masoumeh as "the help," a vague moniker that only indicated what kind of work she did in their home, various phrases from the caption intimate that she had been born into enslavement, even if she retained servant status at some point in her life. Referring to her mother's painting of a Black child crying, the author wrote, "As a child, I'd imagine the girl in the painting to be Masoumeh, separated from her sisters, longing for her own family, wondering how different her life would be, had she not been black." The author ended with a plea asking other Iranians to recognize that the fight against racism was global and that it existed within the Iranian community as well.

While the author of the caption acknowledged racism and Masoumeh's sadness about being separated from her family, the photographs paired with the caption present the author's family as a benevolent one—one that celebrated birthdays and mundane moments together. But the post as a whole presented the author as an expert intimately aware of racism because of her own intimacy with Masoumeh, and the photographs serve as further proof of her reliability because they show that her family treated Masoumeh well, despite her acknowledgment of wondering about her sadness.[20]

The initial comments on the post, from friends, family, and even strangers, focused solely on their family dynamics and less so on the rejection of racism. The feedback from family members included comments like "Haj Masoumeh's existence was a symbol of pure love" and "She was my second mum to me" and other comments, in Persian and in English, that extend the elements of a genre of distortion on the social media platform.

PROPHETIC INFALLIBILITY

On the night of May 23, 1844, at the age of twenty-five, Seyyed ʿAli Mohammad Shirazi adopted the title "the Bab," a designation that would come to represent his new role as prophet and messenger of God. For his followers in Babism and the Baha'i faith, the Bab represented the arrival of the twelfth Shiʿa imam, the Mahdi himself. His proclamation story began with a knock on his front door. That door was opened by an enslaved Black man, Haji Mobarak, whom he had purchased two years earlier.[21]

Abu'l-Qasim Afnan, the grand-nephew of the Bab, wrote about Haji Mobarak and the other enslaved Africans serving the families of the Bab and Baha'u'llah in his book *Black Pearls: Servants in the Household of the Bab and Baha'u'llah*, published first in 1988, and then in 1999 with an introduction by Anthony Lee. Adherents of the Baha'i faith believe the Bab and Baha'u'llah were prophets who ushered in a new age and religion in the nineteenth century.[22] In a later article, Lee noted that while the book was initially met with controversy from the Baha'i community for highlighting enslaved individuals in the households of the prophets, it is seen differently today.[23] Lee acknowledged the disappointment and outrage of African American Baha'is upon learning about the lives of the Bab and Baha'u'llah as having ever enslaved individuals in their households, especially since Baha'u'llah had prohibited the trading of enslaved people in the Kitab-i Aqdas in 1873. Lee, who has dedicated his career to recovering and preserving the lives of these enslaved individuals, argued that some of the reactions "insisted on the erasure of enslaved Africans from the history of the Baha'i religion."[24] Lee also noted that some African American Baha'is were particularly upset and felt that Afnan's accounts were patronizing. It is Afnan's tone and framing that I use here as a comparative to another example of a "genre of distortion," a memoir that documents a Muslim Iranian family (with no purported prophetic or otherwise religiously significant lineage) and the people they enslaved. Where Afnan described the lives and households of prophets he believed to be infallible as a matter of faith, other Iranians also framed their families as infallible, not out of a religious belief but out of a desire to absolve themselves of a guilt-ridden inheritance.

Although Afnan did use the word *slave* in footnotes and asides, the subtitle and narrative of *Black Pearls* insist that these individuals were not truly enslaved: they had a status more similar to that of servants, they were always treated well, they were members of the family, and they loved their enslavers.[25] The text also included explanations for why they would have even enslaved people: that it was customary for wealthy families of their social class, and that Islam's gender boundaries made it difficult for wealthy families to live in their sprawling homes without the labor of enslaved people.[26]

According to Afnan, his great-grandfather Haji Mirza Abo'l Qasem had purchased a five-year-old East African boy in 1828 and named him Mobarak. The boy remained enslaved in his household until 1842, when he was nineteen years old and Abo'l Qasem sold him to his brother-in-law, twenty-three-year-old Seyyed 'Ali Mohammad Shirazi, who was returning to Shiraz after a six-year-long trip to Karbala and Bushehr. Seyyed 'Ali Mohammad Shirazi paid fourteen toman for Mobarak.[27] Despite sharing the exact payment the Bab gave to purchase Mobarak, Afnan's narrative framed them as servants, leaning on the idea that *bardeh* cannot refer to those enslaved in domestic spaces.

As a devout Baha'i, Afnan's belief in the infallibility of the Bab and Baha'u'llah is paramount. Although the wording of the 1873 edict focuses on the slave trade, Bahá'u'lláh is understood to have declared enslavement illegal for Bahá'ís in 1873, ten years after his claim of prophethood in 1863. *Black Pearls*, however, seems to imply that members in the Báb's household kept enslaved people within their home after the edict.[28] Afnan, however, is clear that these individuals were brought into their homes before the prohibition.[29] Afnan's predicament—writing about people enslaved by those he believed were infallible, yet still recognizing that enslavement is wrong and sinful—involves a uniquely difficult tension.[30]

Afnan was not singular in writing about those his family had enslaved. Others also wrote and published about their family's complicity in the slave trade. This narrative is all too familiar, and it often relies on the same kind of language across borders. Enslaving ancestors are framed as only having followed social norms, absolving them of any responsibility in their complicity in the enslavement of others. But even though most people's memories of their forebearers are not underpinned by a religious belief in their prophetic infallibility, their narratives echo the same sentiments of Afnan's—that their families were loving, benevolent enslavers and cherished the enslaved members of their families. Sayeh Dashti's self-published family history, *To Our Children around the World: You Belong*, based on a cassette recording of the author's mother's memories, goes to great lengths to frame those enslaved by her family as family members. Chapter 7 of *To Our Children around the World* is explicitly titled "Black Members of our Family," and two individuals, Sultan and Samanbar (whose name is spelled inconsistently throughout the text), are described as "adopted African children."[31] Throughout the narrative, Dashti produced and packaged memories, casting them in the best possible light to prove the sincerity of her family's love for these individuals, from their arrival in their home to their subsequent treatment and their memories in the afterlife.

The adoption of these children remains questionable: either Dashti was unclear on their status or she intentionally obfuscated it. Her narrative cleared her family, specifically Ammeh ("paternal aunt"), her great-aunt, of any wrongdoing. The enslaved children were first brought to their family by her aunt's second husband:

> This khan brought all his wealth to Ammeh, including two African children he owned. He put the children in Ammeh's "papers" (dowry).
>
> Successive epidemic of cholera killed hundreds in the south of Iran. People of all ages lost their lives, specially the very young white children—most black children survived.

Ammeh had a son with her second husband. Once again she lost her son and her husband to cholera; she and her two black children survived. She decided to devote the rest of her life to serving God and serving her children. She was at her prayer mat most of the day, praying to God.[32]

Dashti's narrative switched from acknowledging that the young Black children were enslaved to shifting to them being adopted. She peddled some unfounded medical racism and ended the section by saying Ammeh decided to "devote the rest of her life to serving her children," reversing one's expectations of how one expects to treat their enslaved.[33]

The matter-of-fact statement of an adoption, however, is curious. Adoptions were not typical in Iran. Dashti adds an additional piece of information in a footnote: "Bibi Batool tried to explain that a woman's papers were different from her dowry. What she tried to say sounded more like adoption papers even though government birth certificates did not exist in Iran at that time. The names of the two black children were written on the first page of Ammeh's Koran, an indication that she was their lawful mother." Even though Dashti specified that it was a "dowry" in the parenthetical aside in text, her footnote negates her explanation and suggests that it was something else altogether, something impossible to translate and impossible to define exactly. It is not beyond the realm of possibility that these children were enslaved and were mentioned in her dowry. (I discussed in chapter 2 how enslaved people were often included in dowries as foundational gifts for a marriage.) Dashti's convoluted explanation rests on a resistance to the most direct explanation—that these children were given to Ammeh as property, that they remained in service to her family for the rest of their lives, and their children were born into service to her family as well. The insistence that her aunt would not keep the children enslaved and would instead raise them as her own is a theme that runs through the memoir that requires undefinable words and relationships.

It is not an exceptional theme, however. Afnan's stories in *Black Pearls* emphasizes that enslaved individuals—Mobarak, Quddus, Isfandiyar, Fiddih, and others—were devoted to their enslaving families and were not really enslaved. For example, after the Bab was executed in Tabriz, the women of his household moved to Karbala, and per Afnan's narrative, they asked Mobarak and the other domestics to join them. The Bab's family never mentioned his execution to Mobarak or the others; instead, they said he was away on a trip to India. Afnan noted Mobarak's devotion to the Bab: for example, he tied a green ribbon on his broom and always looked out for his arrival. Mobarak died waiting for the Bab, who would never return. Afnan offered this story as evidence of Mobarak's dedication to the Bab, whom he is said to have loved deeply and who was deeply loved by the family, despite their decision to never inform him of the Bab's passing.[34]

Afnan explained this secrecy as a reflection of the family's own fears of rumors, and their decision to try to maintain their safety at all costs. According to Afnan, the Bab's family did not trust Mobarak or the other domestics to not share information that may have jeopardized their safety—a lack of trust that distinguished those enslaved from the family.[35] But Afnan's narrative, especially his insistence on Mobarak and the others' devotion to the Bab and Baha'u'llah, makes sense within the broader understanding of enslavement within the Baha'i faith. Baha'u'llah praised the abolition efforts of Queen Victoria in 1869 and would ultimately ban the trading of enslaved people for his followers in 1873.[36] That members of their families had ever enslaved people is a complicated reality that one can make sense of through their believed infallibility, that these individuals were cared for and viewed as members of the family.

What is strange, though, is that Dashti's great-aunt received the same treatment as religious prophets. Dashti wielded the symbolism of the Qur'an and the prayer mat to prove her aunt's religiosity, which Dashti seems to have believed would have negated any possibility of her aunt's enslavement of children. Families that have not reckoned with the weight of enslavement and how their lives have benefited from stolen lives and labor find it more comfortable to cushion memories of their families as infallible, as though they are their own prophets.

It is hard to rewrite the past completely, and Dashti's memoir is replete with examples and hints that these individuals were enslaved. And she even acknowledged that Sultan and Samanbar were enslaved and trafficked on ships from the ports of East Africa.[37] Dashti's contention is not that enslavement never took place in Iran but, rather, that it never took place *within her family*. Throughout the book, she highlighted the various ways they and their children may have been elevated to the status of a family member: their marriages and weddings, their living arrangements, and their inclusion in the patriarch's will. None of these things, however, indicate their freedom. In fact, the continued closeness of their families throughout the generations is the best indicator of their enslavement, as it points toward their lack of mobility and alternate options for work.

Because Dashti was an Iranian living in the United States, the reframing of her family's story allowed her to assert a moral high ground with regard to race and racial relations. She even began her chapter "Black Members of Our Family" with a vignette of her mother chasing down a Black woman in a department store and telling her, "We love our Blacks," deploring the history of racism and anti-Blackness in the United States. Dashti drew on this framing to present her family as distinctly *not* racist despite acknowledging that her mother's words were "inherently prejudiced" and that her family's relationship with "our Blacks" was a nurturing one, overlooking the repeated proprietorial vocabulary used to describe them.[38] The major characteristics that Dashti used to counter any idea that her family enslaved these individuals are all within a legible realm of normative enslavement practices in Iran: enslaving families often arranged for their enslaved domestics to be married; enslaved people were often housed either within the enslaver's home or, in the case of an enslaved family, a separate structure next door; and the enslaved were sometimes mentioned in the will of a patriarch.

Dashti offered a generous reading of her family patriarch's will. Sultan was named as an heir to the will, and Dashti shared it as further proof that her family counted Sultan as one of their own. But the patriarch included the clause that Sultan's family were to "live as free people and always be supported by our family." The will was written in 1939, a decade after the Manumission Law.

Why would this clause be necessary if no one in the family ever viewed Sultan as enslaved, and if everyone viewed him and his children as members of the family?

SERVITUDE

The stories of the enslaving family served the enslaving family. Because of the concerns now surrounding enslavement, the stories are dressed up in a self-serving language of benevolence and generosity to distance parents, uncles, aunts, grandparents, and great-grandparents from culpability in the horrors of enslavement while still claiming it as a status symbol.

___

If we follow Trouillot's four phases of history-making, the distortions can only be addressed at the making of sources, the making of archives, the making of narratives, and then ultimately the making of history. The voices and perspectives of the enslaved and their descendants are typically not represented in these stages for different reasons. At the stage of narrative writing, these seem to boil down to one of two reasons, both related to the erasure of enslavement. Although abolition was a process of erasure, it did not erase the memories of those who had been enslaved. Instead, many were quiet or quieted about their experiences, hushed by the stigma of enslavement. By contrast, the enslavers actively did the erasing, creating alternate histories to explain away the presence of enslaved individuals in their families' homes.

At some point, these narratives from enslaving families all blur together, and it is unhelpful to focus on them. They are self-serving and misleading narratives that intentionally distort the past. When read by other nationalist Iranians, the narrative of the enslaving family is mapped onto Iran, and Iran itself is framed as a benevolent country that could never do harm (although Iranians have and do typically criticize those in political power). These are all narratives and histories derived from sources and archives created and built by enslavers or people in a similar social class. One wonders how these histories might differ if the voices of the enslaved were readily available and not filtered through bureaucratic papers or the albums of their enslaving families.

EPILOGUE
BLACK LIFE IN THE AFTERMATH OF A FORCED INVISIBILITY

Born in Bushehr in 1936, Jahanbakhsh Kurdizadeh grew up leading recitations at religious gatherings for the Shi'i commemorations of 'Ashura and Arba'in.[1] Kurdizadeh's powerful voice and deeply beautiful narrations in honor of the Prophet's grandson Husayn and his family drew people out from all over the southern coast to Bushehr to listen to his *rowzeh*. Like many others in Bushehr, Kurdizadeh was a visibly Black Iranian. He was someone his close friends would call *Siyah* or *Siyahpust*, and those who see his photograph might mistake him for a member of a different African or African diaspora population.

Enslavement and abolition shaped Bushehr, a major port city for the trade of goods and the trafficking of kidnapped Africans into Iran and a home for the British Residency after the eighteenth century. Bushehr's role in the Persian Gulf waxed and waned throughout the nineteenth and twentieth centuries.[2] Wealthy merchant families built out the Behbahani district along the gulf coast, where they lived in homes along with both paid servants or enslaved individuals of African ancestry. Their proximity to the port allowed them to increase their wealth and engage in trade, and the neighborhood grew during the eighteenth and nineteenth centuries. In the twentieth century, trade patterns and political interests changed, and Bushehr stopped being the powerhouse center of the Persian Gulf that it once had been.

After abolition, these wealthy families left the Behbahani district and moved elsewhere. Black freedpeople and their families stayed, and some took over homes once owned by wealthy enslavers.[3] The area came to be associated with Black Iranians. The Behbahani district remains home to an eponymous mosque, with opposing entrances referred to as "Black" and "white."[4]

The Behbahani Mosque has a small side room for storing the *dammam*, a drum used in Bushehri religious services and musical performances.[5] ʿAshura and Arbaʿin services begin with the beating of drums, where the drummers enter from those Black and white entrances, followed by recitations of eulogies, where attendees link together in concentric circles and follow the rhythm of the reciters. Different leaders participate in every phase of the mourning, from coordinating the drumming, to leading the eulogies, to organizing the concentric circles. Photographs of these leaders, some of whom passed on half a century ago, hang above the drums in the *dammam* room (fig. E.1). The generations of photographs narrate the communal history of the mosque after the 1930s.

Against the backdrop of a forced invisibility that erased both the history of enslavement and Black Iranians, these photographs tell a different story of community, family, and preservation. To be clear, I do not know whether anyone photographed here had enslaved ancestors. In a port city like Bushehr, both free and forced patterns of migration connected the East African coast to the Iranian one. But the nature of forced invisibility is such that it erased references to *both* enslavement *and* Black Iranians, regardless of their ancestry, on a national scale. Even today, many Black Iranians can share stories of being mistaken for a foreigner in major metropolitan centers in Iran, such as Tehran, Isfahan, or Mashhad, simply because the locals assume that individuals who are visibly Black must be foreign. Often non-Black Iranians will respond with surprise (or condescension) when they meet a Black Iranian.[6]

But in Bushehr, in the side room of the Behbahani Mosque, a multigenerational story of maintaining the religious services that served the broader community hovers over the hanging drums. Despite the national narrative, Black Iranians continue to live in Iran, maintaining traditions and creating new ones. In central Iran, Black individuals dispersed after abolition, their presence no longer a key fixture of public life. Yet away from Tehran, and away from central Iran, it was harder to cement these erasures because Black communities were integrated into a larger social fabric that existed along the coast. They remained a core part of the

E.1 *Dammam* room at the Behbahani Mosque, marking the mosque's history of *dammam* leaders, sometimes carried within the same family. The third from the left is the father of the third from the right. At far-thest right, the frames also include a still from Naser Taqvayi's *Arba'in*. (Photo by the author, Behbahani Mosque, Bushehr, Iran.)

community, even if their presence was forgotten or erased by people in metropolitan centers.

Any type of forced invisibility or disappearing is never complete, and the racial otherness of Black Iranians was never fully invisibilized. Instead of a direct acknowledgment of their Blackness, however, many will assert that "southerners" have darker skin from their exposure to the hotter sun in the Persian Gulf. These differences are framed as obvious or inconsequential, acknowledged only superficially and only in spaces that do not have national implications. They inform a pattern that tacitly justifies their erasure from history. In a society where racial difference is visually resonant yet almost never openly discussed, these contradictions render the erasures slippery and difficult to pin down.

Yet a case such as Kurdizadeh's—whose ancestry is unknown to me—demonstrates vividly how forced invisibility affected his legacy as a Black Iranian. During his lifetime, Kurdizadeh was a well-known *rowzeh-khwan* in the South. In 1970, Kurdizadeh's recitations drew a larger crowd than usual, one that included director Naser Taqvayi and his crew, who had traveled from Tehran to film a documentary, *Arba'in*. The documentary was part of a larger national trend to create ethnographies about the various regions and minorities across Iran.[7] But *Arba'in* did not circulate much during the 1970s, although it has been screened and reprised several times since. And while the ethnographic documentary does imply some understanding of race or a racial other, it renders Kurdizadeh a regional, minority figure, not an individual of national importance.[8] A few years after Kurdizadeh's death in 1977, however, Kurdizadeh's recitations influenced a popular—if not the most popular—anthem of the Iran-Iraq War (1980–88). Compare Kurdizadeh's eulogy (first) with Kuveitipur's war song (second):

> I fear I may die and not see
> His face anymore,
> Until the lines of Judgment Day,
> Young Akbar,
> *Ah-e-vaveyla*,
> Where is my Akbar,
> The light of my two damp eyes[9]

> Mammad, you weren't there to see,
> The city is now free,

The blood of your peers
Bore fruit,
Ah-o-vaveyla
Where is Jahanara,
The light of our two damp eyes

Kurdizadeh recited the lines in the first recitation in honor of ʿAli Akbar, the son of Husayn who was killed at Karbala from the point of view of his mother. Gholam ʿAli Kuveitipur, who led war songs at the front, sang the lines in the second anthem after the Iranian army drove Iraqi forces out of the city of Khorramshahr in 1982, where Iranian commander Mohammad "Mammad" Jahanara had died a year earlier.

The two songs are remarkably similar not only in their wording but also in their melodies, which Kuveitipur borrowed directly from Kurdizadeh's recitation. Despite these similarities, and despite the nationwide popularity of "Mammad, you weren't there to see," Kurdizadeh has not received an appropriate amount of credit, and Kuveitipur has only acknowledged Kurdizadeh's influence on him in a circuitous manner. While Kurdizadeh and Kuveitipur are both southerners, Kurdizadeh is Black, and Kuveitipur is not.[10] And of the two, only Kuveitipur is a household name across Iran.

Even though Kurdizadeh's work strongly influenced a major cultural production—one that is played on government television and radio outlets every May to commemorate the recapture of Khorramshahr—his person is only ever included in national spaces to represent a peripheral region, a minoritized "other," or a folk tradition, all of which tacitly point to his Blackness without ever referencing it. He is never framed in a way that would allow him to represent or recite on behalf of the Iranian people; only non-Black Iranians, such as Kuveitipur, are ever given such a platform.

Kurdizadeh's case demonstrates plainly how the forced invisibility of abolition was a process that continued throughout the twentieth century and affected all Black Iranians, regardless of their ancestry. The permeative quality of the (willful) erasure is precisely why it is so important to address these histories, to combat a rampant nationalism that frames Blackness in Iran as strange, as an other, or as nonexistent.

GENRES OF RESTORATION

In light of stories like Kurdizadeh's and others who are erased or forgotten from a national perspective, the emergence of social media is a powerful tool for negating hegemonic discourse. Social media has afforded Black Iranians the space to move away from these erasures and to reclaim stories and histories like these as their own. One such pioneering group is the Collective for Black Iranians. Founded by a group of Black and Afro-Iranians, this transnational organization has amplified Black voices and provided accessible histories in their regularly published bilingual content in Persian and English on social media.[11] Iranian social media discourse during the #BlackLivesMatter protests in the summer of 2020 privileged examples of the genre of distortion as reliable sources on race and enslavement in Iran.[12] While the formation of the collective had already been underway, the widespread misinformation and deep interest in Black Iranian histories prompted the group's launch in August 2020.[13]

The work of the collective spans several topics, from their *Siyah Zibast* (*Black Is Beautiful*) series to *Let's Talk about Blackness* and others, all geared toward creating a culture that claims, celebrates, and embraces Blackness as a central identity within the Iranian context. The collective's work has also pushed the boundaries of historical writing by making space for these sources and narratives to be presented from their point of view. Correcting the history of enslavement and acknowledging the ways that it continues to frame Blackness in Iran is key to understanding ongoing racial dynamics in order to move past them.

Among the projects of the collective, one titled *Writing Ourselves* reimagines Qajar-era portraiture to "refocus attention to those who have been erased," placing dignity in being seen.[14] The series takes royal Qajar portraits that included enslaved Black individuals and instead creates a new portrait with them at the center, one bereft of enslavers, demanding that their person be acknowledged and respected, creating a new kind of visibility.

Their work is especially salient because much public discussion of nineteenth-century Iran, the history of enslavement, and the presence of Black Iranians in Iran on social media has been guided via images. For example, the groundbreaking art exhibition *Royal Persian Paintings: The Qajar Epoch, 1785–1925*, curated by Layla Diba with Maryam Ekhtiar at the Brooklyn Museum of Art in 1998–99, and its accompanying volume made

E.2 While eunuchs were often photographed, portrait paintings are rare. (#WritingOurselves, created by the Collective for Black Iranians. Illustrated by Kimia Fatehi in conversation with Priscillia Kounkou Hoveyda [founder] and the author [resident historian]. https.//www. instagram.com/p/CLH_ZCWAZwX/?utm_source=ig_web_copy_link.)

E.3 Refocusing our lens on the enslaved women who were imagined and forgotten. (#WritingOurselves, created by the Collective for Black Iranians. Illustrated by Kimia Fatehi in conversation with Priscillia Kounkou Hoveyda [founder] and the author [resident historian]. https://www.instagram .com/p/COQfFsEAUJf/?utm_source=ig_web_copy_link.)

E.4 and E.5 Popular Qajar-era paintings: Prince ʿAbd al-Samad Mirza and his entourage, held at the Golestan Palace Museum (published in Zoka, *Life and Works of Saniʿ ol-Molk*, 79); "Embracing Lovers Caught by Housemaids" (photo from Sotheby's, *Arts of the Islamic World*).

a case for the importance of the Qajar art, while only briefly mentioning relevant histories or portraits depicting enslaved people or enslavement.[15] Since then, Qajar imagery has become much more popular among people in Iran and in the diaspora. Thumbnails of Qajar portraiture (painted or photographed) pulled from such museum collections or auctions circulate constantly on social media, continuing the erasure of enslaved individuals in the frame.

More recently, in 2016, Pedram Khosronejad published a series of photographs in a *Guardian* piece titled "The Face of African Slavery in Qajar Iran—in Pictures."[16] The photographs are offered without much context, although the accompanying article does mention a few key points: that the history of enslavement is not typically acknowledged and that most enslaved people in Iran were domestics. The article served as the precursor to a number of exhibitions and the publication of his book *Qajar African Nannies*, where captions are separated from the photographs and listed at the end of the book.[17] Despite the lack of much information, these photos are among the most commonly circulated photographs of Iranian examples of enslavement or of Black Iranians on social media. Because these photos are often shared without much context, people have often interpreted these images as proof of the benevolence of enslavement. The refinement of their clothing or luxury of their surroundings have served as a misleading form of evidence that they were not "really" enslaved. The sharing of these historical photographs without appropriate care reinscribes a history of Black Iranians as entirely framed by a gentle enslavement and prevents critical conversations on this history.

Reframing these histories remains critical to writing the past. These are histories that have lingered without proper attention, despite having been built on sources, narratives, and archives that were formed at the expense of enslaved and freed Black people. At this point, some of these histories have been forgotten, some have been erased, and others are willfully ignored. It is for this reason that the collective and other scholars, artists, and activists have taken to returning to these moments, photographs, spaces, and places and to honor those forgotten. Their histories, like that of Kurdizadeh and others who came before him, need to be written and rewritten: new genres of restoration that push for a different kind of visibility.

AN EPILOGUE BUT NOT AN ENDING

I struggled with naming this section: Is it a conclusion? An afterword? An epilogue? All of these imply an ending, but the work here is ongoing. Until we can say we remember that little girl in that first photograph, the one whose name has been forgotten and replaced multiple times over; until we can say we remember her and others like her; until we can say we remember the Yaquts, the work remains unfinished. I spent over half this book describing what forgetting looks like. But what can remembering look like?

NOTES

INTRODUCTION

1   There were other Yaquts as well, enslaved in other parts of the Indian Ocean world and beyond, their lives not bound by these centuries. See Nicolini, "Western Indian Ocean as Cultural Corridor," for a discussion of Yaqut bin ʿAmbar al-Habashi, a eunuch and the appointed governor of Zanzibar under Omani rule. In earlier centuries, it appears that enslaved people were also named Yaqut, most notably Yaqut al-Mustaʿsimi, the well-known calligrapher of the last Abbasid caliph in the thirteenth century.

2   File 280-1-5, Sazman-i Asnad, Tehran; "File 5/190 V Manumission of Slaves at Muscat: Individual Cases," British Library, India Office Records (hereafter IOR) and Private Papers, IOR/R/15/1/219, in *Qatar Digital Library*, https://www.qdl.qa/archive/81055/vdc_100000000193.0x0000c0 (accessed September 10, 2019).

3   Zdanowski, *Speaking with Their Own Voices*, 147, 155, 158, 159.

4   For a discussion of pearl diving and enslavement in the Gulf region, see Hopper, *Slaves of One Master*.

5   Naming practices across the Middle East seemed to have favored flowery names for enslaved women and gem-oriented names for enslaved men, as well as other names describing positive attributes. See Toledano, *As If Silent and Absent*, for more on similar naming practices in the Ottoman Empire.

6   Sharpe, *In the Wake*, 12.

7   See Trouillot, *Silencing the Past*.

8   I use *Iran* and *Iranians* here to refer to the inhabitants of the Iranian plateau, roughly along the borders of the modern nation-state. I recognize the problems of using *Iran* or *Iranian* as a modern identifier as delineated by Mana Kia, as it risks essentialization, especially as I refer to practices in the Achaemenid Empire in a book about modern Iran in the nineteenth and twentieth centuries. Unfortunately, as Kia has noted, modern nationalism has created a mirage of continuity that is ahistorical and incorrect. Kia, *Persianate Selves*, 5–8. In addition to the inelegance of alternatives to

Iran and *Iranians*, I consistently come up against rebuttals to my research that are rooted in this ahistorical and incorrect mirage of the past that reify Iran as a singular space never tainted with the stain of slavery, and thus, find myself forced to address these claims. For example, contrary to the common nationalist refrain "But Cyrus the Great freed all the slaves!," which I discuss further in chapter 4, enslavement has existed in a multitude of forms in the Iranian plateau. Similarly, modern claims that the practice of enslavement was only "imported" later to Iran by way of the Arab invasion or Portuguese imperialism are also untrue. Dandamayev, section 1, "Achaemenid Period," in "Barda and Barda-Dari."

9 The patterns and types of enslavement practiced throughout Iran and the broader region varied broadly per time period. Examples of military enslavement have been most readily studied, but other forms of domestic or labor-intensive forms of enslavement also existed. For a broad overview, see Dandamayev, "Barda and Barda-Dari," which is divided into the following sections: the Achaemenid period, the Sassanian period, the Islamic period up to the Mongol invasion, the period from the Mongols to the abolition of slavery, and military slavery in Islamic Iran. Throughout this time and into the twentieth century, Iranians were enslavable in the surrounding region as well. See Eden, *Slavery and Empire in Central Asia*; Najmabadi, *Story of Daughters of Quchan*.

10 The term *elite* here is not meant to conjure positive or notable imagery. I use it to refer to people who are either royalty or connected to the court. In discussions about the dynamics of enslavement, the vocabulary around certain terms and labels tends to favor the oppressors (for example, *master* instead of *enslaver*). I have tried to avoid as much of this language as possible, but I could not find an adequate alternative for *elite*, as it is a bit more expansive than the typical terms that are used in relation to enslavement.

11 Mirzai cited a British official in their use of the term *menial*. Mirzai, *History of Slavery*, 18, 93, 117.

12 See Hopper, *Slaves of One Master*; Sabban, "Encountering Domestic Slavery"; Mathew, *Margins of the Market*.

13 Most eunuchs described as "Black" at the Safavid court (1501–1736) were South Asian, as opposed to Caucasian eunuchs who were "white." Babaie et al., *Slaves of the Shah*, 158. See also Babayan, "Eunuchs, iv. The Safavid Period."

14 For centuries, major Persian poets such as Ferdowsi, Hafez, Rumi, and Nezami associated the adjective *Black* with different groups, including the *Hindu* (South Asian), *Habashi* (Abyssinian), and *Zangi* (Zanzibari). For some examples, see Khaleghi-Motlagh, *Abu'l Qasem Ferdowsi*, 2:15, l. 196; Dastgirdi, *Kitab-i Khusraw va Shirin*, 355–56; Foruzanfar, *Kulliyat-i Shams-i Tabrizi*, 5:230, poem 2499, l. 26444.

15 It is important to note that Iranians did not typically use the continental adjective or noun—that is, *African*—to refer to these individuals. It is for

this reason that I typically use the term *Black* throughout the manuscript and opt to use *African* or *East African* only when necessary for clarification.

16 Gloria Wekker describes white innocence as "an important and apparently satisfying way of being in the world. It encapsulates a dominant way in which the Dutch think of themselves, as being a small, but just, ethical nation; color-blind, and thus free of racism." Wekker, *White Innocence*, 2.

17 Apart from a few examples from prerevolutionary Iran (Naser Taqvayi's *Bad-i Jinn* and *Arba'in*, among others), the 2000s have seen a rapid spike in the production of these documentaries, beginning with Behnaz Mirzai's *Afro-Iranian Lives* (2007) and *The African-Baluchi Trance Dance* (2012), Kamran Heidari's *Dingomaro* (2013), Farhad Varahram's *Siyahan-i Junub-i Iran* (2014), and Mahdi Ehsaei's photo series *Afro-Iran: The Unknown Minority* (2016).

18 Mirzai has attempted to reconstruct this data as much as possible throughout her book. See Mirzai, *History of Slavery*.

19 Here I am drawing on Campt's pivotal works for understanding Black photography, drawing our attention to the haptic and sonic textures of photographs and their various layers that create meaning. Campt, *Listening to Images*; Campt, *Image Matters*.

20 "Children of Yamin al-Saltanah," Bahman Bayani Collection, *Women's Worlds in Qajar Iran*, http://www.qajarwomen.org/en/items/31e137.html (accessed January 10, 2015); Turkchi and Tatari, *Asnad-i banuvan dar durih-yi Mashrutiyyat*, 311.

21 In an accompanying photograph, which I discuss in chapter 2, each of the individuals is numbered directly on the photograph, although no image of the verso is provided there either. "Amir Heshmat Family," Bahman Bayani Collection, *Women's World in Qajar Iran*, http://www.qajarwomen.org/en/items/31e137.html.

22 In *Dispossessed Lives*, Marisa Fuentes describes analyzing archival fragments on the lives of enslaved women and the importance of mining the archives for what they include and do not include. That same methodology is imperative in the Iranian context as well.

23 "Sale document of a black slave, 1891," Yazd Document Center and Library, *Women's Worlds in Qajar Iran*, http://www.qajarwomen.org/en/items/13122A31.html.

24 "The Library, Museum, and Archives Center of the Islamic Parliament" ("Kitabkhunih, Muzih, va Markaz-i Asnad-i Majlis-i Shura-yi Islami"), hereafter referred to as Kitabkhunih-yi Majlis or Majles Library.

25 Conversation with an archivist, Kitabkhunih-yi Majlis, Tehran, 2015.

26 When looking back on this, I am often struck by how similar it was to Maria Elena Martinez's experience of researching *limpieza de sangre* in Spain, and the reactions of archivists to her research. Martinez, *Genealogical Fictions*, 7.

27 Mirzai, *History of Slavery*, 24, 109. I discuss the term *kaka Siyah* and its racist vestiges more in depth in chapters 1 and 5. See also Wendy DeSouza's

critique of Mirzai's approach, which she identifies as one that "exonerates a nation-state from its slaving past." DeSouza, "Race, Slavery, and Domesticity in Late Qajar Chronicles."

28   Zilfi, *Women and Slavery*, xii.

29   Zilfi, *Women and Slavery*, 139; Lewis, *Race and Slavery in the Middle East*. For a succinct description of the problems with Lewis's argument as well as the revisionist histories that followed in the broader Muslim world, see Ware, *Walking Qur'an*, 23–24. This mode of thinking about race in the Middle East as either irrelevant or ahistorical still persists. See Alex Lubin's interview with Ussama Makdisi: Makdisi, "Coexistence, Sectarianism, and Racism."

30   See Cakmak, "Citizens of a Silenced History"; El Hamel, *Black Morocco*; Moore, "Superstitious Women"; Tolan-Szkilnik, *Maghreb Noir*; Troutt Powell, *Tell This in My Memory*; Walz and Cuno, *Race and Slavery in the Middle East*; Wingham, "Arap Bacı'nın Ara Muhaveresi"; and Willoughby, "Opposing a Spectacle of Blackness," among others. The reticence around discussing race extends into African Studies as well. Young and Weitzberg have traced the broader hesitancy around discussing race, racialization, and racism (while also noting the scholarly exceptions) in African Studies and have called for a more rigorous analysis in this area. Young and Weitzberg, "Globalizing Racism and De-Provincializing Muslim Africa." For works on premodern race in adjacent Islamic societies, see Arvas, "Early Modern Eunuchs"; and Schine, "Race and Blackness in Premodern Arabic Literature," among others. For a study of Middle East imperialism in Africa, see Mostafa Minawi, *Ottoman Scramble for Africa*.

31   Natalia Molina advances the idea that race is relational in its social constructions, which I argue is also true in the Iranian and broader Middle Eastern context. Molina, *How Race Is Made in America*.

32   Motlagh, "Translating Race" and *Burying the Beloved*.

33   Zia Ebrahimi, *Emergence of Iranian Nationalism*; Maghbouleh, *Limits of Whiteness*. For more on the history of whiteness in the broader Middle Eastern diaspora, see Gualtieri, *Between Arab and White* and *Arab Routes*. For discussions of Iranian nationalism, see also Zakir Isfahani, *Farhang va siyasat-i Iran*.

34   Most premodern Persian poetry placed Persian speakers as "between" Turks and Greeks (described as "white") and Africans and South Asians (described as "black").

35   Notes from fieldwork in Fereydunshahr, Isfahan, 2014; Sipiani, *Dibachih*.

36   H. Afshar, "Age, Gender, and Slavery," 909, 912. I discuss Afshar's narrative and its implications more deeply in chapter 6.

37   Khosronejad, *Qajar African Nannies*.

38   Motlagh, "Translating Race," 51.

39   Conversation with Tatari, Kitabkhunih-yi Majlis, Tehran, 2015.

40 Questions of modernity during the nineteenth and twentieth centuries, and especially during Reza Shah's rule, has been a major genre of study. See Marashi, *Nationalizing Iran*; Amin, *Making of the Modern Iranian Woman*; Grigor, *Building Iran*; Kashani-Sabet, *Frontier Fictions*; and Koyagi, *Iran in Motion*, among others.

41 I discuss this further in chapter 4.

42 Sazman-i Asnad website, https://www.nlai.ir, http://www.nlai.ir/history. Farzin Vejdani's *Making History in Iran* outlines some of the other ways Reza Shah and his government worked to usher in a new understanding of history and historiography in Iran.

43 National Archives and Library of Iran, "Sazman-i Asnad va Kitabkhanih-yi Milli-yi Iran" (Sazman-i Asnad), Tehran. See the Sazman-i Asnad website, https://www.nlai.ir, http://www.nlai.ir/history.

44 See Hathaway, "Wealth and Influence of an Exiled Ottoman Eunuch."

45 Ceyda Karamursel's scholarship explores the question of property from the same period in the Ottoman context, in an examination of the property of enslaved people (otherwise assumed to have been property before their manumission. See Karamursel, "Shiny Things and Sovereign Legalities."

46 Bsheer, *Archive Wars*, 5. Bsheer's *Archive Wars* explores these themes of organization and destruction and their connection to the secularization of the state.

47 There is one archive in Tehran that may be the exception, the archive of the Ministry of Foreign Affairs. Unfortunately, however, I was not given access to the collection.

48 Zavier Wingham, "Notes from the Field," Middle East Librarian Association (MELA) Social Justice Lecture Series, September 24, 2020.

49 Hopper, *Slaves of One Master*, 11; Zdanowski, *Speaking with Their Own Voices*.

50 I discuss an example of this in chapter 1.

51 Mira Schwerda, "Seen and Unseen," Association for Iranian Studies, August 5, 2016.

52 Odumosu, "Crying Child."

53 Drake, "Blood at the Root."

54 Drake, "Blood at the Root," 4.

55 Drake, "Blood at the Root," 13.

56 Browne, *Dark Matters*. The only exception here is when their visibility would have marked them for abolition efforts, which I discuss in chapter 1.

57 Benjamin, *Race after Technology*, 99.

58 Hartman, *Wayward Lives*.

59 I appreciate the care that Drake, Odumosu, and Samuels put into their methodology concerning reprinting photography: omitting entirely, blurring, and cropping, respectively. Drake, "Blood at the Root"; Odumosu, "Crying Child"; Samuels, "Examining Millie and Christine McKoy."

60 Princewill takes inspiration from the real-life account of Jamila, one of many remaining accounts of enslaved people from the early twentieth century in this region. Princewill, *In the Palace of Flowers*.

61 The founding members of the collective are Priscillia Kounkou Hoveyda (founder), Alex D. Eskandarkhah, Homayoun Fiamor, Pardis Nkoy, Parisa Nkoy, and Norman Soltan Salahshour (cofounders).

62 For more on the work of the collective, see the epilogue.

63 Kounkou Hoveyda invited me to serve as the resident historian of the Collective for Black Iranians in August 2020, where I have worked with artists to illustrate historical research on Black life in Iran and the broader Indian Ocean world.

PART I. ENSLAVEMENT

1 G. Nashat, "Anis-al-Dawla."

2 Whether a king's affection could truly free someone of their enslavement and servitude is a central question that some have grappled with when examining the life of Roxelana/Alexandra, who was enslaved and renamed Hurrem (in Persian, Khorram, or "Happy") by Sultan Suleiman at the Ottoman court. For more on her and her ascent to power, see Peirce, *Imperial Harem* and *Empress of the East*.

3 Album 215, no. 13, Golestan Palace Photo Archive, Tehran.

4 The inscription at the top of the photograph reads "*mahbub-e Anis od-Dowleh.*" *Mahbub*, derived from *hobb*, an Arabic term for "love," may also be translated as "favorite." This translation raises more questions, namely, favorite what exactly? Album 215, no. 13, Golestan Palace Photo Archive, Tehran.

5 As I've mulled over the photograph's inscription, I am reminded over and over of Toni Morrison's *Beloved*, and I am left wondering if the mothers of these little beloveds ever learned of their fate, enslaved at the Qajar court.

CHAPTER 1. GEOGRAPHIES OF BLACKNESS AND ENSLAVEMENT

1 Ittihadiyih and Saʿdvandian, *Amar-i Dar al-Khilafih-yi Tihran*, 28. See also section 1, "In Iran," in "Census"; Ricks, "Slaves and Slave Trading in Shiʾi Iran." For other examples from Naser ed-Din Shah's rule, see Rustayi and Ahmadi-Rahbarian, *Kitabchih-yi aʿdad-i nufus-i ahali-yi Dar al-Iman-i Qom*.

2 IOR/R/1/15/157, British Library, London. Several scholars, including Niambi Cacchioli, Anthony Lee, and Hideaki Suzuki, have written on Khyzran's story from different perspectives. See Cacchioli, "Disputed Freedom"; Lee, "Half the Household Was African"; and Suzuki, *Slave Trade Profiteers*, 101.

Through the Collective for Black Iranians, I have worked with Priscillia Kounkou-Hoveyda and Mina Jafari to illustrate and animate her story. See *"We Are Here*: Exhibition Featuring Works from Afro-Iranians in Philadelphia, US," bbcpersian, October 2, 2021, https://www.youtube.com/watch?v=LI8An_Lp-nA.

3   In the document, his name is spelled "Kummal." IOR/R/1/15/157.

4   The British, to justify such a move, took Sheikh Khuleefa bin Saeed Mahmood Sultan's word at face value. He had claimed that he had enslaved Walladee several years prior. "Translated substance of extract from a letter from Moolla Ahmed," IOR/R/1/15/157, British Library, London. Rightly, Cacchioli notes that the missives do not mention any evidence for the sheikh's claim. Cacchioli, "Disputed Freedom," 1.

5   Farahani, *Safarnamih-yi Farahani*, 197. The negotiation of ethnic terms and geographies between Arabic, Persian, and Swahili is not unique to the Persian Gulf coast or the Iranian interior. Prita Meier discusses the various ethnic (and racialized) terms that were commonly used, abandoned, or changed in nineteenth-century Zanzibar. See Meier, *Swahili Port Cities*, chap. 1.

6   See Wingham's work on how an imagined geography informs the *Arap Baci* in the Ottoman and modern Turkish contexts. Wingham, "Arap Bacı'nın Ara Muhaveresi," 178.

7   Gilroy, *Black Atlantic*. Hiba Ali has worked on framing the Black Indian Ocean through her art and practice as well. Hiba Ali, "Black Indian Ocean Reading List," 2020, https://hibaali.info/projects/black-indian-ocean. See also Bishara, "Many Voyages of *Fateh al-Khayr*." Mathew's *Margins of the Market* explores the Arabian Sea from the perspective of trafficking and free trade.

8   Scholars have highlighted how people from all around the Indian Ocean were enslaved and trafficked elsewhere in the region, even throughout the nineteenth century. Similarly, East Africans were engaged in both free and forced labor throughout the region. See Zdanowski, *Speaking with Their Own Voices*; Hopper, *Slaves of One Master*; Mirzai, *History of Slavery*, and others.

9   Mirzai (*History of Slavery*, 104–5) describes enslavement in Iran as egalitarian and dismisses race as irrelevant. See my introduction, above, where I further discuss scholarship on race in the Middle East.

10 The British applied similar tactics around the world, stationing patrols to prevent the slave trade by water in particular. Benjamin Reilly argues that these patrols were largely ineffective and did little to decrease the presence of slavery. Reilly, "Well-Intentioned Failure."

11 Domestic forms of enslavement were common across the Qajar and Ottoman empires during the nineteenth century. For a more detailed discussion of enslavement in the late Ottoman period, see Toledano, *As If Silent and Absent*.

12 Kurtynova-D'Herlugnan, *Tsar's Abolitionists*, 78. The Ottomans relied on the forced migration of Circassians out of the Caucasus and the creation of a refugee population during the 1850s–1860s as sources of enslavement. Toledano, *As If Silent and Absent*, 36. For more on Ottoman abolition throughout the nineteenth and early twentieth centuries, see Cakmak, "Citizens of a Silenced History"; Erdem, *Slavery in the Ottoman Empire*; Karamursel, "Transplanted Slavery, Contested Freedom" and "Uncertainties of Freedom." Mirzai notes that enslaved Caucasians were immediately claimed by the Russian embassy in Tehran. Mirzai, *History of Slavery*, 38. See also Eden, *Slavery and Empire in Central Asia*.

13 Because of their drastically diminished numbers in the nineteenth century, I have only come across one photograph of an enslaved South Asian woman at the Qajar court. "Zaʿfiran Baji," Album 362, Golestan Palace Photo Archive.

14 In his preface to Afnan, *Black Pearls* (xiii), Lee discusses the importance of the 1873 decree in Kitab-i Aqdas. Mirzai also discusses the importance of abolition for the Baha'i faith, although she misidentifies Baha'u'llah as the Bab's half-brother and as the leader of all Babis. Mirzai, *History of Slavery*, 160–61. I look forward to future research studies that examine the impact of the decree through the lens of social history.

15 Hopper, *Slaves of One Master*, 24; Mirzai, *History of Slavery*, 59. Stephenson's work considers the networks of smaller ports that dotted the coastline of the gulf, encouraging smuggling contraband and as well as engaging in licit forms of trade. Stephenson, "Rerouting the Persian Gulf."

16 In the Maghrebi context and the broader Muslim world, M'hamed Oualdi has argued for a similarly nuanced understanding of abolition in the region and argues that European intervention alone cannot be credited for the abolition of enslavement. See Oualdi, *Slave between Empires*, chap. 1.

17 Vanessa Martin has also discussed British economic interests in the Persian Gulf, particularly in Bushehr and Kharg. See Martin, *Qajar Pact*, chap. 2.

18 Kia offers a deep and incisive examination of the term *ethnicity* and fictive genealogies in the premodern Persianate world. See Kia, *Persianate Selves*.

19 The census counted 756 Black *ghulam* and 3,014 Black *kaniz* out of the total population of 147,256. Servants were reported as 13,885 in number. Ricks, "Slaves and Slave Trading in Shi'i Iran." In his article, Anthony Lee combined the percentage of general servants with the number of enslaved Black men and women and referred to the total percentage of 12 percent as reflective of the Black population in Tehran. This combination is somewhat misleading, as the general servant population in this census was likely to have not been Black, hence the separate, unracialized category. See Lee, "Half the Household Was African."

20 Though it sounds clunky in English, *gholam-e siyah* and *kaniz-e siyah* are best translated as "Black enslaved men" and "Black enslaved women," respectively, as *Black* here was a qualifier and not the noun.

21 Great Britain, Foreign and Commonwealth Office, *British and Foreign State Papers*, 465.

22 Hertslet, *Treaties Concluded between Great Britain and Persia*, 54. Persian-language documents and translations of English-documents all seem to use *Siyah-ha* as the equivalent for *Negroes*. See ʿAlipour, *Asnad-i bardih-furushi*. Lady Sheil, the wife of the British envoy to Persia, wrote that the Russians also helped convince the government to move forward with the decree. Sheil, *Glimpses of Life and Manners of Persia*, 243. For more on Sheil's writings, see Otsby, "'There Are in Persia Many Subjects Not Accessible to Female Inquiry.'"

23 Decree sent from the Governor of Fars to the Governor of Bushehr in July 1848, in Hertslet, *Treaties Concluded between Great Britain and Persia*, 56.

24 Great Britain, Foreign and Commonwealth Office, *British and Foreign State Papers*, 468.

25 By this time, the British were familiar with the practices of enslavement in Iran not only through diplomacy but also through literature. James Morier's widely popular *Hajji Baba of Ispahan* includes references to the enslavement of Black people in Iran. Morier, *Adventures of Hajji Baba of Ispahan*, 8–9. To read more about a Persian contemporary of Morier's, a man named Mirza Abul Hassan Khan, and his experience in England, see Cloake, *Persian at the Court of King George, 1809–10*. The British also pressured the Ottomans to abolish the slave trade, deploying a similar tactic of focusing on trafficking rather than enslavement. The Ottomans banned the trafficking of Africans into the empire in 1856. Enslavement, however, remained legal. Toledano, *As If Silent and Absent*, 10. For a case study on the British seizure of a boat carrying enslaved Abyssinians in the Persian Gulf, see Martin, "Abyssinian Slave Trade to Iran."

26 Martin, *Qajar Pact*, 155.

27 ʿAlipour, *Asnad-i bardih-furushi*.

28 ʿAlipour, *Asnad-i bardih-furushi*, 69–71. Abbas Amanat describes the kidnapping and enslaving of Iranians from Khurasan to be enslaved and sold in Central Asia as "a major menace to the Qajar government." Amanat, *Pivot of the Universe*, 15. Afsaneh Najmabadi's *Story of Daughters of Quchan* focuses on the specific enslavement of Iranian women and children during the Constitutional Revolution, which I discuss in more depth in chapter 2. Najmabadi, *Story of Daughters of Quchan*.

29 Letter from Amir Kabir dated August 1850, in Al-i-Davud, *Asnad va namih-hayi Amir Kabir*, 141–42.

30 See ʿAlipour, *Asnad-i bardih-furushi*, 36, 44, 52; Hertslet, *Treaties Concluded between Great Britain and Persia*, 12, 41; Mirzai, *History of Slavery*, 153.

31 Zekrgoo, *Sacred Art of Marriage*, 22.

32 Naghmeh Sohrabi has argued that this genre of travel writing during the late nineteenth century was both "institutionalized and developed into a tool of state propaganda." Sohrabi, *Taken for Wonder*, 4. For more on pilgrimage

to Mecca during the nineteenth and early twentieth centuries, see Can, *Spiritual Subjects*; and Low, *Imperial Mecca*.

33 Farmayan, "Farahani, Mirza Mohammad-Hosayn."

34 Farahani, *Shi'ite Pilgrimage to Mecca*, 226–27. Farmayan, who translated Farahani's text into English in 1993, elided the key descriptor *va sabzeh*, "and olive skin." See Farahani, *Safarnamih-yi Farahani*, 197; Farahani, *Shi'ite Pilgrimage to Mecca*, 226–27.

35 Farahani's quote reflects how the Middle Passage is marked by the conversion of a free person to an enslaved person. Jessica Marie Johnson has described this as a reduction from captives to *piece d'Inde*, a measure of potential labor. Johnson, *Wicked Flesh*, 80. In this case, Farahani was reducing them from individuals to markers of prestige.

36 *A Glossary of Anglo-Indian Colloquial Words* was first published in 1886 and later reprinted. Yule and Burnell, *Glossary of Anglo-Indian Colloquial Words*; Wills, *In the Land of the Lion and the Sun*, 326. Yule and Burnell's *Glossary* cites an 1883 publication of the book.

37 Sheil, *Glimpses of Life and Manners of Persia*, 243.

38 Wills, *In the Land of the Lion and the Sun*, 326–27. The definition of *Bombassi*, for example, is taken verbatim from Wills. Yule and Burnell, *Glossary of Anglo-Indian Colloquial Words*, 77.

39 As Nur Sobers-Khan has noted in the Ottoman context, these terms demonstrate the "understanding of whom it was permissible to enslave, or of who was an archetypal 'slave' rather than specifying where slaves genuinely originated with any precision, much less how an enslaved individual may have perceived his own origins or identity." Sobers-Khan, *Slaves without Shackles*, 106.

40 Farahani, *Safarnamih-yi Farahani*, 197.

41 This also speaks to the increased presence of children born into enslavement within Iran, as a result of the difficulties of trafficking people, and how their ancestors' homelands were seen as irrelevant or were forgotten.

42 In the Shirazi dialect, it was typically pronounced as *kako*, whereas other dialects of Persian pronounce it as it is written, especially when used as a racial slur. In dialects of Persian spoken in Afghanistan, *kaka* refers to one's paternal uncle.

43 In an encounter with a eunuch, Zell ol-Sultan writes his name in his journal as "Kaka Sa'id" rather than "Agha Sa'id Khwajeh," noting, "Besyar kaka-ye zaban fahmi bud." Zill al-Sultan, *Khatirat-i Zill al-Sultan*, 2:474–75.

44 The commonality of the term has led some, including Mirzai, to argue that it is simply a term of intimacy. Instead of recognizing "my *kakas*" as a phrase expressing one's proprietary ownership over the enslaved group, she simply translates it as "my brothers." Mirzai, *History of Slavery*, 24, 109.

45 "Holy law" here refers to the regulations of slavery found within the Qur'an and relevant hadiths. Farahani, *Shi'ite Pilgrimage to Mecca*, 128.

46 These stories are quite common throughout the late nineteenth and twentieth centuries. For example, Chehabi has noted that Mohammad Mossadeq's grandfather had traveled to Mecca and purchased an enslaved young woman, bringing her to Iran and manumitting her later. Chehabi, "Mohammad Mossadeq and the 'Standard of Civilization,'" 7. One should note that pilgrims to Mecca were also vulnerable to enslavement, even later in the twentieth century. See Zdanowski, *Speaking with Their Own Voices*, 34.

47 Ardakani, "'Ala'-al-Molk, Hajji."

48 Ambraseys and Melville, *History of Persian Earthquakes*, 53–54.

49 Based on information provided to guests, the dates of the structures are as follows: 'Abbasi House, 1829–34; 'Ameri House, mid-nineteenth century; Borujerdi House, 1857; and Tabataba'i House, 1880. House tours in Kashan, January 2016. See Wegmann's *Persian Nights* for modern photographs and reviews of some of these now-renovated spaces.

50 Jateen Lad discusses similar corridors (although much more complex and expansive) as a part of the architecture of Topkapi Palace and demonstrates how the layout informed the enslavement of eunuchs. Lad, "Panoptic Bodies."

51 Kashan House visit, December 2015. See Haji-Qassemi, *Ganjnameh*; Haeri, "Kashan v. Architecture," section 4, "Historic Mansions."

52 House Tour, January 2016.

53 This is a popular story shared with tourists who visit the home. House tour, January 2016.

54 Hensel and Gharleghi, "Iran," 36.

55 This is true of homes in Tehran, Isfahan, Kashan, Bushehr, and beyond.

56 Amanat, *Pivot of the Universe*, 436; Sattari and Nameghi, "Photography Studio of the Naseri Harem," 280–81; Mu'taqidi and Namvar Yikta, *Az Bagh-i Gulistan*, 204–8. Leila Pourtavaf has shown how the guests of the Qajar harem would have "ranged from the tens to the hundreds," on a daily basis, with some staying for long-term periods. Pourtavaf, "Reimagining Royal Domesticity," 172.

57 *Sharaf*, 1888, no. 65, cited in Karimi, *Domesticity and Consumer Culture in Iran*, 25. *Khoddam* is a vague term that could have referred to both paid and unpaid (free or enslaved) servants.

58 Sattari and Nameghi, "Photography Studio of the Naseri Harem," 281.

59 Robin Mitchell describes a similar notion of elaborate dress of enslaved or servant Africans in eighteenth-century France as well. R. Mitchell, *Venus Noire*, 23. Tamara J. Walker explores the clothing of enslaved people in Peru and argues that they were also reflections of their own agency and expressions of honor. Walker, *Exquisite Slaves*. This was undoubtedly true on some level in Iran as well, but the specific visibility of enslavement made it such that Iranian enslavers would have paid attention to the appearance of the

people they enslaved, especially for special occasions, in person and in photographs, as I discuss in chapter 2.

60   C. C. Rice, *Persian Women and Their Ways*, 200.

61   C. C. Rice, *Persian Women and Their Ways*, 47.

62   Although several scholars have written about the higher prestige of enslaved Caucasians in the Middle East, by the late nineteenth century this was rare and not a real possibility beyond the royal family in Iran.

63   *Gholam-e Siyah* is also pronounced as *gholam Siyah*.

64   Sheil, *Glimpses of Life and Manners of Persia*, 244.

65   This practice was continued after the Manumission Law of 1929 as well. Shirazi, "Review of *Tarabnameh*."

66   Hopper, "Liberated Africans in the Indian Ocean World," 271.

67   Sheil, *Glimpses of Life and Manners of Persia*, 243. It would not be until 1910–11 that internal British papers would warn against using *slave* and *Negro* interchangeably, with the explanation that there is a large free Black population in the Gulf and that many slaves are actually not from Africa but, rather, are from the Makran coast in Baluchistan. "Manumission of Slaves: Notes for Guidance on Persian Coast," IOR/R/15/1/215, p. 57, British Library, London.

68   Thank you to Razan Idris and Lindsey Stephenson for suggesting these possibilities.

69   Hopper, *Slaves of One Master*, 114.

70   Zdanowski, *Speaking with Their Own Voices*.

71   Hopper, *Slaves of One Master*, 11. Hopper has also written on liberated Africans who were relocated, "renamed, reclothed, converted to foreign religions, taught new languages, and placed in arranged marriages," sent to missions or put to work on plantations. Hopper, "Liberated Africans," 275.

72   "Expenses incurred as a result of slaves taking refuge in consulates and agencies," IOR/R/15/1/215, p. 112, British Library, London.

73   A document from 1910 outlines the grounds for manumission: "1) enslavement after conclusion of agreement not to import slaves, 2) cruelty." In other words, a seemingly "well-treated" enslaved person did not have the grounds for freedom. Further, the document continued, in the case of those who have been enslaved for a longer period, they are more likely to compromise with their enslavers, and that should be encouraged. See IOR/R/15/1/215, doc. 54, p. 3/33.

74   As Hopper has written, "No group of recaptive Africans was ever simply released on shore near the point of capture." Hopper, "Liberated Africans," 275.

75   MSS Brit Emp S 22 G 94, Bodleian Libraries, Oxford University.

76   MSS Brit Emp S 22 G 94, Bodleian Libraries, Oxford University.

77   Redhouse, *Diary of HM the Shah of Persia*, 215.

78   Redhouse, *Diary of HM the Shah of Persia*, 18; Mustawfi, *Safarnamih-yi Nasir al-Din Shah*, 19. For a discussion of this travelogue in particular, see Sohrabi, *Taken for Wonder*, chap. 4.

79 Redhouse, *Diary of HM the Shah of Persia*, 19; Mustawfi, *Safarnamih-yi Nasir al-Din Shah*, 19. Shahbazi has identified Aqa Baqer as a relative of a statesman who later was given a governorship. However, it feels unlikely that this Aqa Baqer is the same person—the list of names is clearly written in order of status and power, and the free people in the list are all addressed by their royal or court given titles, not by "Aqa + first name," which would have been too informal of an address. Daryush Shahbazi, "Aqa Baqir," *Tehrannameh*, https://tehrannameh.com/list/آقا-باقر/ (accessed November 3, 2021).

80 Ittihadiyih and Sa'dvandian, *Amar-i Dar al-Khilafih-yi Tihran*, 28.

81 Glassman, *War of Words, War of Stones*, 36; Meier, *Swahili Port Cities*, 14.

CHAPTER 2. LIMITS IN FAMILY AND PHOTOGRAPHY

1 File 296-26454, Sazman-i Asnad, Tehran.

2 The lack of vowelization on the name *S-l-m-i* has made its transliteration difficult. I have opted to transliterate it as *Selmi*, but it may also have been *Salmi*, *Salma*, or *Solami*.

3 For examples of this, see chapter 6.

4 Motlagh discusses four terms: *manzel* (house), *'ayal* (burden), *siyah-bakht* (unlucky), and *madkhul* (that which is entered). The only term that conveys some intimacy, but only on a vulgar level, is *madkhul*. Motlagh, *Burying the Beloved*, 9. Najmabadi argues that changes in terminology around the household/family structure reflect the difference between "household-centered merging of two familial groups . . . to a conjugal, couple-centered one." Najmabadi, *Familial Undercurrents*, 127.

5 Both men and women were considered the "owners" of the enslaved individuals in their home. Two patterns seem to emerge, that men purchased enslaved people on their travels, or women requested enslaved people from their husbands, either in their dowries or after their marriage, to help with the maintenance of the household. Future scholars may choose to examine these relationships more closely in terms of power and privilege, as Stephanie Jones-Rogers does in *They Were Her Property*. See also Brown, *Good Wives, Nasty Wenches*.

6 In some ways, these photographs operate in direct contrast to those analyzed by Tina Campt's *Image Matters*, which examines family photographs as a space for establishing community and identity.

7 Campt, *Listening to Images* and *Image Matters*.

8 Notably, I have not come across "family" portraits that include children born to enslaved mothers and free fathers from this period, even though those children would have claimed similar legal status (in both freedom and inheritance) to their other siblings from the same father.

9 For examples of Qajar-era marriage contracts, see Zekrgoo, *Sacred Art of Marriage*.

10 Floor, *Social History of Sexual Relations in Iran*, 60–61.

11 Afary, *Sexual Politics in Modern Iran*, 21–22.

12 While it would be impossible to list all of the marriage contracts that included enslaved individuals as part of their dowers, I wanted to include two examples from the early to mid-nineteenth century for context. The dower from the marriage of Bibi Fatimeh and Agha Mohammad Hosayn in 1819 included a hundred Tabrizi toman, twenty *mesqal* gold, one *kaniz-e Habashi* worth thirty toman, and some silk. File 999-29986, Sazman-i Asnad, Tehran; and the dower from the marriage of Saheb Baygum Khanum and Abo'l Hosayn in 1847: "one hundred and fifty *ashrafi* toman minted with Mohammad Shah Qajar's name, one hundred and fifty *mesqal* of pure unminted gold . . . and one *gholam-e Habashi* for the price of thirty toman, and one *jariyeh-ye Habashi* for the price of thirty toman." "Aghd-namih, 1263 Q," File 296/16904, Sazman-i Asnad, Tehran.

13 File 210/597, Sazman-i Asnad, Tehran.

14 Behdad, *Camera Orientalis*, 106–7.

15 I. Afshar, "Early History of Photography."

16 Sattari and Nameghi, "Photography Studio of the Naseri Harem," 281.

17 Sattari and Nameghi, "Photography Studio of the Naseri Harem," 278. Schweiller argues that the volume of harem photographs indicates the dominance of women at court, describing the photographs as an attempt "to reign them in." Schweiller, *Liminalities of Gender and Sexuality*, 58. See also Pourtavaf, "Reimagining Royal Domesticity."

18 Photographs guarded by descendants of the former ruling family reveal a different aesthetic. Schweiller has published a few of these photographs, held by the Kimia Foundation. Schweiller, *Liminalities of Gender and Sexuality*, 102, 135–44. Presumably these photographs also existed at the palace archives, either they are not made available to researchers because of decency codes or because they have since been destroyed.

19 He also labeled 'Aziz os-Soltan and Hassan Khan. As children, their appearances changed rapidly and required labeling. Album 210, no. 25, Golestan Palace Photo Archive, Tehran.

20 'Aziz os-Soltan was born in 1879 and seems to be between six and eight years old in these photographs, which places some of these photos in the mid-1880s. Amanat, "'Aziz-Al-Soltan." Naser ed-Din Shah gave him the title "'Aziz os-Soltan" in 1886, but we cannot use this as a sure measure of when the photographs were taken, as the shah was known for returning to earlier photographs and annotating them after some time had passed. See chapter 3.

21 Sattari and Nameghi, "Photography Studio of the Naseri Harem," 277.

22 Album 210, photos 1-4, 7-3, 25, 29. Golestan Palace Photo Archive, Tehran.

23 This was true in other Middle East contexts as well. See Sheehi, "Glass Plates and Kodak Cameras," 263.

24 Steven Sheehi has highlighted similar patterning of photographs in the Ottoman Arab world, where even a torn photo of a woman can be reconstructed based on the presumed presence of other family members in the photograph. Sheehi, *Arab Imago*, xxx–xxxii. See also Schweiller, *Liminalities of Gender and Sexuality*, 106. Zeynep Devrim Gursel has explored how Ottoman Armenian families continued to wield family portraits for their purposes even after immigration to the United States, where they were used to project their notions of whiteness and belonging. Gursel, "Classifying the Cartozians."

25 Paid servants, if photographed, were also shown standing.

26 Abrahamian, *Iran between Two Revolutions*, 81–92.

27 See Kashani-Sabet, *Conceiving Citizens*; Rostam-Kolayi, "Origins of Iran's Modern Girls' Schools"; and Koyagi, "Modern Education in Iran."

28 See Afary, *Sexual Politics in Modern Iran*; Amin, *Making of the Modern Iranian Woman*; Kashani-Sabet, *Conceiving Citizens*; and Najmabadi, *Women with Mustaches*.

29 Beth Baron has examined the role of enslaved Circassian women in Egypt at this time through this lens. See Baron, *Egypt as a Woman*, 17–39.

30 Najmabadi, *Story of Daughters of Quchan*.

31 Munis al-Dawlih, *Khatirat*, 300. Protestors sat *bast* in the British embassy during the Constitutional Period, in mosques, and in other venues where Iranian government officials did not have the authority to arrest people or force them to leave. Abrahamian, *Iran between Two Revolutions*, 84–91. Taking *bast*, a hallmark of constitutional protests, protected Narges's safety temporarily.

32 Munis al-Dawlih, *Khatirat*, 300–304. The escape of enslaved women from their households was reported in newspapers as well, indicating a tension around the ability of enslaved women to run away. "Vanished Female Slave, 1909," Iran-i naw, *Women's Worlds in Qajar Iran*, http://www.qajarwomen .org/en/items/15158F28.html.

33 I am often reminded of how Narges's inheritance—freedom—was intangible compared to other kinds of inheritances that have been denied children of free fathers and enslaved mothers: for example, Amanda, whose story Imani Perry has used to describe the architecture of patriarchy. Amanda was the daughter of a free man and enslaved mother, the product of rape and sexual vulnerability, much like Narges. Even though Amanda's father would go on to name Amanda as the main heir to his estate in Georgia, her inheritance was contested by forty-nine people. I. Perry, *Vexy Thing*, 7.

34 Gomez, *Exchanging Our Country Marks*; Troutt Powell, *Tell This in My Memory*.

35 Johnson, *Wicked Flesh*, 155.

36 Narges's experience of being born free and yet treated as enslaved has parallels with examples from the Atlantic world, see Barragan's *Freedom's*

Captives, where Barragan has discussed the experience of Magdalena, a young girl born to a "free womb" who, despite her alleged freedom, endured violent treatments typically reserved for enslaved people. Similarly, Johnson opens chapter 5 of *Wicked Flesh* with the story of Charlotte from 1751. The parallels and divergences between Charlotte's and Narges's lives demonstrate the depth of Black femme freedom, where two women, both born to enslaved Black mothers and free (enslaving) non-Black fathers, had to escape enslavement and plead for their lives. The difference here is that Narges was born free, as she inherited her father's standing, and Charlotte was not, as she inherited her mother's standing. Both, however, had to establish their freedom for themselves. Johnson, *Wicked Flesh*, 153–86.

37   Algar, "ʿAbdallah Behbahani."

38   Abrahamian, *Iran between Two Revolutions*, 80; Keddie, *Religion and Rebellion in Iran*, 79.

39   Kasravi, *Tarikh-i Mashrutih-yi Iran*, 48; Abrahamian, *Iran between Two Revolutions*, 83.

40   Tabatabaʾi is said to have done the same as well. Abrahamian, *Iran between Two Revolutions*, 88.

41   Abrahamian, *Iran between Two Revolutions*, 96–97.

42   Dehkhoda noted that *Shah Siyah* was used by Behbahani's detractors. Dehkhoda, "Shah Siyah," *Lughat-namih*, https://www.vajehyab.com /dehkhoda/شاه-سیاه (accessed February 4, 2014).

43   Moderates promptly attributed the murder to Taqizadeh. Abrahamian, *Iran between Two Revolutions*, 106–7.

44   Sadr-i Hashim, *Tarikh-i jaraʾid va majallat-i Iran*, 265–66. *Danesh* was later renamed *Shekufeh* in 1913 and continued printing until 1917. Ringer, "Rethinking Religion," 48. *Danesh*'s editor, Dr. Kahhal, emphasized education for all women, even advocating for men to read the journal to women who cannot read. Kashani-Sabet, *Conceiving Citizens*, 127.

45   *Danish*, no. 1 (1910): 9–10; *Danish*, no. 5 (1910): 2–3; *Danish*, no. 7 (1910): 4–7.

46   *Dadeh-ye ʿaziz-e man, dadeh-am, dadeh khanum*; Taj al-Saltanih, *Khatirat*, 9. For more on literary examples of the Black nanny, see Vafa, "Race and the Aesthetics of Alterity."

47   Taj al-Saltanih, *Khatirat*, 9.

48   "Will of Maʿsumah Nizam Mafi," Mansoureh Ettehadieh, *Women's Worlds in Qajar Iran*, http://www.qajarwomen.org/en/items/13104A41.html (accessed May 4, 2014); "Will of Mirza Masʿud Shaykh," Bahram Sheikholeslamni, *Women's Worlds in Qajar Iran*, http://www.qajarwomen.org/en/items /1016A199.html (accessed May 4, 2014). The wet nurse was also the subject of a poem. In a handwritten comedic poem for her nurse, an upper-class educated woman wrote about her marital problems. Having left her childhood home, the author addresses her nurse, complaining about her difficult transition to her new stage in life. The irony in complaining

about one's plight to her nurse, who had limited resources, added to the humorous effect, creating a dramatic expression of married life with no viable resolution. The newlywed's poem confessed her problems not to her mother but, rather, to her nurse, an unintimidating figure who was obligated to listen. "Tasnif-i Dayyih Dayyih jan," Nosrat Mozaffari, *Women's Worlds in Qajar Iran*, http://www.qajarwomen.org/en/items/1023A135.html (accessed May 5, 2014).

49 In Shi'i fiqh, the wet nurse creates a special relationship with the children she breastfeeds and carries a similar status to one's mother. Children nursed for a sustained period of time by anyone besides their mother were considered close family or *mahram*. *Mahramiyyat* laws denote who is legally marriageable. Those who are *mahram* cannot be married—immediate families, for example (parents and children, siblings, aunts/uncles, and nieces/nephews), are all *mahram* to each other. The word is derived from *h-r-m*, related to *haram*, meaning "forbidden," "inviolable," or "sacred."

50 Willis and Krauthamer, *Envisioning Emancipation*, 8.

51 For a related overview of European-inspired tastes within the domestic sphere, see Tanavoli, *European Women in Persian Houses*.

52 "*Vali Sayf od-Din khodesh az aksesh behtar ast, kheyli suratesh siyah shodeh, sayeh oftadeh.*" "Group portrait: Standing: Abu al-Qasim (child of one of the house servants); seated from the left: 'Alinaqi Ghaffari, Badi' al-Zaman Ghaffari, and Sayf al-Din Ghaffari," Iran Khanum and Amirdokht Ghaffari, *Women's Worlds in Qajar Iran*, http://www.qajarwomen.org/en/items/16178A30.html.

53 Conversations in Kerman, 2015.

54 For other similar photographs of enslaved children standing next to enslaving children, see Khosronejad, *Qajar African Nannies*.

55 "Amir Heshmat Family," Bahman Bayani Collection, *Women's Worlds in Qajar Iran*, http://www.qajarwomen.org/en/items/31e137.html. For a discussion of this young girl's name in the archival record, see the introduction. The dehumanizing language of comparing slaves to cockroaches operated beyond the confines of the Persian language: in Turkish, cockroaches are *karafatma*, or *Black Fatima*, a reference to the common label for enslaved African women.

56 Even if these photographs were intended for members of the family and not for public consumption, the women still covered their hair not only because of the presence of the photographer but also as a reflection of their status.

57 The age difference is easily tracked by looking at the little girl in relation to the other children, for example, the girl labeled as Ihtiram al-Saltanah. In figure 2.7, Ihtiram al-Saltanah stands to the left of the little girl. In figure 2.8, Ihtiram al-Saltanah is seated on the right. She seems to have aged and matured as much as the little girl, although her appearance is notably not dramatically different.

58 Willis and Krauthamer, *Envisioning Emancipation*, 8.

59 Wexler, *Tender Violence*, 60.

60 Conversations in Kerman, 2015.

CHAPTER 3. PORTRAITS OF EUNUCHS AND THEIR AFTERLIVES

1 I modified Eskandari-Qajar's translation slightly, replacing *progeny* with *descendants*. 'Azod al-Dowleh, *Life at the Court of the Early Qajar Shahs*, 47; 'Azud al-Dawlih, *Tarikh-i 'Azudi*, 43.

2 Mohammad Khan Qajar is often referred to as both *Aqa* and *Agha*. I have opted for *Agha* here, because of its commonality in English transliteration, not because it is more correct.

3 In a moment of political chaos after Nader Shah's death in 1747, Agha Mohammad Khan's father, Mohammad Hassan, attempted to seize Astarabad in northeastern Iran. Nader Shah's heir, Adel Shah retaliated by capturing and castrating Agha Mohammad Khan at the young age of five. In the years following his castration, Agha Mohammad Khan attempted to seize Astarabad as well, but the failed incursion led to him being sent to Tehran as Karim Khan's hostage. Only after Karim Khan's death in 1779 was Agha Mohammad Khan Qajar able to lead an insurrection against the Zand dynasty and establish his dominion over Iran in 1789. J. R. Perry, "Aga Mohammad Khan Qajar."

4 'Azod al-Dowleh, *Life at the Court of the Early Qajar Shahs*, 336.

5 Amanat, "Fath-'Ali Shah Qajar."

6 Eunuchs were part and parcel of court life in the Ottoman and Mughal empires, as well as other royal and nonroyal spaces around the world, despite the ban on castration in Islamic law. Freamon, *Possessed by the Right Hand*, 509. Several extant hadith either mention Prophet Muhammad's ban on castration or his warning to those who castrate enslaved individuals: that they themselves should be castrated as a punishment. Serena Tolino, "Castration," in *The Encyclopedia of Islamic Bioethics*, Oxford Islamic Studies Online, http://oxfordislamicstudies.com/print/opr/t9002/e0288 (accessed December 10, 2021). Despite this, there are several examples from the Islamic world of castrations taking place; see the work of Taef El-Azhari, who includes the story of the Seljugid commander Zengi I (r. 1127–46), who castrated boys if he found them attractive or as retribution against their fathers. El-Azhari, *Queens, Eunuchs, and Concubines*, 334. One should note that the banning of castration did not necessarily indicate an interest in ending the tradition of court eunuchs. For example, in 1715, Sultan Ahmet III issued a decree to Egypt banning castration. The decree was geared toward new instances of castrations, as the royal court still sent requests for eunuchs in 1722 and 1737 asking for eunuchs whose enslavers had recently passed away. Smith, *Islam and the Abolition of Slavery*, 93.

7   Eunuchs were not solely enslaved in service of the harem, but the harem necessitated their presence. Their other responsibilities indicated their enslavers' prestige.

8   I. Afshar, "Early History of Photography."

9   See Najmabadi, *Women with Mustaches*, 26; Schweiller, *Liminalities of Gender and Sexuality*, 4.

10 In the premodern Ottoman context, Abdulhamit Arvas has also argued that eunuchs represented a distinct gender of their own. Arvas, "Early Modern Eunuchs." This is counter to Jane Hathaway's understanding, where she describes them as "not so much a third gender but an arrested male gender." Hathaway, *Beshir Agha*, 8. Of course, the question of trans and nonbinary individuals highlights the fragility of the gender binary. See Najmabadi, *Professing Selves*. Note that Najmabadi's focus on sex change and trans experiences only runs from the 1920s onward and does not discuss eunuchs or forced castrations. Najmabadi, *Professing Selves*, 39.

11 In the Qajar context, Najmabadi has argued that an individual's masculinity rested on whether or not they would be the penetrating individual in a sexual act, regardless of whether the sexual partner has a penis or vagina, and similarly, that one's femininity was determined by their penetration. Najmabadi, *Women with Mustaches*. In the case of eunuchs, some would have been able to maintain an erection, while others would not. Because of the range of possibilities of their castrations and their ability to penetrate or be penetrated, this becomes a difficult standard to use to determine their gendered status.

12 Princewill, *In the Palace of Flowers*, 134–37.

13 Abbas Amanat described the presence of eunuchs as key for maintaining royal *namus* or honor. Amanat, *Pivot of the Universe*, 436. In an exposition of the Topkapi Palace, Jateen Lad has demonstrated how the rule of the eunuch extends beyond these sexual anxieties, although their presence is still animated by it to some degree. Lad, "Panoptic Bodies."

14 Extant copies in various languages from the fourteenth century onward reveal that although the individual stories told by Shaherzad differ, the frame story has remained remarkably consistent. The best-known stories from *One Thousand and One Nights*, including Aladdin and Sinbad, were likely added in the eighteenth century. Mahdi, *Arabian Nights*; Galland, *Les mille et une nuits*. Most recently, Yasmine Seale and Paulo Lemos Horta have published a new annotated translation, *Annotated Arabian Nights*.

15 Folios 23–24, ʿAbd al-Latif Tasuji, illustrated by Saniʿ al-Mulk, *Hizar va yik shab*, Manuscript Library, Golestan Palace Photo Archive, Tehran.

16 Amanat, *Pivot of the Universe*, 66.

17 Zoka, *Life and Works of Saniʿ ol-Molk*, 36.

18 The use of contemporary dress is particularly interesting, as Collaco draws on Tavakoli-Targhi to describe a kind of "time-distancing," where the Qajars "would contemporize themselves by casting off their traditional Persian

dress in favor of European modes." Collaco, "Crafting Time through Dress," 42. The *1001 Nights* manuscript involves a bit of both, creating a more realistic depiction of the cosmopolitanism of the Qajar court amid depictions of monsters and other mythical beings.

19   The companion to this chair was Mahd 'Olya's favorite seat, where Naser ed-Din Shah photographed her and other members of the harem as well. The pair of chairs is on display at the Golestan Palace Museum. Visited June 2014.

20   Polak, *Persien*, 1:259. Abbas Amanat frames Bashir Khan's declaration of changing diapers as a boastful phrase of intimacy, rather than a declaration of subordination. Amanat, *Pivot of the Universe*, 36–37. I differ here and would argue that the situation does not reflect intimacy and, rather, demonstrates how intimacy did not save those enslaved from the cruelty of their enslavers.

21   Schweiller suggests that these portraits were taken in 1865. Schweiller, *Liminalities of Gender and Sexuality*, 188. Based on Atabay's index of royal photography, I believe these photographs were part of a series of people who were freed in 1872. Atabay, *Fihrist-i album-hayih kitabkhanih-yih saltanati*, 110.

22   The name *Bashir* (*Beshir*) was also used for eunuchs elsewhere. Jane Hathaway has written about el-Hajj Beshir Agha (1717–46), the Ottoman court eunuch. Hathaway, *Beshir Agha*. Shaun Marmon also makes mention of a certain Bashir al-Tanami in 1435 under the Mamluks. See Marmon, *Eunuchs and Sacred Boundaries*, 42.

23   "Adam-e ma'qul, aram, va khubi bud." I'timad al-Saltanih, *Ruznamih-yi khatirat-i I'timad al-Saltanih*, 526–27. Many thanks to Camron Amin for his suggestion to consider the passive/active forms of the term.

24   A desire to be buried in Najaf is one that reflected his piety and belief in Shi'i Islam. Sabri Ates had discussed the difficulties of cross Iranian-Ottoman burials, particularly at Shi'i shrines in his article. Ates, "Bones of Contention," 512–32.

25   There are exceptions to this, where some eunuchs had married despite their castrations. One assumes their wives would have received their inheritance. Agha Bashir was one example, who had been married to a widower of Mohammad Shah. See Polak, *Persien*, 1:258.

26   Another Agha Javaher served at Mozaffar ed-Din Shah's court and was reported to have been invested in politics and even the Constitutional Revolution. See Vanzan, "Eunuchs."

27   Prepubescent boys who had not experienced hormonal changes were typically chosen for castrations. Despite the discrepancy between the different accounts of how fatal the surgery was, it was, clearly, a major surgery. Hathaway suggests that the places with the highest rates of survival were places that were accustomed to performing castrations regularly. Hathaway, *Beshir Agha*, 32.

28 Toledano, "Imperial Eunuchs of Istanbul," 382. Eve Troutt Powell and John Hunwick have compiled texts describing the castration of young enslaved boys in Egypt during the nineteenth century. See Hunwick and Troutt Powell, *The African Diaspora in the Mediterranean Lands of Islam*, 92–93, 99–101, 105.

29 Mirzai suggests that only one of ten boys survived the operation, based on a British report from 1847. Mirzai, *History of Slavery*, 114n146.

30 Manuchehr Khan, a Georgian eunuch at the court of Fath 'Ali Shah, was said to have been purchased by Mohammad Shah Qajar as a young boy and castrated in Iran. Diba and Ekhtiar, *Royal Persian Paintings*, 229. 'Azod od-Dowleh remembered Manuchehr Khan as a favored eunuch at his father's court. 'Azod al-Dowleh, *Life at the Court of the Early Qajar Shahs*, 49; 'Azud al-Dawlih, *Tarikh-i 'Azudi*, 43.

31 Taj al-Saltana, *Crowning Anguish*, 130.

32 "Photograph of Agha Davud, 40 days after a wrestling match with a slave girl," album no. unknown, Golestan Palace Photo Archive, Tehran. It is unclear whether they had wrestled because of a disagreement or as a source of amusement for the royal family.

33 Zell os-Sultan recalled the interaction: "Kaka Sa'id apologized, flattered me, and I told him and ensured him that at no point am I interested in revenge, even in the slightest rudeness or dishonor, and I even told the *kaka*: give him this on my behalf, and God willing I will not make you black in the face [dishonor you] in the presence of your master, and make Moshir understand this. The *kaka* was of Shiraz and funny, he joked with me so much that 'My sir, God has colored me, don't you color me too!' Because this is a saying in Shiraz where they say, 'don't color me' [don't dishonor me]. I gave the diamond ring to the *kaka* and in my heart and soul I assured him [that nothing was wrong] and let him go." Zill al-Sultan, *Khatirat-i Zill al-Sultan*, 2:474–75. For more on Zell os-Soltan, see Walcher, *In the Shadow of the King*.

34 Mirzai has noted that Josef Polak noted the last Caucasian eunuch's death in his memoir of his stay in Tehran as a court physician. Mirzai, *History of Slavery*, 114; Polak, *Persien*, 1:256.

35 "Group Portrait: Naser ed-Din Shah and His Eunuchs," Myron Bement Smith Collection, Freer Gallery of Art and Arthur M. Sackler Gallery Archives (hereafter Freer-Sackler Archives), FSA A.4 2.12.GN.51.02, https://collections.si.edu/.

36 'Azod al-Dowleh, *Life at the Court of the Early Qajar Shahs*, 34.

37 Feuvrier, *Trois ans à la cour de Perse*, 63.

38 See Najmabadi, *Women with Mustaches*.

39 "Yusuf of the court" referred to the Caucasian eunuch Agha Bahram and was a reference to the legendary beauty of Prophet Joseph. 'Azod al-Dowleh, *Life at the Court of the Early Qajar Shahs*, 34. "Our partner" referred to Manuchehr Khan, a high-ranking Georgian eunuch at the court. 'Azod

al-Dowleh, *Life at the Court of the Early Qajar Shahs*, 49; ʿAzud al-Dawlih, *Tarikh-i ʿAzudi*, 43.

40 ʿAzod al-Dowleh, *Life at the Court of the Early Qajar Shahs*, 49.

41 "Group Portrait: Naser ed-Din Shah and His Eunuchs," Myron Bement Smith Collection, Freer-Sackler Archives, FSA A.4 2.12.GN.51.02, https://collections.si.edu/.

42 "Agha Sarvar Khan Iʿtimad al-Haram," *Women's Worlds in Qajar Iran*, http://www.qajarwomen.org/fa/people/4811.html (accessed June 10, 2022).

43 Taj os-Saltaneh writes that the chief eunuch was tasked to beat anyone who did not greet her appropriately when she was a baby. Taj al-Saltanih, *Khatirat*, 8.

44 Feuvrier, *Trois ans à la cour de Perse*, 155.

45 Taj al-Saltana, *Crowning Anguish*, 121–22.

46 Hathaway, *Beshir Agha*, 34.

47 Hathaway, *Beshir Agha*, 34.

48 Muʿayyir al-Mamalik, *Yaddasht-hayi az zindagani*, 18.

49 "Amin al-Aqdas and Agha Muhammad Khan," album no. unknown, Golestan Palace Photo Archive, Tehran.

50 "Yusif Khan, Agha Muhammad Khan," Golestan Palace Photo Archive, Tehran. This photograph was used on the cover of Behdad's *Camera Orientalis*.

51 For example, a brief research note accompanying the group photograph opens with the sentence "Aqa Mohammad Khan Khaja was one of Nasir al-Din shah's favorite Eunuchs [*sic*] who was also very well trusted by the court," by Shabnam Rahimi-Golkhandan, curatorial research specialist at the Freer-Sackler Archives. "Group Portrait: Nasir al-Din Shah and His Eunuchs," Myron Bement Smith Collection, Freer-Sackler Archives, FSA A.4 2.12.GN.51.02, https://collections.si.edu/.

52 Many thanks to Nahid Mozaffari for sharing his "nickname" and showing me these photographs.

53 Willis and Krauthamer, *Envisioning Emancipation*; Wexler, *Tender Violence*.

54 Several scholars have written on Akhundzadeh and his social commentary. Camron Amin discusses this play and its commentary on restrictions placed on women. Amin, *Making of the Modern Iranian Woman*, 26–27. See also Zia Ebrahimi, *Emergence of Iranian Nationalism*, 43–53; Gould, "Critique of Religion as Political Critique," 171–84; K. Rice, "Forging the Progressive Path," chap. 4.

55 Qarachih-Daghi cited character-building as his main goal in translating the works into Persian. The 1978 edition of Akhundzadeh's *Tamsilat* in Persian includes the letters sent between Qarachih-Daghi and Akhundzadeh, as well as a translator's note. Akhundzadih, *Tamsilat, shish namayishnamih va yik dastan*, 7–25.

56 In addition to the pieces mentioned here, Akhundzadeh also faulted Muslims for buying castrated boys from Meccan markets. In one of his works, two characters, Prince Kamal od-Dowleh and Prince Jamal ol-Dowleh

wrote letters to each other complaining about the horrifying practice of
castrating young boys and selling the ones who survived. See Afary, *Sexual
Politics in Modern Iran*, 114–15.

57 Motlagh, "Translating Race," 52; Algar, "Akundzada."

58 Taj os-Saltaneh describes her brother's excesses in her memoir. Taj al-
Saltanih, *Khatirat*.

59 *L'assiette au beurre*, July 22, 1905, 258, https://gallica.bnf.fr/ark:/12148
/bpt6k1048198t/f2.item.

60 There are others illustrated as well, including François-Marie-Benjamin
Richard wearing nothing but shoes and a miter, perhaps representing
the recent law separating church and state under the Third Republic.
L'assiette au beurre, July 22, 1905, 264–65, https://gallica.bnf.fr/ark:/12148
/bpt6k1048198t/f2.item.

61 Eunuchs had also accompanied royal retinues on their European tours.
'Aziz Khan went to Europe in 1890 to accompany a wife of the shah for an
optical surgery. See Feuvrier, *Trois ans à la cour de Perse*, 63.

62 Odumosu, *Africans in English Caricature*, 29.

63 Karim Shireh-yi's long-standing popularity has ensured his portrayal in
later period dramas/comedies based in the Qajar court. "Soltan-e sahebgeran
(TV Mini-Series 1974–)," IMDb, http://www.imdb.com/title/tt0830855/ (accessed December 15, 2017); Bonine and Keddie, *Modern Iran*, 372.

64 Beeman, *Iranian Performance Traditions*, 3.

65 "Arpee Album: Photograph of Three Men and a Sleeping Lion in Chain,"
FSA A2011.03 A.01a. For more on Sevruguin's career and legacy, see Bohrer,
Sevruguin and the Persian Image.

66 Schwerda has discussed how Sevruguin was known to paint or draw over
glass plates to achieve his preferred image. Schwerda, "Iranian Photography," 88.

67 Both father and son were given the titles *Sani' os-Saltaneh* during their ap-
pointments at the royal court respectively. Tahmasbpur, *Nasir al-Din Shah-i
'Akkas*, 39.

68 Portrait representations of eunuchs from Naser ed-Din Shah's court,
however, made it clear that their visuality had always been a source of
comedy. Rather than presenting eunuchs as significant members of the
court, Sani' ol-Molk, the chief royal painter, manipulated size and stature
in his works to present caricatures that visually conjured their ineptitude
or impotence for comedic effect. For example, see *Taqi Khan-e Biqavareh*,
"the misshapen Taqi Khan" (1859), which mocked the son of Mohammad
'Ali Khan, commander of the Royal Arsenal. Five African and Caucasian
eunuchs appear around him, all about half his height and looking up at
him. Because the satire here targeted Taqi Khan's size, Sani' ol-Molk had
miniaturized the eunuchs for additional comedic effect, especially as they
were known for their height. Taqi Khan, "the misshapen" son of Mohammad 'Ali Khan, Commander of the Royal Arsenal, watercolor on paper,

38.5 by 47.3 cm, inscribed "His Majesty commanded Sani' ol-Molk to make this painting in 1276 [1859]," held at the Golestan Palace Museum; Yahya Zoka, *Life and Works of Sani' ol- Molk*, 76.

69 Lott, *Love and Theft*, 25. The rise of blackface minstrelsy in Iran seems to co-incide with its rise in the United States, and some scholars have discussed the export of Jim Crow minstrelsy to other parts of the world. See, for example, Thelwell, *Exporting Jim Crow*. In the Iranian case, I have not been able to locate clear connections to the United States, although foreign emissaries, photographers, and others often stayed at the Qajar court. Even if the shows were somehow inspired by US or European blackface minstrelsy, I show how the Iranian shows were patterned precisely on Iranian circumstances of enslavement and eunuchs specifically.

70 For more on the discourse of Aryanism, see chapter 4.

71 I mention in chapter 5 that after abolition, freedmen no longer joined circus troupes, likely indicative of the alternative and less humiliating economic opportunities available to them. But during the Qajar era it seems troupes visiting the Qajar court typically included one or two Black men. Elizabeth Dyer examined a similar phenomenon in colonial Kenya, where she argued that Black actors joined theaters as both performers and audience members, wielding these social spaces to assert themselves as cultural interpreters while being shut out of formal and institutional-ized centers of power. Dyer, "Dramatic License." Similarly, Nicholas R. Jones has examined *habla de negros* in Spain during the 1500s–1700s and has argued that Black Africans animated their agency through this genre. Jones, *Staging* Habla de Negros. Based on my sources—these photographs and their continued legacy today—I am not able to argue for the empower-ment of Black freedmen through this genre, although a future researcher may be able to delve into these troupes and their dynamics more deeply.

72 Hartman, *Scenes of Subjection*, 23.

73 See chapter 2 for more on Seyyed 'Abdollah Behbahani and the phrase *Shah Siyah*.

74 It is important to note that the Black men in the troupe were not cas-trated. Album 189, no. 60, Golestan Palace Photo Archive, Tehran.

75 Glass plate no. 432, Golestan Palace Photo Archive, Tehran. Given that all three individuals in this photograph are dressed in loincloths and that their participation or partial nudity may have been coerced, I have opted to omit this photograph. See also Samuels, "Examining Millie and Christine McKoy."

76 The rise of the freak show in Iran coincides with other similarly raced/rac-ist freak shows around the world. Sarah Baartman's shows in Europe were similarly framed around whether her body was "normal." R. Mitchell, *Venus Noire*, 30–32. See also Samuels, "Examining Millie and Christine McKoy."

77 These photographs are held at the Golestan Palace Photo Archive.

78 Afshar, *Ruznamih-yi khatirat-i I'timad al-Saltanih*, 163.

79 Mu'ayyir al-Mamalik, *Yaddasht-hayi az zindagani*, 56.

80 Haji Firuz had been appointed to Naser ed-Din Shah's mother, Mahd
    'Olya. File 295-157, Sazman-i Asnad, Tehran.

81 Per naming practices surrounding royal eunuchs, this individual was not
    the only "Haji Firuz" at the Qajar court.

PART II. ERASURE

1 For more on Shaykh Khaz'al and Arabistan, see Stephenson, "Rerouting
   the Persian Gulf," 2–24, 124.

2 Reza Shah mentioned these traditional animal sacrifices, called *qurbani*, at
   various points of his travelogue to Khuzestan. The meat of these sacrifices would typically be distributed to the needy. Pahlavi, *Safarnamih-yi
   Khuzistan; Safarnamih-yi Mazandaran*, 114.

3 *Bastigan*, or "a member of their household," here served as a euphemism
   for an enslaved person. *Karbalayi* is a title of respect given to someone who
   has performed pilgrimage at Karbala.

4 The story came up in my conversations with Bashiri in Bushehr,
   December 2015.

5 "After a few minutes we arrived at the bazaar [between the shrines of
   Imam Hussain and Hazrat-e Abbas] . . . in fifty places, they slaughtered
   sheep as *qurbani*. In the middle of the bazaar, an Iranian spice merchant
   who had laid his son and daughter down yelled, 'Because you have given
   life to the nation of Iran . . . and because I have nothing to offer besides
   these two children, I have to dedicate them to you.' . . . He picked up the
   knife and put it against the throat of one of his children, and I had to
   hurry to prevent it, I picked up the child from in front of him and kissed
   them and caressed them, and I spoke warmly with the spice merchant."
   Pahlavi, *Safarnamih-yi Khuzistan; Safarnamih-yi Mazandaran*, 197.

6 *Muzakirat-i Majlis*, 26th Assembly, 18 Bahman 1307 (Tehran), 409.

CHAPTER 4. HISTORIES OF A COUNTRY THAT NEVER ENSLAVED

1 *An Introduction to the Art of Black Africa*, 14.

2 The language of the catalog, which included references to Aimé Césaire
   and Leopold Senghor, very much reflected contemporary debates and
   discussions among Black thinkers about the importance of Black art and
   culture after independence. Savoy, *Africa's Struggle for Its Art*, 4–7.

3 Jamshid Behnam, introduction to *An Introduction to the Art of Black Africa*, 19.

4 This was the case with families in Kerman, who still, after several generations, have ties with the family their family had once enslaved after
   resettling in Bam. Conversations in Kerman, 2015. When I asked if I could

meet these individuals, the room erupted in a series of reasons it would be impossible or futile for me to do so.

5 This seems to have been very common, although families will describe them differently to cushion the stigma of enslavement.

6 There are several preabolition examples where this was the case, such as Khyzran, whom I discuss in chapter 1, whose enslaver told her to stay home to prevent British officials from granting her freedom in 1856. This is because in Khyzran's case, the British presence in the South was predicated on the patrolling of enslaved people who had recently been trafficked via the Persian Gulf, which rendered it different than major urban areas in other parts of Iran. It is reasonable to believe this happened after abolition as well. In chapters 2 and 6, I reference some possible instances of this.

7 For more on the process of naming during the Reza Pahlavi period, see Chehabi, "Reform of Iranian Nomenclature."

8 Mirzai suggests that names like *Kakai* reflects "their adaptation of traditional terminologies to new social and legal realities." Mirzai, *History of Slavery*, 204. As I mentioned in chapter 1, instead of recognizing "my *kakas*" as a phrase expressing one's proprietary ownership over the enslaved group, Mirzai simply translates it as "my brothers." Mirzai, *History of Slavery*, 24, 109. *Kakai* is a slur that can mean "brother," but demeaned Black men in intimate terms. See chapters 1 and 5 for a discussion of *kaka* as a racist slur. Mirzai's analysis neglects the very real possibility that some people may not have chosen their names themselves. Afifa Ltifi's work has examined naming practices among freedpeople in the Tunisian context. Ltifi, "Black Tunisians and the Pitfalls of Bourguiba's Homogenization Project."

9 Racial categories were not used in census reports throughout the twentieth century. Elling and Harris, "Difference in Difference," 2257. This is similar in the Turkish case as well, as Afro-Turks fell under the categories of *Muslim* and *Turk*. See Toledano, *As If Silent and Absent*.

10 Sharpe, *In the Wake*, 113.

11 See chapter 6 for a deeper discussion on the use of *we*.

12 Record 714533, file 6/54/25/1/1530 ح, September 1926, Kitabkhunih-yi Majlis, Tehran; "Slavery Convention of Geneva," *International Conciliation* (Carnegie Endowment for International Peace, no. 236), September 25, 1926.

13 Record 714533, file 6/54/25/1/1530 ح, September 1926, Kitabkhunih-yi Majlis, Tehran; "Slavery Convention of Geneva," *International Conciliation* (Carnegie Endowment for International Peace, no. 236), September 25, 1926.

14 *Muzakirat-i Majlis*, 26th Assembly, 18 Bahman 1307 (Tehran), 409.

15 *Muzakirat-i Majlis*, 26th Assembly, 18 Bahman 1307 (Tehran), 398.

16 Even Persian translations of British records from the 1910s used *kaniz* instead of *bardeh* to describe a slave woman, Saeedeh bint Mabrook. "Case concerning a slave woman named Saeedeh bint Mabrook," file 1(86), 1913, Iran Shinasi, Bushehr, Iran.

17 'Alipour, *Asnad-i bardih-furushi*, 44, 52.

18 One could also argue that the use of *bardeh* reflected the trajectory of nationalism in Iran, much of which was rooted in the de-Arabization and Westernization of the language. People like Akhundzadeh and Mirza Aqa Khan Kermani had suggested language reforms for Persian for decades, but Reza Pahlavi's government implemented the active purging of Arabic words from Persian. See Zia Ebrahimi, *Emergence of Iranian Nationalism*, 41–72. *Kaniz* and *gholam*, both derived from Arabic for "treasure" and "young boy," respectively, were cast aside in favor of *bardeh*. The ministry's language and Parliament's approval of it reflected a turn toward a Western-style understanding of enslavement.

19 Though there is some precedent for the phrase *kanizak-forushi* ("the selling of female slaves"), it did not serve as an all-encompassing term in the way *bardeh-forushi* did.

20 Parvin, "*Ettela'at*"; "Bardih-furushi" ("Slave Trade"), *Ittila'at*, 18 Bahman 1307 (February 7, 1929), 1.

21 *Muzakirat-i Majlis*, 26th Assembly, 18 Bahman 1307 (Tehran), 410.

22 "Bardih-furushi" ("Slave Trade"), *Ittila'at*, 18 Bahman 1307 (February 7, 1929), 1.

23 "Slavery That Still Lingers in the Countries of the East: Persia Takes the Lead in Abolishing Human Bondage and Other Lands Discourage It," *New York Times*, April 21, 1929, 149.

24 "The Persian Gulf, Piracy, and the Slave Trade," *Times*, January 5, 1931, xv.

25 See chapter 1 for Khyzran's story.

26 *Anglo-Persian Slavery Convention*, April 4, 1929, L/PS/10/1278, British Library, London.

27 The British Residency remained in Bushehr until 1946, when it was moved to Bahrain. Onley, "Raj Reconsidered," 44–62.

28 Letter from British Residency & Consulate-General, November 30, 1929, Cases in Persian Balochistan file 377, British Legation (Tehran), Public Records Office, National Archives, London. See also Mirzai, *History of Slavery*, 43–46.

29 "Manumission of Slaves: Notes for Guidance on Persian Coast," IOR/R/15/1/215, p. 112, British Library, London.

30 Memorandum sent from the British Residency and Consulate-General in December 1932, IOR/R/15/1/215, British Library, London.

31 Although I do not focus on the Baluch/Baloch in this book, their enslavement through the nineteenth and twentieth centuries is an important subject of study that can further shed light on patterns of racism and racialization during this period.

32 *Ruznameh-yi Shafaq-i Surkh*, November 19, 1929, p. 2, column 1.

33 File 240-34788, Sazman-i Asnad, Tehran.

34 The Street Widening Act, passed on November 13, 1933 (22 Aban 1312), proved controversial, as it required the destruction of homes and other

private structures to make room for the wide European-style streets. Karimi, *Domesticity and Consumer Culture in Iran*, 52.

35   Grigor, *Building Iran*, 132.

36   Karimi, *Domesticity and Consumer Culture in Iran*, 63; Amin, *Making of the Modern Iranian Woman*, chap. 5.

37   Marefat, "Building to Power," 76.

38   Grigor, *Building Iran*, 139; "Golestan Palace," United Nations Educational, Scientific and Cultural Organization, http://whc.unesco.org/en/list/1422 (accessed September 10, 2013).

39   Mu'ayir al-Mamalik, *Yaddasht-hayi az zindagani*, 11; Eskandari-Qajar, "Dust 'Ali Khan," 183.

40   Marefat attributes the consolidation of separate gendered areas into spaces for the entire family in part to the *kashf-e hijab* decree of 1936, which declared public veiling by women illegal. Marefat argued that the decree rendered rigid gender segregation in private spaces unnecessary since women were already uncovered in public. While this may have been true, the removal of enslaved people and servants made these spaces unwieldy. Without a specific person to serve as the go-between in these distinctly separate spaces, the family would have been scattered and isolated from one another. The new social norms allowed for a more fluid consolidation. Spaces, however, still remained gendered—for example, the men of the family still used the *mehmankhaneh* to entertain their guests, much like the *biruni*. Marefat, "Building to Power," 199.

41   The distinction between pre- and postabolition homes is not that they were all made uniform (though that trend begins later) but that the characteristics and spaces of the home that accommodated enslaved individuals were eliminated. It is important to note that although these rooms and characteristics were found in larger preabolition Iranian homes across the plateau, different cities had their own distinctive features. In the desert city of Kashan, for example, the lower floor of the home was built underground to make use of the cooler temperatures. In the port city of Bushehr, these homes tended to be narrower and taller. Karimi describes how older characteristics of Iranian homes were incorporated into modern units with a Bauhaus aesthetic which prioritized practicality over prestige. Karimi, *Domesticity and Consumer Culture in Iran*, 61–62.

42   Marefat. "Building to Power," 197.

43   See Wegmann, *Persian Nights*.

44   When thinking about these structures and their presentation in Iran, I am reminded of Celia Naylor's work on the Rose Hall Plantation in Jamaica, where the museum tours focus entirely on the life and death of Annie Palmer, an enslaving white woman whose ghost is said to now haunt the plantation, completely supplanting and obscuring any reference to the people who were enslaved there. Naylor, *UnSilencing Slavery*, 2–3.

45 This was certainly not the first dictionary of Persian, but it was the first modern dictionary of Persian that reflected some of the linguistic changes taking place in Persian at that time. For Qajar-era dictionaries, see Vejdani, *Making History in Iran*.

46 Dihkhoda and Mu'in, *Lughat-Namih*, 865–66. The dictionary also includes a separate definition for *bardeh* that follows the more typical format for Dihkhoda's entries.

47 *Tarikh-i 'umumi va Iran*, vol. 1.

48 *Gone with the Wind* represents one of the best examples of the popularity of American cultural products during this time, and it has remained a popular movie in Iran long after its release. Both the book and the film were translated into Persian; *Sinama-yih Iran* magazine named the film one of the best-dubbed films in Persian. "Bihtarin-hayih tarikh-i dublih-yi Iran" ("Best Works from the History of Dubbing in Iran"), *Sinama-yih Iran*, February 2006, 110–20. The book's classic status among Iranian audiences continues to prevail over other novels and films, including a serialized 1,700-word language reader for intermediate readers of English. M. Mitchell, *Gone with the Wind*.

49 "Shurish-i nizhadi dar Amrika bih shiddat yaft" ("The Racial Uprising in America Grows More Intense"), *Ittila'at*, 18 Farvardeen 1347 (April 6, 1968), 1–2.

50 Many thanks to Shaherzad Ahmadi for sharing these newspaper articles with me and encouraging me to write about them when we were early graduate students. Much of this section on Malcolm X and Black Americans was developed in Baghoolizadeh, "Seeing Black America in Iran." When announcing Malcolm X's assassination, *Ettela'at* mistakenly printed that he had been murdered on January 21 instead of February 21. "Malcolm X, the Leader of the Black Muslims Was Killed," *Ittila'at*, 3 Isfand 1343 (February 24, 1965), 1. Kashani-Sabet also included *Ettela'at*'s coverage of Malcolm X's assassination in her review essay. See Kashani-Sabet, "Anti-Aryan Moment." Brent Hayes Edwards has written on Black internationalism and how translations of Black American works and thought moved globally, although during an earlier time period. Edwards, *Practice of Diaspora*, 7. For those interested in the specifics of translation from the West into Iran, see Milad Odabaei's work. Odabaei, "Slip of the Philosopher." For more on the life and death of Malcolm X, see Marable, *Malcolm X*; Payne and Payne, *Dead Are Arising*.

51 "Payruvan-i 'Malkum' rahbar-i maqtul-i musalmanan-i siyahpust-i Amrika az jasad-i u kih dar tabut qarar darad binawbat didan mikunan" ("Followers of Malcolm, the slain leader of Black Muslims in the US, line up to view his body in the casket"), *Ittila'at*, 8 Isfand 1343 (February 27, 1965), 13.

52 Malcolm X, trans. Jafar Madani, "Sar guzasht-i man" ("My Story"), *Ittila'at*, 10 Isfand 1343 (March 1, 1965), 1, 13.

53 Malcolm X, trans. Jafar Madani, "Sar guzasht-i man" ("My Story"), *Ittila'at*, 10 Isfand 1343 (March 1, 1965), 1, 13.

54 Malcolm X, "Malcolm X/My Story," *Observer*, February 28, 1965, 11, and March 7, 1965, 21.

55 Malcolm X, trans. Jafar Madani, "Sar guzasht-i man" ("My Story"), *Ittila'at*, 16 Isfand 1343 (March 7, 1965), 11, and 20 Isfand 1343 (March 11, 1965), 15.

56 Malcolm X, trans. Jafar Madani, "Sar guzasht-i man" ("My Story"), *Ittila'at*, 18 Isfand 1343 (March 9, 1965), 11.

57 "Masjid-i New York munfajir gardid va gunbad-i an atash girift" ("New York's Mosque Was Blown Up and Its Dome Caught on Fire"), *Ittila'at*, 4 Isfand 1343 (February 23, 1965), 1.

58 Following Malcolm's assassination, *Ettela'at* published reports about the threats on King's life, highlighting the violent threats on the lives of those who spoke about racial justice in the United States. "Martin Luther King tahdid biqatl shud" ("Martin Luther King Has Been Threatened with Murder"), *Ittila'at*, 4 Isfand 1343 (February 23, 1965), 4.

59 "Ella Mae Collins," *Ittila'at*, 9 Isfand 1343 (February 28, 1965), 16; "Betty Shabazz," *Ittila'at*, 5 Isfand 1343 (February 24, 1965), 16; "Tazahurat-i Siyahan aghaz shud" ("The Blacks' Protests Have Begun"), *Ittila'at*, 5 Isfand 1343 (February 24, 1965), 4.

60 Malcolm X, "Malcolm X/My Story," *Observer*, March 7, 1965, 21.

61 It is important to note that the coverage of Malcolm X's death and coverage of race relations in the United States overlapped with Iran's Nowruz holiday, which was celebrated in Tehran with a blackface minstrel. The Nowruz editions of the paper included Haji Firuz caricatures in the same editions that attempted to edify the Iranian public about the problem of racism in the United States. "Sar guzasht-i man—Malkum," ("My Story—Malcolm"), "Shumarih makhsus-i nowruz" ("Special Nowruz edition"), *Ittila'at*, 22 Isfand 1343 (March 13, 1965), 15, 18.

62 Haley, *Autobiography of Malcolm X*; Iks, *Malkum Iks: Gangistiri kih rahbar-i Musalman-i Amrika shod* (trans. Abbasi). Other presses have also published translations of the autobiography. Ihya Press published its translation by Farhad Khurrami in 1979 under the title *Siyah mikhurushad: Malcolm X (The Black Seethes: Malcolm X)*. Amir Kabir Press also published a translation by Ghulam Husayn Kishavarz and released its third edition in 2001.

63 Haley, *Autobiography of Malcolm X*.

64 Kiyanush, *Az Klasik ta mudirn*.

65 L. Thompson, "Vernacular Transactions."

66 "Bidunbal-i qatl-i Luther King" ("Following Luther King's Murder"), *Ittila'at*, 17 Farvardin 1347 (April 6, 1968), 1.

67 "Shikaf bayn-i Siyah va sifid chigunih pur mishavad?" ("How Will the Schism between Black and White Be Filled?"), *Ittila'at*, 24 Farvardin 1347 (April 13, 1968), 8.

68 "Carmichael, Siyahpusti kih mikhwahad Amrika ra atash bizanad" ("Carmichael, the Black Who Wants to Set America on Fire"), *Ittila'at*, 25 Farvardin 1347 (April 14, 1968), 8.

69 "Masjid-i New York munfajir gardid va gunbad-i an atash girift" ("New York's Mosque Was Blown Up and Its Dome Caught on Fire"), *Ittila'at*, 4 Isfand 1343 (February 23, 1965), 1.

70 Cohen, *Duke Ellington's America*, 411. Photographs of white police officers handling Black protestors were also widely shared in Iran. "1343: Saal-i tashanuj va buhran dar jahan" ("1343: A year of tension and struggle around the world"), *Ittila'at*, 29 Esfand 1343 (March 20, 1965), 10.

71 A note on the first page of the undated manuscript *Man yik ghahriman-i Siyah hastam*, file 264-6559, Sazman-i Asnad, Tehran.

72 Because "Muhammad 'Ali" is a common first name in Iran, Iranians took to fondly calling him Mohammad Ali Clay, keeping his former last name as a part of his identity. Iranians in Iran were not alone in seeing Black American struggles as part in parcel with their own. Manijeh Moradian explores these connections in the US diaspora context in *This Flame Within*.

73 Author's private collection.

74 United Nations, "International Day for the Elimination of Racial Discrimination," http://www.un.org/en/events/racialdiscriminationday/background.shtml (accessed April 29, 2016).

75 It is important to note that the Islamic Republic was invested in the South African antiapartheid movement. Streets in Tehran were renamed "Mandela" and "Africa" to honor Nelson Mandela and general anticolonial movements in the continent.

76 A revealing example that highlighted Malcolm X's enduring recognizability in the early years of the Islamic Republic is found in Marjane Satrapi's *Persepolis*. In 1983, teenage Satrapi was stopped by the women's branch of the Guardians of the Revolution for sporting a Michael Jackson pin. Satrapi tried to convince them that the pin was not the singer but, rather, "Malcolm X, the leader of Black Muslims in America." They were not convinced; they only let her go after she cried about a fake stepmother and threats of being sent to an orphanage. Satrapi, *Persepolis*, 133.

77 Akkad, *The Message*.

78 The following year the Iranian government issued a stamp featuring two African children in honor of World Racial Day. Author's private collection.

79 I use *America/n* here not necessarily to refer to the Americas but to mimic the use of *American* in Persian when referencing the United States.

80 See Zia Ebrahimi, *Emergence of Iranian Nationalism*; Ansari, *Perceptions of Iran*.

81 See Steele, *Shah's Imperial Celebrations of 1971*.

82 Many thanks to Amy Motlagh for suggesting that perhaps the emphasis on *Black Africa* was also to distinguish it from North Africa, namely Egypt, the birthplace of the Shah's first wife, Princess Fawzia.

83 Steele, *Shah's Imperial Celebrations of 1971*, 1.

84 Cyrus Cylinder translation presented to the United Nations by Princess Ashraf (Mohammad Reza Shah's sister), UN Archives, doc. S-0882-0002 -02-00001. Many thanks to Amy Malek for providing me with this source.

85 Dandamayev, "Barda and Barda-Dari," section 1, "Achaemenid Period." The Cyrus Cylinder is now held at the British Museum. For a scholarly translation of the cylinder, see "The Cyrus Cylinder," record no. 90920, British Museum, https://www.britishmuseum.org/collection/object/W_1880-0617 -1941; and Wiesohofer, *Ancient Persia*.

86 This version of the Cyrus Cylinder is posted on an English-language plaque in Balboa Park in San Diego, California. See the work of Amy Malek for more on diaspora Iranians and their work around the Cyrus Cylinder.

87 "Amadan-i jaru barqi bih Tihran va giriftan-i aks-i yadigari," ʿAbbasi House, Kashan, December 2015.

88 Shadi Ghadirian, *Untitled* (*Qajar Series*), Los Angeles County Museum of Art, Los Angeles, CA.

CHAPTER 5. ORIGINS OF BLACKFACE IN THE ABSENCE OF BLACK PEOPLE

1 While I have capitalized *Siyah* when referring to Black people, I have left *siyah-bazi* and *siyah* (the character in a *siyah-bazi*) lowercase, in the same way "blackface" is lowercased in English.

2 There are few examples of women starring as protagonists in *siyah-bazi*, including the 2016 television series *Dandun tala* (*Golden Tooth*), directed by Davud Mir-Bagheri, which chronicles the story of a woman who wanted to play the role of the main *siyah* in face of pressures against her in the male-dominated field. Women who appear in blackface roles typically play a secondary role, such as a love interest. In direct contrast with Iran, the main blackface character in Turkey is the *arap baci*, a caricature of an enslaved Black woman. See Wingham, "Arap Bacı'nın Ara Muhaveresi"; Willoughby, "Opposing a Spectacle of Blackness."

3 Baghoolizadeh, "Myths of Haji Firuz."

4 Muʿayyir al-Mamalik, *Yaddasht-hayi az zindagani*, 56; "Irsal-i dastkhat-i Nasir al-Din Shah dar murid-i haramsara," file 295-157, Sazman-i Asnad, Tehran.

5 A. Thompson, *Blackface*; Reyes, "Performativity and Representation."

6 See chapter 3 for an in-depth discussion of these troupes at the Qajar court.

7 Beeman, *Iranian Performance Traditions*, 137. Some shows would include the *sholi* character, "the loose one," which may have developed out of the Caucasian eunuch, although the reference is generally a vague one.

8 Bayzai, *Namayish dar Iran*, 172–73. Even stranger, the cover of the book has isolated one of the individuals from the miniatures, a turbaned Black man. Bayzai, *Namayish dar Iran*, note on cover.

9   The film follows the story of Bashu, a young boy from southern Iran who escapes a bombardment and accidentally ends up in a northern Iranian village during the Iran-Iraq War. His Blackness is highlighted throughout the film, including scenes where a woman tries to buy several bars of soap to wash the darkness off his skin. Ultimately, Bashu becomes a key member of their family, a metaphor for the importance of Iranian unity. Bayzai, *Bashu: The Little Stranger*. See also Naficy, *A Social History of Iranian Cinema*, 4:35–36.

10 He has also suggested that Karim engaged in whiteface makeup, where the black clown was quick and agile and the white clown was *sholi*, slow, and stupid. Beeman, *Iranian Performance Traditions*, 137.

11 Iraj Emami allows for the possibility that the clowns may have imitated the accents of former Black enslaved people and cited Reza Khaki's 1977 presentation *The Development of the Black-Face Clowns in Traditional Iranian Theater* (Iranian Center for Performing Traditions, Shiraz Art Festival, International Seminar on Improvisatory Theater, August 19, 1977). Emami, "Evolution of Traditional Theatre," 88.

12 S. Afshar, ʿAli jinab-i siyah, 48. Maheri is also credited by others, including Shiva Masʿudi. Masʿudi, *Karnamih-yi talkhagan*, 171.

13 S. Afshar, ʿAli jinab-i siyah, 47–48.

14 S. Afshar, ʿAli jinab-i siyah, 48.

15 S. Afshar, ʿAli jinab-i siyah, 48.

16 S. Afshar, ʿAli jinab-i siyah, 45.

17 See chapter 3 for a discussion on the voices of eunuchs. Similarly, Eve Troutt Powell has shown how accents were heightened in racial comedies in nineteenth-century Egypt. Troutt Powell, *A Different Shade of Colonialism*, chap. 2.

18 Baghoolizadeh, "Myths of Haji Firuz."

19 Akhavan-Salis, *Arghanun*, 77.

20 Vaziri, "Thaumaturgic, Cartoon Blackface."

21 "Poupée de chiffon, tunique de soie artificielle," 1979, Musée du quai Branly—Jacques Chirac, http://www.quaibranly.fr/fr/explorer-les -collections/base/Work/action/show/notice/799998-poupee-de-chiffon -tunique-de-soie-artificielle/page/1 (accessed February 4, 2019); "Poupée représentant un bateleur du Nouvel an," 1960s, Musée du quai Branly— Jacques Chirac, http://www.quaibranly.fr/fr/explorer-les-collections/base /Work/action/show/notice/73391-poupee-representant-un-danseur/page /1 (accessed February 4, 2019). Many thanks to Mira Xenia Schwerda for alerting me to these dolls.

22 Collection of the author, 1995–2015. After the crackdown on blackface minstrelsy under the Islamic Republic, many shows continued their performances without blackening the *siyah*'s face. In these instances, the role of the blackened face is diminished in live action, as other characteristics, such as accent or comportment, can communicate the racialized caricature in the absence of blackface.

23 Until recently, a doll or an illustration without a blackened face may not have even been recognizable as a Haji Firuz but could instead have been mistaken for any doll wearing a red outfit. This may be changing as some are keen to save Haji Firuz's character from claims of racism by removing the blackened face, even if the entirety of the character is racist.

24 Tawfiq, *Tawfiq chigunih Tawfiq shud*, 1; Javadi, "Towfiq (Tawfiq) Newspaper."

25 Tawfiq, *Tawfiq chigunih Tawfiq shud*, 1; Javadi, "Towfiq (Tawfiq) Newspaper."

26 Shiraz, a major city in southern Iran, was once a hub for the trafficking of African slaves via the Persian Gulf coast. While it is written *kaka* in Persian, it is most often pronounced *kako* in the Shirazi dialect.

27 As mentioned earlier in chapter 1, this was especially in areas outside Shiraz, where *dada* referred to brothers and *kaka* referred exclusively to enslaved Black men. The plural *kaka-ha* was also used to describe a group of enslaved Black men.

28 Tawfiq, *Tawfiq chigunih Tawfiq shud*, 27. Abbas Towfigh ('Abbas Tawfiq; I have preserved this transliteration of his name for citation purposes, though he uses "Abbas Towfigh" in the United States) also describes how, officially, he and his brothers only received approval to publish the satirical after they promised authorities that the name of their magazine would be *Fokahi* (*Humorous*). And while the issues typically did have "ruznameh-ye fokahi" printed at the top, it was in a small script and almost unnoticeable next to the large, stylized *Towfiq*.

29 Tawfiq, *Tawfiq chigunih Tawfiq shud*, 26–27.

30 Tawfiq, *Tawfiq chigunih Tawfiq shud*, 50. Gishniz is herself a caricature of a woman from a lower socioeconomic background. Her blue-and-yellow-patterned chador wrapped revealingly around her curvy body, her red heels that do not match her outfit, and even the lipstick that peeks out from under her chador all are intended as visual cues of someone who lacks class, education, and any sense of a "modern" identity. See Amin, *Making of the Modern Iranian Woman*.

31 Marwa Elshakry's *Reading Darwin* demonstrates how eugenics debates and racist comparisons of Black people as related to apes entered Egypt after 1900. This may also have been one of the trajectories from which it entered Iran. Elshakry, *Reading Darwin in Arabic*, 245–47.

32 Tawfiq, *Tawfiq chigunih Tawfiq shud*, 50.

33 One might note that the references to monkeys are now also deployed in *siyah-bazi* theater. Take, for example, Behnam Bayzai's *Tarabnameh* (2016), where the childhood name of the *siyah* character, Mobarak, was *antar* or "monkey." Shirazi, "Review of *Tarabnameh*."

34 *Tawfiq*, no. 24, 10 Shahrivar 1349 (September 1, 1970).

35 Javadi, "Towfiq (Tawfiq) Newspaper."

36 Mas'udi, *Karnamih-yi talkhagan*, 221–24; *Yaqut*, Tehran, 1979–80. I am grateful to Hushidar Mortezaie for providing me with a copy of the periodical.

37 See the introduction and chapter 2 for examples of others named Yaqut.

38 See the works and writings of Saʿdi Afshar, Bayzai, Mohammad Hosayn Naserbakht, and others.

39 An earlier version of this section on the narratives that developed around Haji Firuz appears in Baghoolizadeh, "Myths of Haji Firuz."

40 Wekker, *White Innocence*, 140; Hall, *Representation*, 245.

41 Khomeini was exiled in November 1964 and returned to Iran in January 1979. From Najaf and Paris, he gave speeches where he linked the shah's rule to the United States until he returned for the revolution. Abrahamian, *Iran between Two Revolutions*, 445, 461.

42 Negative feelings about these policies went beyond the regulation of Haji Firuz, as the scope of censorship and redlining extended (and continues to extend) beyond music/dancing and touched all forms of art and other creative expressions. See Atwood, *Underground*; Bajoghli, *Iran Reframed*; Karimi, *Alternative Iran*; and Siamdoust, *Soundtrack of the Revolution*.

43 The original form of Siavash, "Siiauuarsan," was derived from the Avestan for "the one with the black stallions." Skjærvø, "Kayanian," section 6, "Siiauuarsan, Siyawaxs, Siavas."

44 Bahar's work has had a long-term impact on the discourse. As recently as 2021, Javad Insafi has written a defense of Haji Firuz using this same logic. "Insafi: Siyah-bazi hich irtibat-i ba dawran-i bardih dari nadarad," *Theater. ir* (24 Aban 1400, November 15, 2021), https://theater.ir/fa/149477.

45 See Khaleghi-Motlagh, *Abu'l Qasem Ferdowsi*.

46 Omidsalar, "Haji Firuz."

47 H. K., "Dar guzasht-i Saʿdi Afshar, akharin bazmandih-yi nasl-i siyah bazi" (30 Farvardeen 1392, April 19, 2013), https://www.dw.com/fa-ir/در-گذشت-سعدی-افشار-آخرین-باز-مانده-نسل-سیاه‌باز‌ان/a-16758519.

48 "Sadi Afshar Stresses Need to Teach the Youth Siah-Bazi," *Payvand News*, November 8, 2009, http://www.payvand.com/news/09/nov/1081.html.

49 Insafi, *Siyah Bazi az nigah-i yik siyah baz*, 23; Nasirbakht, "Tahavulat-i namayish-hayi shadi-avar-i Irani dar duran-i Qajar," February 2, 2021, https://tv.theater.ir/theater/تحول-نمایشهای-شادیآور-ایرانی-در-دوره-قاجار.

50 Kimiyai's 1971 film *Dash Akol* is based on a short story by Sadegh Hedayat.

51 Khazaʾi acknowledges that *zaban-i kakai* is derived directly from mimicking enslaved Africans at the Qajar court and their accented Persian. Khazaʾi, *Sabk-i bazigari va zindigi*, 121–39.

52 The announcement was made by M. R. Javadi Yeganeh, deputy mayor of Tehran for social and cultural affairs. M. R. Javadi Yeganeh (@javadimr), tweet, March 22, 2021, 5:45 p.m., https://twitter.com/javadimr/status /1373979204577062921.

53 The post from the Collective for Black Iranians was created under the direction of Priscillia Kounkou Hoveyda, which summarized my research alongside a Nowruz visual by Mina Jafari. Collective for Black Iranians (@BlackIranians), "My Master, hold your head up high, / My Master, why don't you laugh? / It's Nowruz, it's one day a year! These are the words sung

by Haji Firuz every year. Not anymore . . . ," Twitter, March 22, 2021, 10:27 a.m., https://twitter.com/BlackIranians/status/1374004734227476482. Javadi Yeganeh shared posts from the collective and referenced my broader scholarship (including "Myths of Haji Firuz") alongside that of Behnaz Mirzai in his defense of the ban. Baghoolizadeh, "Myths of Haji Firuz"; M. R. Javadi Yeganeh (@javadimr), tweet, March 22, 2021, 8:58 a.m., https://twitter.com/javadimr/status/1374027827012632581; M. R. Javadi Yeganeh (@javadimr), tweet, March 22, 2021, 10:17 p.m., https://twitter.com/javadimr/status/1374228879552942082.

54 The emotionality of these arguments are reminiscent of reactions Wekker has had to hear white Dutch people share in defense of Zwarte Piet / Black Pete. Wekker asks, "I am wondering what is at stake here?" when reflecting on the level of hostility expressed by them. Wekker, *White Innocence*, 141. I find myself wondering the same.

55 Although many across the Persianate world celebrate Nowruz during the spring equinox, Haji Firuz only appears in Iranian-centric celebrations.

CHAPTER 6. MEMORIES AND A GENRE OF DISTORTION

1 "*Black People of Iran*: Documentary on the Lives of Afro-Iranians," film screening and Q&A with Farhad Varahram (the film's director) and Roya Arab, Zoom event, School of Oriental and African Studies, January 18, 2021, https://www.soas.ac.uk/about/event/black-people-iran-documentary-lives-afro-iranians-southern-coasts-iran. Varahram, *Siyahan-i Junub-i Iran*.

2 January 2016, Kerman. See chapter 4 for the parliamentary debates.

3 January 2016, Kerman. As I reflect on this conversation several years later, I remember being shocked at the callousness of the statement, a stark difference to the complete denials of enslavement that I had become accustomed to in the course of my fieldwork. This person noticed my visible reaction and resorted to a different form of casual racism to explain their harshness as enslavers. "They had Arab ancestry," he shrugged, as though that would account for violence, and moved on to a discussion of the ways his family differed as he shared their family album. This story is a common one in Kerman, and other Kermanis often referred to this family when learning about my research. "Oh, you work on slavery? Have you heard of the khan who sewed his slave's mouth for being cheeky?"

4 Trouillot, *Silencing the Past*, 26.

5 Kendra T. Field explores memory, family history, and institutionalized archives from a Black and Indigenous perspective in the US context. See Field, "Privilege of Family History."

6 See chapter 4 for an examination of this narrative.

7 Wingham has rightfully critiqued the use of *we* in the context of Ottoman and Middle East Studies more broadly in contexts that ignore histories

of enslavement and the African diaspora. Wingham, "Arap Bacı'nın Ara Muhaveresi," 180.

8 These individuals were colloquially referred to as *noon-rakhti*, or "food and clothing," which referred to their labor in exchange for room and board.

9 It is no doubt possible that some of these relationships started out as voluntary but later became involuntary if the person was not able to leave, resulting in cruel and inhumane conditions that amount to enslavement. This is not the typical scenario shared with me, however.

10 Recently, a few scholars from Iran and other parts of the Middle East have begun to push toward an honest examination of their families' complicity in the history of enslavement. I look forward to seeing how these works will change these patterns.

11 AIS conference, Vienna, August 5, 2016.

12 Motlagh, *Burying the Beloved*, 59–61.

13 H. Afshar, "Age, Gender, and Slavery," 908.

14 H. Afshar, "Age, Gender, and Slavery," 910–11.

15 H. Afshar, "Age, Gender, and Slavery," 910, 909.

16 H. Afshar, "Age, Gender, and Slavery," 909.

17 H. Afshar, "Age, Gender, and Slavery," 912. Motlagh also noted the limited domestic options available to Sonbol Baji in Afshar's home. Motlagh, *Burying the Beloved*, 60.

18 Various studies of enslaving family photo albums reveal that photographs of enslaved domestics with their enslavers is not unique to Iran. See chapter 2.

19 Motlagh, "Translating Race." The photograph appears in Khosronejad, *Qajar African Nannies*, 51.

20 @Stillchill.mindfulness, June 1, 2020, https://www.instagram.com/p/CA52GmL n9iC/?utm_source=ig_web_copy_link". The account has since been deleted.

21 Afnan, *Black Pearls*, 7, xix.

22 After the Bab's declaration, his adherents came to be known as Babis, and their religion Babism. Since Baha'u'llah's declaration of prophethood in 1863, many Babis converted to the Baha'i faith, while others either maintained their faith or joined the 'Azali Babis. For more, see Cole, *Modernity and the Millennium*.

23 Lee, "Half the Household Was African."

24 Lee, "Half the Household Was African," 37n52. Anthony Lee has written extensively on the lives of the enslaved in the homes of the Bab and Baha'u'llah. See Lee, "Half the Household Was African"; "Enslaved African Women in Nineteenth-Century Iran"; and "Haji Mobarak." The Baha'i faith has a long history of addressing race and racism head-on, as evidenced by the journey that 'Abdu'l-Baha, Baha'u'llah's son and successor, made to the United States in the early twentieth century and his reflections on and interactions with Black Americans and the NAACP. See Mottahedeh, *'Abdu'l Baha's Journey West*. The international Baha'i community continues to actively advocate for racial justice as a core principle of the faith, publishing articles,

videos, and other forms of media on the subject. See *The Baha'i Faith*, www.
bahai.org and others.

25 Afnan, *Black Pearls*, 3. Lee also refers to these individuals as slaves or
enslaved in his own writings. Lee, "Half the Household Was African" and
"Enslaved African Women in Nineteenth-Century Iran."

26 Lee takes it a step further in the introduction and even argues that Muslim
societies made it necessary to enslave people due to gender separations
and general household chores—a questionable proposition, given that the
majority of Muslims, as well as a majority of Iranians in the nineteenth
century, did not, in fact, enslave others. Instead, this was a practice of the
wealthy and the elites. "In such a society, domestic slaves were absolutely
necessary to carry on the normal business of any household and to maintain the respectability of the family." Afnan, *Black Pearls*, xxiii.

27 Afnan, *Black Pearls*, 5.

28 Afnan offers stories about individuals who continued to live in the Bab's
household after the 1873 prohibition (e.g., Fiddih), but he does not elaborate on whether they were still enslaved or had been freed at this point.
Afnan, *Black Pearls*, 23.

29 Afnan, *Black Pearls*, 3fn.

30 This tension is shared by Muslims in the modern period as well, who have
come to agree that enslavement is wrong but have to grapple with enslavement by the Prophet Muhammad, his companions, and descendants.

31 Dashti switches between two spellings of her name, "Samanber" and
"Samanbar."

32 Dashti, *To Our Children around the World*, 89.

33 Dorothy Roberts has written extensively on the dangers of medical racism
that pitches Black people as somehow stronger, more resistant to pain,
or somehow anatomically different and unique from other people. See,
among other works, Roberts, *Fatal Invention* and *Killing the Black Body*.

34 Afnan, *Black Pearls*, 17–18.

35 A more cynical read of their secrecy revolves around the norms of enslavement in Iran during this period: often, when an enslaver died, those who
were enslaved received their freedom.

36 Afnan, *Black Pearls*, xii–xiii.

37 Dashti, *To Our Children around the World*, 94.

38 Dashti, *To Our Children around the World*, 87 ("inherently prejudiced"), 86,
87, 91 ("our Blacks").

EPILOGUE

1 Ideas from this section on Kurdizadeh's life and legacy were developed in
Baghoolizadeh, "From Religious Eulogy to War Anthem." 'Ashura marks
the Battle of Karbala (680 CE), where the Umayyad army killed nearly every

male relative of the Prophet, including his grandson Husayn, and arrested the women of the family. Shiʿa Muslims commemorate the battle by reciting eulogies every year.

2 Martin, *Qajar Pact*, 29–31. A number of scholars have written on the history of the Persian Gulf in the nineteenth and twentieth centuries, especially from an economic or urban perspective. See Atabaki, "From ʿAmaleh (Labor) to Kargar (Worker)"; Boodrookas and Keshavarzian, "Forever Frontier of Urbanism"; Kamrava, *Gateways to the World* (for more on Iran, see chapters by Keshavarzian, Alaedini, and Javaheripour); Stephenson, "Rerouting the Persian Gulf"; and Elling and Razak, "Oil, Labour and Empire."

3 Several of these homes have been renovated in recent decades into museums, restaurants, boutique hotels, or cultural institutional buildings.

4 *Vurudi-ye Siyahha* and *vurudi-ye sefidha*, respectively.

5 Some Bushehris attribute the origin of the *dammam* to East Africa.

6 Kounkou Hoveyda, "Writing Ourselves into Existence with the Collective for Black Iranians." I also note this phenomenon in my article "Seeing Black America in Iran."

7 Baghoolizadeh, "From Religious Eulogy to War Anthem," 444.

8 Baghoolizadeh, "From Religious Eulogy to War Anthem." Parisa Vaziri has written about Blackness in *Arbaʾin* from a film studies perspective as well. Vaziri, "Arbaʾīn and Bakhshū's Lament."

9 Since the rise of the internet, several different versions of this eulogy can be found, as is customary for these commemorations. Kurdizadeh's version includes the lines "tarsam bemiram nabinam / ruye an degar / ta saff-e mahshar / nawjavan Akbar / ah-e-vaveyla / ku Akbar-e man / nur-e do chashman-e tar-e man."

10 Kuveitipur's last name translates to "son of a Kuwaiti" and hints at a foreign and potentially Arab heritage. By contrast, Kurdizadeh's last name offers an ethnic lineage native to Iran, "descendant of a Kurd." The comparison between the two names and their vastly differing connotations indicates that visible racial appearance trumps other secondary associations. Stephenson's work on migration networks between Iran, Kuwait, and Bahrain in the early twentieth century offers explanations for Kuveitipur's surname and demonstrates how notions of "Arab" or "Iranian" are not as distinct as nationalists would like to assume today. Stephenson, "Rerouting the Persian Gulf."

11 The term *Black Iranian* can be understood expansively to include not only those who are often referred to as Afro-Iranian, or *Irani-ye Ifriqai-tabar*, but also those born to a non-Black Iranian parent and a non-Iranian African/African diaspora parent.

12 See chapter 6 for a discussion on genre of distortion.

13 Kounkou Hoveyda invited me to serve as the resident historian for the collective in August 2020.

14 In this series, Kounkou Hoveyda asked artist Kimia Fatehi and me to recreate the historical portraits.

15 Abbas Amanat's chapter overview of Qajar history, for example, focuses largely on political history. Amanat, "Qajar Iran." Maryam Ekhtiar's chapter, "From Workshop to Bazaar to Academy," acknowledges the presence of unpaid, enslaved artisans at the royal court: "Priority was given to those who had acquired skills through apprenticeship in the royal workshops, sons of master craftsmen in the royal workshops, and unpaid artisans such as prisoners of war and slaves (slave painters)." Ekhtiar, "From Workshop to Bazaar to Academy," 54. The volume does include an image of Manuchehr Khan, a Georgian eunuch and a note on his life, in the examples offered throughout the book. Diba and Ekhtiar, *Royal Persian Paintings*, 229.

16 Denise Hassanzade Ajiri, "Face of African Slavery in Qajar Iran—in Pictures," *Tehran Bureau*, January 14, 2016, https://www.theguardian.com /world/iran-blog/2016/jan/14/african-slavery-in-qajar-iran-in-photos.

17 Khosronejad, *Qajar African Nannies*.

BIBLIOGRAPHY

ARCHIVES

Albumkhanih-yi Kakh Gulistan (Golestan Palace Photo Archive), Tehran, Iran
Astan-i Quds-i Razavi, Imam Reza Shrine Complex, Mashhad, Iran
Bibliothèque Nationale de France, Paris, France
Bodleian Libraries, Oxford University, Oxford, United Kingdom
British Library, London, United Kingdom
Bunyad-i Iran Shinasi, Bushehr, Iran (Iranian Studies Association in Bushehr)
Freer Gallery of Art and Arthur M. Sackler Gallery Archives, Washington, DC
Kamal al-Mulk Museum, Bagh-i Nigaristan, Tehran, Iran
Kitabkhanih, Muzih, va Markaz-i Asnad-i Majlis-i Shura-yi Islami (Kitabkhunih-
     yi Majlis or Majles Library), Tehran, Iran
League of Nations Archives, Geneva, Switzerland
Los Angeles County Museum of Art, Los Angeles, CA
Musée du quai Branly–Jacques Chirac, Paris, France
National Archives, London, United Kingdom
Sazman-i Asnad va Kitabkhanih-yi Milli-yi Iran (Sazman-i Asnad or National
     Archives and Library), Tehran, Iran
United Nations Archives, New York, NY
Women's Worlds in Qajar Iran (digital archive), Harvard University, Cambridge, MA

HOMES, MOSQUES, AND OTHER ARCHITECTURAL STRUCTURES

Bagh-i Firdaws (Bagh-e Ferdows), Tehran, Iran
Bunyad-i Iran-Shinasi, Bushehr, Iran
Imarat-i Mas'udiyih, Tehran, Iran
Kakh Gulistan (Golestan Palace Museum), Tehran, Iran
Khanih-yi 'Abbasian ('Abbasi House), Kashan, Iran
Khanih-yi 'Amiriha ('Ameri House), Kashan, Iran
Khanih-yi Burujirdiha (Borujerdi House), Kashan, Iran
Khanih-yi Tabataba'iha (Tabataba'i House), Kashan, Iran
Masjid-i Bihbahani (Behbahani Mosque), Bushehr, Iran

PERIODICALS

Danish (Danesh)
Ittila'at (Ettela'at)
L'assiette au beurre
Muzakirat-i Majlis
New York Times
Observer
Shafaq-i Surkh (Shafaq-e Sorkh)
Sur-i Israfil
Tawfiq (Towfiq)
Times (United Kingdom)
Yaqut

PUBLISHED TEXTS

Abrahamian, Ervand. *Iran between Two Revolutions*. Princeton, NJ: Princeton University Press, 1982.

Afary, Janet. *The Iranian Constitutional Revolution, 1906–1911*. New York: Columbia University Press, 1996.

Afary, Janet. *Sexual Politics in Modern Iran*. Cambridge: Cambridge University Press, 2009.

Afkhami, Amir Arsalan. *A Modern Contagion: Imperialism and Public Health in Iran's Age of Cholera*. Baltimore, MD: Johns Hopkins University Press, 2019.

Afnan, Abu'l-Qasim. *Black Pearls: Servants in the Households of the Bab and Baha'ullah*. Edited by Anthony Lee. Los Angeles: Kalimat Press, 1999.

Afshar, Haleh. "Age, Gender, and Slavery in and out of the Persian Harem: A Different Story." *Ethnic and Racial Studies* 23, no. 5 (2000): 905–16.

Afshar, Iraj. "Some Remarks on the Early History of Photography." In *Qajar Iran: Political, Social, and Cultural Change, 1800–1925*, edited by Edmund Bosworth and Carole Hillenbrand, 261–90. Costa Mesa, CA: Mazda, 1983.

Afshar, Sa'di. *'Ali jinab-i siyah: Zindigi va khatirat-i Sa'di Afshar*. Edited by Lalih 'Alam. Tehran: Puyandih, 2012.

Ahmad Ibn Fath 'Ali. *Tarikh-i 'Azudi, dar sharh-i halat-i zawjat va banin va banat-i khaqan*. Bombay, 1888/1889.

Akhavan-Salis, Mahdi. *Arghanun: Majmu'ih Sh'ir*. Tehran: Murvarid, 1951.

Akhundzadih, Fath 'Ali. *Tamsilat, shish namayishnamih va yik dastan*. Translated by Muhammad Ja'far Qarachih-Daghi. Tehran: Shirkat-i Sahamiyi Khwarazmi, 1978.

Akkad, Moustapha, dir. *The Message*. 3 hrs., 26 mins. Filmco International Productions, 1976.

Alaedini, Pooya, and Mehrdad Javaheripour. "Urban Dynamics in Iranian Port Cities: Growth, Informality, and Decay in Bandar Abbas." In *Gateways to the World: Port Cities in the Persian Gulf*, edited by Mehran Kamrava, 217–44. Oxford: Oxford University Press, 2016.

al-Dawlih, Munis. *Khatirat-i Munis al-Dawlih*. Edited by Sirus Sa'dvandian. Tehran: Kitabkhanih va Markaz-i Asnad-i Majlis-i Shura-yi Islami, 2001.

Algar, Hamid. "'Abdallah Behbahani." *Encyclopaedia Iranica*, 2011. Accessed July 21, 2017. http://www.iranicaonline.org/articles/abdallah-Bihbahani.

Algar, Hamid. "Akundzada." *Encyclopaedia Iranica*, 2011. Accessed July 21, 2017. https://iranicaonline.org/articles/akundzada-playwright.

al-i-Davud, Sayyid 'Ali. *Asnad va namih-hayi Amir Kabir*. Tehran: Sazman-i Asnad va Kitabkhanih-yi Milli, 2011.

'Alipour, Nargis. *Asnad-i bardih-furushi va man'-i an dar 'asr-i Qajar*. Tehran: Kitabkhanih va Markaz-i Asnad-i Majlis Shura-yi Islami, 2011.

al-Saltana, Taj. *Crowning Anguish: Memoirs of a Persian Princess from the Harem to Modernity*. Translated by Abbas Amanat. Washington, DC: Mage, 1993.

al-Saltanih, I'timad. *Ruznamih-yi khatirat-i I'timad al-Saltanih*. Edited by Iraj Afshar. Tehran: Amir Kabir, 2010.

al-Saltanih, Taj. *Khatirat-i Taj al-Saltanih*. Edited by Masumih Ittihadiyih and Sirus Sa'dvandian. Tehran: Nashr-i Tarikh-i Iran, 1999.

Alvandi, Roham, ed. *The Age of Aryamehr, Late Pahlavi Iran and Its Global Entanglements*. London: Gingko Library, 2018.

Amanat, Abbas. "'Aziz-Al-Soltan." *Encyclopaedia Iranica*, 1988. Accessed August 5, 2017. http://www.iranicaonline.org/articles/aziz-al-soltan-golam-ali-khan.

Amanat, Abbas. "Fatḥ-'Ali Shah Qajar." *Encyclopaedia Iranica*, 1999. Accessed November 11, 2016. http://www.iranicaonline.org/articles/fath-ali-shah-qajar-2.

Amanat, Abbas. *Iran: A Modern History*. New Haven, CT: Yale University Press, 2017.

Amanat, Abbas. *Pivot of the Universe: Nasir al-Din Shah and the Iranian Monarchy, 1831–1896*. New York: I. B. Tauris, 1997.

Amanat, Abbas. "Qajar Iran: A Historical Overview." In *Royal Persian Paintings: The Qajar Epoch, 1785–1925*, edited by Layla S. Diba with Maryam Ekhtiar, 14–29. New York: Brooklyn Museum of Art in association with I. B. Tauris, 1998.

Ambraseys, Nicholas N., and Charles Peter Melville. *A History of Persian Earthquakes*. Cambridge: Cambridge University Press, 1982.

Amin, Camron. *The Making of the Modern Iranian Woman: Gender, State Policy, and Popular Culture, 1865–1946*. Gainesville: University Press of Florida, 2002.

Andreeva, Elena. *Russia and Iran in the Great Game: Travelogues and Orientalism*. New York: Routledge, 2007.

Ansari, Ali, ed. *Perceptions of Iran: History, Myths and Nationalism from Medieval Persia to the Islamic Republic*. London: Bloomsbury, 2013.

Ardakani, H. Mahbubi. "'Ala'-al-Molk, Hajji." *Encyclopaedia Iranica*, 1/7, 783–84. Updated version. Accessed May 15, 2014. http://www.iranicaonline.org/articles/ala-al-molk-hajji-mirza-abdallah-khan-d.

Arvas, Abdulhamit. "Early Modern Eunuchs and the Transing of Gender and Race." *Journal of Early Modern Cultural Studies* 19, no. 4 (2019): 116–36. https://doi.org/10.1353/jem.2019.0040.

Atabaki, Touraj. "From ʿAmaleh (Labor) to Kargar (Worker): Recruitment, Work Discipline, and Making of the Working Class in the Persian/Iranian Oil Industry." *International Labor and Working-Class History* 84, no. 1 (2013): 159–75.

Atabay, Badri. *Fihrist-i album-hayi kitabkhanih-yi saltanati.* Tehran: Chapkhanih-yi Ziba, 1976.

Ates, Sabri. "Bones of Contention: Corpse Traffic and Iranian-Ottoman Rivalry in Iraq." *Comparative Studies of Asia, Africa, and the Middle East* 30, no. 3 (2010): 512–32.

Atwood, Blake. *Underground: The Secret Life of Videocassettes in Iran.* Cambridge, MA: MIT Press, 2021.

ʿAzod al-Dowleh, Soltan Ahmad Mirza. *Life at the Court of the Early Qajar Shahs: Tarikh-e ʿAzodi.* Translated by Manoutchehr M. Eskandari-Qajar. Washington, DC: Mage, 2014.

ʿAzud al-Dawlih. *Tarikh-i ʿAzudi, shahr hal-i zanan va dukhtaran va pisaran va mutizamin si va shish saal saltanat va nava dar ahval-i Fath ʿAli Shah.* Edited by Kuhi Kirmani. Tehran: Intisharat-i Sarv, 1984.

Babaie, Sussan, Kathryn Babayan, Ina Baghdiantz-McCabe, and Massumeh Farhad. *Slaves of the Shah: New Elites of Safavid Iran.* New York: I. B. Tauris, 2004.

Babayan, Kathryn. "Eunuchs, iv. The Safavid Period." *Encyclopaedia Iranica*, 1998. Accessed August 5, 2015. https://iranicaonline.org/articles/eunuchs#iv.

Baghoolizadeh, Beeta. "From Religious Eulogy to War Anthem: Kurdizadeh's 'Layla Bigufta' and Blackness in Late Twentieth-Century Iran." *Comparative Studies of South Asia, Africa, and the Middle East* 41, no. 3 (2021): 441–54.

Baghoolizadeh, Beeta. "The Myths of Haji Firuz: The Racist Contours of the Iranian Minstrel." *Lateral* 10, no. 1 (2021). https://doi.org/10.25158/L10.1.12.

Baghoolizadeh, Beeta. "Seeing Black America in Iran." *American Historical Review* (2023).

Bajoghli, Narges. *Iran Reframed: Anxieties of Power in the Islamic Republic.* Stanford, CA: Stanford University Press, 2019.

Baron, Beth. *Egypt as a Woman: Nationalism, Gender, and Politics.* Berkeley: University of California Press, 2005.

Barragan, Yesenia. *Freedom's Captives: Slavery and Gradual Emancipation on the Colombian Black Pacific.* Cambridge: Cambridge University Press, 2022.

Bayzai, Bahram, dir. *Bashu: Gharibih-yi Kuchak (Bashu: The Little Stranger).* 120 mins. Kanun-i Parvarish-i Fikri, 1989.

Bayzai, Bahram. *Namayish dar Iran.* Tehran: Chap-i Kavian, 1965.

Beeman, William O. *Iranian Performance Traditions.* Costa Mesa, CA: Mazda, 2011.

Behdad, Ali. *Camera Orientalis: Reflections on Photography of the Middle East.* Chicago: University of Chicago Press, 2016.

Behdad, Ali. "Royal Portrait Photography in Iran: Constructions of Masculinity, Representations of Power." *Ars Orientalis* 43 (2013): 32–45.

Benjamin, Ruha. *Race after Technology: Abolitionist Tools for the New Jim Code.* Cambridge, UK: Polity, 2019.

Bishara, Fahad. "The Many Voyages of *Fateh al-Khayr*: Unfurling the Gulf in the Age of Oceanic History." *International Journal of Middle East Studies* 52, no. 3 (2020): 397–412.

Bohrer, Frederick, ed. *Sevruguin and the Persian Image: Photographs of Iran, 1870–1930*. Seattle: University of Washington Press; Washington, DC: Arthur M. Sackler Gallery, 1999.

Bonine, Michael E., and Nikki Keddie. *Modern Iran: The Dialectics of Continuity and Change*. Albany: SUNY University Press, 1981.

Boodrookas, Alex, and Arang Keshavarzian. "The Forever Frontier of Urbanism: Historicizing Persian Gulf Cities." *International Journal of Urban and Regional Research* 43, no. 1 (2019): 14–29.

Brown, Kathleen M. *Good Wives, Nasty Wenches, and Anxious Patriarchs: Gender, Race, and Power in Colonial Virginia*. Chapel Hill: University of North Carolina Press, 1996.

Browne, Simone. *Dark Matters: On the Surveillance of Blackness*. Durham, NC: Duke University Press, 2015.

Bsheer, Rosie. *Archive Wars: The Politics of History in Saudi Arabia*. Stanford, CA: Stanford University Press, 2020.

Cacchioli, Niambi. "Disputed Freedom: Fugitive Slaves, Asylum, and Manumission in Iran (1851–1913)." UNESCO Culture, *The Slave Route*, 2008.

Cakmak, Ezgi. "Citizens of a Silenced History: The Legacy of African Slavery and Racial Contours of Citizenship in the Late Ottoman Empire and Early Turkish Republic, 1857–1933." PhD diss., University of Pennsylvania, 2022.

Calmard, J. "Bast." *Encyclopaedia Iranica*, 1988. Accessed September 25, 2016. https://iranicaonline.org/articles/bast-sanctuary-asylum.

Campt, Tina. *Image Matters: Archive, Photography, and the African Diaspora in Europe*. Durham, NC: Duke University Press, 2012.

Campt, Tina. *Listening to Images*. Durham, NC: Duke University Press, 2017.

Can, Lale. *Spiritual Subjects: Central Asian Pilgrims and the Ottoman Hajj at the End of Empire*. Stanford, CA: Stanford University Press, 2020.

Chehabi, Houchang. "Mohammad Mosaddeq and the 'Standard of Civilization.'" Paper presented at the Thirteenth Biennial Conference of the Association for Iranian Studies, Salamanca, August 30–September 2, 2022.

Chehabi, Houchang. "The Reform of Iranian Nomenclature and Titulature in the Fifth Majles." In *Converging Zones: Persian Literary Tradition and the Writing of History: Studies in Honor of Amin Banani*. Costa Mesa, CA: Mazda, 2012.

Cloake, Margaret Morris, trans. *A Persian at the Court of King George, 1809–10: The Journal of Mirza Abul Hassan Khan*. Exeter, UK: David & Charles, 1988.

Cohen, Harvey G. *Duke Ellington's America*. Chicago: University of Chicago Press, 2010.

Cole, Juan. *Modernity and the Millennium: The Genesis of the Baha'i Faith in the Nineteenth-Century Middle East*. New York: Columbia University Press, 1998.

Collaco, Gwendolyn. "Crafting Time through Dress: A Pastiche of Periods and Regions." In *An Album of Artists' Drawings from Qajar Iran*. Cambridge, MA: Harvard Art Museums, 2017.

Dandamayev, Muhammad A. "Barda and Barda-Dari." *Encyclopaedia Iranica*, 1988. Accessed November 13, 2015. https://iranicaonline.org/articles/barda-i.

Dashti, Sayeh. *To Our Children around the World: You Belong*. Xlibris, 2016.

Dastgirdi, Vahid. *Kitab-i Khusraw va Shirin: Hakim Nizami Qumi Shahir bih Ganjavi*. Tehran: Ibn-i Sina, 1954.

Dehkhoda, Ali Akbar. *Charand-o Parand: Revolutionary Satire from Iran, 1907–1909*. Translated by Janet Afary and John R. Perry. New Haven, CT: Yale University Press, 2016.

de Planhol, Xavier. "Busehr, i. the City." *Encyclopaedia Iranica*, 1990. Accessed February 6, 2018. https://www.iranicaonline.org/articles/bushehr-01-city.

DeSouza, Wendy. "Race, Slavery and Domesticity in Late Qajar Chronicles." *Iranian Studies* 53, nos. 5–6 (2020): 821–45.

Diba, Layla, with Maryam Ekhtiar, eds. *Royal Persian Paintings: The Qajar Epoch, 1785–1925*. New York: Brooklyn Museum of Art in association with I. B. Tauris, 1998.

Dihkhoda, ʿAli Akbar, completed by Muhammad Muʿin. *Lughat-namih*. Tehran: Chapkhanih-yi Dawlati-yi Iran, 1958.

Drake, Jarrett Martin. "Blood at the Root." *Journal of Contemporary Archival Studies* 8, article 6 (2021). https://elischolar.library.yale.edu/jcas/vol8/iss1/6/.

Dyer, Elizabeth. "Dramatic License: Histories of Kenyan Theater, 1895–1964." PhD diss., University of Pennsylvania, 2017.

Eden, Jeff. *Slavery and Empire in Central Asia*. Cambridge: Cambridge University Press, 2018.

Edwards, Brent Hayes. *The Practice of Diaspora*. Cambridge, MA: Harvard University Press, 2003.

Ehlers, Eckart, and Willem Floor. "Urban Change in Iran, 1920–1941." *Iranian Studies* 26, nos. 3–4 (1993): 251–75.

Ehsaei, Mahdi. *Afro-Iran: The Unknown Minority*. Berlin: Kehrer, 2016.

Ekhtiar, Maryam. "From Workshop to Bazaar to Academy: Art Training and Production in Qajar Iran." In *Royal Persian Paintings: The Qajar Epoch, 1785–1925*, edited by Layla S. Diba with Maryam Ekhtiar, 50–66. New York: Brooklyn Museum of Art in association with I. B. Tauris, 1998.

El-Azhari, Taef. *Queens, Eunuchs, and Concubines in Islamic History, 661–1257*. Edinburgh: Edinburgh University Press, 2019.

El Hamel, Chouki. *Black Morocco: A History of Slavery, Race, and Islam*. Cambridge: Cambridge University Press, 2013.

Elling, Rasmus, and Kevan Harris. "Difference in Difference: Language, Geography, and Ethno-Racial Identity in Contemporary Iran." *Ethnic and Racial Studies* 44, no. 12 (2021): 2255–81.

Elshakry, Marwa. *Reading Darwin in Arabic, 1860–1950*. Chicago: University of Chicago Press, 2014.

Emami, Iraj. "The Evolution of Traditional Theatre and Development of Modern Theatre in Iran." PhD diss., University of Edinburgh, 1987.

Erdem, Hakan. *Slavery in the Ottoman Empire and Its Demise, 1800–1909*. London: Palgrave Macmillan, 1996.

Eskandari-Qajar, Manoutchehr M. "Dust 'Ali Khan Mo'ayyer al-Mamalek: Scion of a Once Powerful Family; Witness to the End of an Era." *Anthropology of Contemporary Middle East and Central Eurasia* 5, nos. 1–2 (2021): 175–213.

Farahani, Muhammad Husayn. *Safarnamih-yi Farahani*. Edited by Mas'ud Gulzari. Tehran: Firdawsi, 1982.

Farahani, Mohammed Hosayn. *A Shi'ite Pilgrimage to Mecca, 1885–1886: The Safarnameh of Mirza Mohammad Hosayn Farahani*. Translated by Hafez Farmayan. Austin: University of Texas Press, 1990.

Farmayan, Hafez. "Farahani, Mirza Mohammad-Hosayn." *Encyclopaedia Iranica*, 1999. Accessed February 11, 2017. http://www.iranicaonline.org/articles/farahani.

Feuvrier, Jacques. *Trois ans à la cour de Perse*. Paris: F. Juven, 1899.

Field, Kendra T. "The Privilege of Family History." *American Historical Review* 127, no. 2 (2022): 600–633.

Floor, Willem. *A Social History of Sexual Relations in Iran*. Washington, DC: Mage, 2015.

Freamon, Bernard. *Possessed by the Right Hand: The Problem of Slavery in Islamic Law and Muslim Cultures*. Leiden: Brill, 2019.

Fuentes, Marisa. *Dispossessed Lives: Enslaved Women, Violence and the Archive*. Philadelphia: University of Pennsylvania Press, 2018.

Galland, M. *Les mille et une nuits*. Paris: Ledentu, 1832.

Gilroy, Paul. *The Black Atlantic*. Cambridge, MA: Harvard University Press, 1995.

Glassman, Jonathan. *War of Words, War of Stones: Racial Thought and Violence in Colonial Zanzibar*. Bloomington: Indiana University Press, 2011.

Gomez, Michael. *Exchanging Our Country Marks*. Chapel Hill: University of North Carolina Press, 1998.

Gould, Rebecca. "The Critique of Religion as Political Critique: Mirza Fath 'Ali Akhundzada's Pre-Islamic Xenology." *Intellectual History Review* 26, no. 2 (2016): 171–84.

Great Britain, Foreign and Commonwealth Office. *British and Foreign State Papers*. Vol. 37. London: HMSO, 1862.

Grigor, Talinn. *Building Iran: Modernism, Architecture, and National Heritage under the Pahlavi Monarchs*. New York: Periscope/Prestel, 2009.

Gualtieri, Sarah. *Arab Routes: Pathways to Syrian California*. Stanford, CA: Stanford University Press, 2019.

Gualtieri, Sarah. *Between Arab and White: Race and Ethnicity in the Early Syrian American Diaspora*. Berkeley: University of California Press, 2009.

Gursel, Zeynep Devrim. "Classifying the Cartozians: Rethinking the Politics of Visibility alongside Ottoman Subjecthood and American Citizenship." *Photographies* 15, no. 3 (2022): 349–80.

Haeri, Mohammad Reza. "Kashan v. Architecture." *Encyclopaedia Iranica*, 2012, 16/1, 23–29. Accessed December 30, 2012. http://www.iranicaonline.org/articles/kashan-v4-historic-mansion.

Hafiz. *Divan-i Khwajih Shams al-Din Muhammad Hafiz-i Shirazi*. Edited by Qasim Ghani. Tehran: Kitabfurushi-yi Zavvar, 1959.

Haji-Qassemi, Kambiz, ed. *Ganjnameh: Cyclopaedia of Iranian Islamic Architecture*, vol. 4: *Mansions of Esfahan*. Translated by Claude Karbassi. Tehran: Shahid Behesht University Press, 1998.

Haley, Alex, ed. *The Autobiography of Malcolm X*. New York: Grove Press, 1966.

Hall, Stuart, ed. *Representation: Cultural Representations and Signifying Practices*. London: Sage, 1997.

Hartman, Saidiya. *Scenes of Subjection: Terror, Slavery, and Self-Making in Nineteenth-Century America*. New York: Oxford University Press, 1997.

Hartman, Saidiya. *Wayward Lives, Beautiful Experiments: Intimate Histories of Social Upheaval*. New York: W. W. Norton, 2019.

Hathaway, Jane. *Beshir Agha: Chief Eunuch of the Ottoman Imperial Harem*. Oxford: Oneworld, 2005.

Hathaway, Jane. *The Chief Eunuch of the Ottoman Harem: From African Slave to Power-Broker*. Cambridge: Cambridge University Press, 2018.

Hathaway, Jane. "The Wealth and Influence of an Exiled Ottoman Eunuch in Egypt: The Waqf Inventory of ʿAbbas Agha." *Journal of the Economic and Social History of the Orient* 37, no. 4 (1994): 293–317.

Hayes, Brent Edwards. *The Practice of Diaspora: Literature, Translation, and the Rise of Black Internationalism*. Cambridge, MA: Harvard University Press, 2003.

Heidari, Kamran, dir. *Dingomaro*. 45 mins. 3w Production, 2013.

Hensel, Michael, and Mehran Gharleghi, eds. "Iran: Past, Present and Future." *Architectural Design*, no. 217 (2012): 36.

Hertslet, Sir Edward. *Treaties, &c. Concluded between Great Britain and Persia and between Persian and Other Foreign Powers, Wholly or Partially in Force on the 1st April, 1891*. London: Harrison and Sons, 1891.

Hopper, Matthew. "Liberated Africans in the Indian Ocean World." In *Liberated Africans and the Abolition of the Slave Trade, 1807–1896*, edited by Richard Anderson and Henry B. Lovejoy, 271–94. Rochester, NY: University of Rochester Press, 2021.

Hopper, Matthew. *Slaves of One Master: Globalization and Slavery in Arabia in the Age of Empire*. New Haven, CT: Yale University Press, 2015.

Horta, Paulo Lemos, and Yasmine Seale. *The Annotated Arabian Nights: Tales from 1001 Nights*. New York: Liveright, 2021.

Hunwick, John, and Eve Troutt Powell. *The African Diaspora in the Mediterranean Lands of Islam*. Princeton, NJ: Markus Wiener, 2002.

Iks, Malkum (Malcolm X). *Malkum Iks*. Translated by Ghulam Husayn Kishavarz. Tehran: Amir Kabir, 2001.

Iks, Malkum (Malcolm X). *Malkum Iks: Gangistiri kih rahbar-i Musalman-i Amrika shod*. Translated by Ali Abbasi. Tehran: Miras-i Ahl-i Qalam, 2016.

Iks, Malkum (Malcolm X). *Siyah mikhurushad: Malkum Iks (The Black Seethes: Malcolm X)*. Translated by Farhad Khurrami. Tehran: Ihya Press, 1979.

Insafi, Javad. *Siyah bazi az nigah-i yik siyah baz*. Isfahan: Nashr-i Hujjat, 1997.

An Introduction to the Art of Black Africa. Exhibition catalog. Tehran: Sponsored by the Shahbanu Farah Foundation, Farabi University, National Iranian Radio and Television, 1977.

Ittihadiyih, Maʿsumih, and Sirus Saʿdvandian, eds. *Amar-i Dar al-Khilafih-yi Tihran.* Tehran: Nashr-i Tarikh-i Iran, 1989.

Javadi, Hasan. "*Towfiq (Tawfiq)* Newspaper." *Encyclopaedia Iranica,* 2017. Accessed April 13, 2017. http://www.iranicaonline.org/articles/towfiq-newspaper.

Johnson, Jessica Marie. *Wicked Flesh: Black Women, Intimacy, and Freedom in the Atlantic World.* Philadelphia: University of Pennsylvania Press, 2020.

Jones, Nicholas R. *Staging* Habla de Negros: *Radical Performances of the African Diaspora in Early Modern Spain.* University Park: Penn State University Press, 2019.

Jones-Rogers, Stephanie E. *They Were Her Property: White Women as Slave Owners in the American South.* New Haven, CT: Yale University Press, 2019.

Kamrava, Mehran, ed. *Gateways to the World: Port Cities in the Persian Gulf.* Oxford: Oxford University Press, 2016.

Karamursel, Ceyda. "'In the Age of Freedom, in the Name of Justice': Slaves, Slaveholders, and the State in the Late Ottoman Empire and Early Turkish Republic, 1857–1933." PhD diss., University of Pennsylvania, 2015.

Karamursel, Ceyda. "Shiny Things and Sovereign Legalities: Expropriation of Dynastic Property in the Late Ottoman Empire and Early Turkish Republic." *International Journal of Middle East Studies* 51, no. 3 (2019): 445–64.

Karamursel, Ceyda. "Transplanted Slavery, Contested Freedom, and Vernacularization of Rights in the Reform Era Ottoman Empire." *Comparative Studies in Society and History* 59, no. 3 (2017): 690–714.

Karamursel, Ceyda. "The Uncertainties of Freedom: The Second Constitutional Era and the End of Slavery in the Late Ottoman Empire." *Journal of Women's History* 28, no. 3 (2016): 138–61.

Karimi, Pamela. *Alternative Iran: Contemporary Art and Critical Spatial Practice.* Stanford, CA: Stanford University Press, 2022.

Karimi, Pamela. *Domesticity and Consumer Culture in Iran: Interior Revolution of the Modern Era.* London: Routledge, 2013.

Kashani-Sabet, Firoozeh. "The Anti-Aryan Moment: Decolonization, Diplomacy, and Race in Late Pahlavi Iran." *International Journal of Middle East Studies* 53, no. 4 (2021): 691–702.

Kashani-Sabet, Firoozeh. *Conceiving Citizens: Women and the Politics of Motherhood in Iran.* New York: Oxford University Press, 2011.

Kashani-Sabet, Firoozeh. *Frontier Fictions.* Princeton, NJ: Princeton University Press, 1999.

Kasravi, Ahmad. *Tarikh-i Mashrutih-yi Iran.* Tehran: Majid, 1999.

Keddie, Nikki R. *Religion and Rebellion in Iran: The Tobacco Protest of 1891–92.* New York: Routledge, 1966.

Keshavarzian, Arang. "From Port Cities to Cities with Ports: Towards a Multiscalar History of Persian Gulf Urbanism in the Twentieth Century." In *Gateways* to the World: Port Cities in the Persian Gulf, edited by Mehran Kamrava, 33–56. Oxford: Oxford University Press, 2016.

Khaleghi-Motlagh, Djalal. *Abu'l Qasem Ferdowsi: The Shahnameh (The Book of Kings)*. New York: SUNY Press, 2007.

Khaza'i, Muhammad Riza. *Sabk-i bazigari va zindigi-yi hunari-yi Sa'di Afshar*. Tehran: Anjuman-i Honar-hayi Namayishi-yi Tihran, 2014.

Khazeni, Arash. *Tribes and Empire on the Margins of Nineteenth-Century Iran*. Seattle: University of Washington Press, 2009.

Khosronejad, Pedram. *Qajar African Nannies: African Slaves and Aristocratic Babies*. Stillwater: Iranian and Persian Gulf Studies Program at Oklahoma State University, 2017.

Kia, Mana. *Persianate Selves: Memories of Place and Origin before Nationalism*. Stanford, CA: Stanford University Press, 2020.

Kiyanush, Mahmud, trans. and ed. *Az klasik ta mudirn*. Tehran: Intishirat-i Ishrafi, 1967.

Kounkou Hoveyda, Priscillia. "Writing Ourselves into Existence with the Collective for Black Iranians." Interview by Beeta Baghoolizadeh. MERIP 29, no. 299 (2021). https://merip.org/2021/06/writing-ourselves-into-existence-with -the-collective-for-black-iranians/.

Koyagi, Mikiya. *Iran in Motion: Mobility, Space, and the Trans-Iranian Railway*. Stanford, CA: Stanford University Press, 2021.

Koyagi, Mikiya. "Modern Education in Iran during the Qajar and Pahlavi Period." *History Compass* 7, no. 1 (2009). https://doi.org/10.1111/j.1478-0542.2008.00561.x.

Kurtynova-D'Herlugnan, Liubov. *The Tsar's Abolitionists: The Slave Trade in the Caucasus and Its Suppression*. Leiden: Brill, 2010.

Lad, Jateen. "Panoptic Bodies: Black Eunuchs as Guardians of the Topkapi Harem." In *Harem Histories: Envisioning Places and Living Spaces*, edited by Marylin Booth. Durham, NC: Duke University Press, 2010.

Lee, Anthony. "Enslaved African Women in Nineteenth-Century Iran: The Life of Fezzeh Khanom of Shiraz." *Iranian Studies* 45, no. 3 (2012): 417–37.

Lee, Anthony. "Haji Mobarak." *Encyclopaedia Iranica*, 2016. Accessed September 25, 2017. https://iranicaonline.org/articles/mobarak-haji.

Lee, Anthony. "Half the Household Was African: Recovering the Histories of Two African Slaves in Iran, Haji Mubarak and Fezzeh Khanum." UCLA *Historical Journal* 26, no. 1 (2015): 17–38.

Lewis, Bernard. *Race and Slavery in the Middle East*. Oxford: Oxford University Press, 1990.

Lott, Eric. *Love and Theft: Blackface Minstrelsy and the American Working Class*. Oxford: Oxford University Press, 1993.

Low, Michael Christopher. *Imperial Mecca: Ottoman Arabia and the Indian Ocean Hajj*. New York: Columbia University Press, 2020.

Ltifi, Afifa. "Black Tunisians and the Pitfalls of Bourguiba's Homogenization Project." POMEPS *Studies* 40 (2020): 69–72.

Lutz, Catherine, and Jane Collins. *Reading* National Geographic. Chicago: University of Chicago Press, 1993.

Maghbouleh, Neda. *Limits of Whiteness: Iranian-Americans and Everyday Politics of Race*. Stanford, CA: Stanford University Press, 2017.

Mahdi, Muhsin. *Arabian Nights*. Translated by Husain Haddawy. New York: W. W. Norton, 1995.

Makdisi, Ussama. "Coexistence, Sectarianism and Racism—an Interview with Ussama Makdisi." Interview by Alex Lubin. MERIP 299, no. 29 (2021). https://merip.org/2021/06/coexistence-sectarianism-and-racism-an-interview-with-ussama-makdisi/.

Marable, Manning. *Malcolm X: A Life of Reinvention*. London: Penguin, 2011.

Marashi, Afshin. *Nationalizing Iran: Culture, Power and the State, 1870–1940*. Seattle: University of Washington Press, 2008.

Marefat, Mina. "Building to Power: Architecture of Tehran, 1921–1941." PhD diss., MIT Department of Architecture, 1988.

Marmon, Shaun. *Eunuchs and Sacred Boundaries in Islamic Society*. Oxford: Oxford University Press, 1995.

Martin, Vanessa. "The Abyssinian Slave Trade to Iran and the Rokeby Case, 1877." *Middle Eastern Studies* 58, no. 1 (2022): 201–13.

Martin, Vanessa. *The Qajar Pact: Bargaining, Protest, and the State in Nineteenth-Century Persia*. London: I. B. Tauris, 2005.

Martinez, Maria Elena. *Genealogical Fictions: Limpieza de Sangre, Religion, and Gender in Colonial Mexico*. Stanford, CA: Stanford University Press, 2008.

Mashayekhi, Abdulkarim. *Yad-i Abu Shahr: ʿAks-hayi qadim-i Bushehr*. Bushehr: Iran Shinasi, 2015.

Masʿudi, Shiva. *Karnamih-yi talkhagan*. Tehran: Nay, 2016.

Mathew, Johan. *Margins of the Market: Trafficking and Capitalism across the Arabian Sea*. Berkeley: University of California Press, 2016.

Matthee, Rudi, and Willem Floor. *The Monetary History of Iran: From the Safavids to the Qajars*. New York: I. B. Tauris, 2013.

Mawlawi, Jalal al-Din Muhammad. *Kulliyat-i Shams-i Tabrizi*. Edited by Badiʿ al-Zaman Furuzanfar. Tehran: Amir Kabir, 2000.

Meier, Prita. *Swahili Port Cities: The Architecture of Elsewhere*. Bloomington: Indiana University Press, 2016.

Minawi, Mostafa. *The Ottoman Scramble for Africa: Empire and Diplomacy in the Sahara and the Hijaz*. Stanford, CA: Stanford University Press, 2016.

Mirzai, Behnaz, dir. *The African-Baluchi Trance Dance*. 27 mins. Social Sciences and Humanities Research Council of Canada, 2012.

Mirzai, Behnaz, dir. *Afro-Iranian Lives*. 45 mins. Self-published, 2007.

Mirzai, Behnaz. *A History of Slavery and Emancipation in Iran, 1800–1929*. Austin: University of Texas Press, 2017.

Mitchell, Margaret. *Gone with the Wind (Bar bad raftih)*. Translated by Muhammad Sadiq Shariʿati. Tehran: Guyish-i Naw, 2008.

Mitchell, Robin. *Venus Noire: Black Women and Colonial Fantasies in Nineteenth-Century France*. Athens: University of Georgia Press, 2020.

Molina, Natalia. *How Race Is Made in America: Immigration, Citizenship, and the Historical Power of Racial Scripts*. Stanford, CA: Stanford University Press, 2014.

Moore, Taylor. "Superstitious Women: Race, Magic, and Medicine in Egypt (1875–1950)." PhD diss., Rutgers University, 2020.

Moradian, Manijeh. *This Flame Within: Iranian Revolutionaries in the United States*. Durham, NC: Duke University Press, 2022.

Morgan, Jennifer. *Laboring Women: Reproduction and Gender in New World Slavery*. Philadelphia: University of Pennsylvania Press, 2004.

Morier, James. *The Adventures of Hajji Baba of Ispahan*. New York: Random House, 1937.

Morrison, Toni. *Beloved*. New York: Knopf, 1987.

Motlagh, Amy. *Burying the Beloved*. Stanford, CA: Stanford University Press, 2011.

Motlagh, Amy. "Translating Race: Simin Daneshvar's Negotiation of Blackness." *Iran Namag* 5, no. 3 (2020): 46–66.

Mottahadeh, Negar, ed. ʿAbduʾl Bahaʾs Journey West: The Course of Human Solidarity. London: Palgrave Macmillan, 2013.

Muʿayyir al-Mamalik, Dust ʿAli Khan. *Yaddasht-hayi az zindagani-yi khususi-yi Nasir al-Din Shah*. Tehran: Naqsh-i Jahan, 1983.

Mustawfi, ʿAbdullah, ed. *Safarnamih-yi Nasir al-Din Shah bih farang*. Tehran: Intisharat-i Mashʿal, 1362.

Muʿtaqidi, Kiyanush, and Nami Namvar Yikta. *Az Bagh-i Gulistan ta Kakh-i Gulistan*. Tehran: Danyar, 2022.

Naficy, Hamid. *A Social History of Iranian Cinema*. Vol. 4. Durham, NC: Duke University Press, 2012.

Najmabadi, Afsaneh. *Familial Undercurrents: Untold Stories of Love and Marriage in Modern Iran*. Durham, NC: Duke University Press, 2022.

Najmabadi, Afsaneh. *Professing Selves: Transsexuality and Same-Sex Desire in Contemporary Iran*. Durham, NC: Duke University Press, 2013.

Najmabadi, Afsaneh. "Reading for Gender through Qajar Paintings." In *Royal Persian Paintings: The Qajar Epoch, 1785–1925*, edited by Layla S. Diba with Maryam Ekhtiar, 76–89. New York: Brooklyn Museum of Art in association with I. B. Tauris, 1998.

Najmabadi, Afsaneh. *Story of Daughters of Quchan: Gender and National Memory in Iranian History*. Syracuse: Syracuse University Press, 1998.

Najmabadi, Afsaneh. *Women with Mustaches and Men without Beards: Gender and Sexual Anxieties of Iranian Modernity*. Berkeley: University of California Press, 2005.

Nashat, G. "Anis-Al-Dawla." *Encyclopaedia Iranica*, 2011. Accessed February 11, 2016. https://www.iranicaonline.org/articles/anis-al-dawla-d.

Naylor, Celia. *UnSilencing Slavery: Telling Truths about Rose Hall Plantation, Jamaica*. Athens: University of Georgia Press, 2022.

Nicolini, Beatrice. "The Western Indian Ocean as Cultural Corridor: Makran, Oman, and Zanzibar through Nineteenth Century European Accounts and Reports." MESA *Bulletin* 37, no. 1 (2003): 20–49.

Odabaei, Milad. "The Slip of the Philosopher and the Sinking of the Ship: Translation, Protest, and the Iranian Travails of Learned Politics." *HAU: Journal of Ethnographic Theory* 10, no. 2 (2020): 561–78.

Odumosu, Temi. *Africans in English Caricature, 1769–1819: Black Jokes, White Humour.* London: Harvey Miller, 2017.

Odumosu, Temi. "The Crying Child: On Colonial Archives, Digitization, and Ethics of Care in the Cultural Commons." *Current Anthropology* 61, no. 22 (2020): 289–302.

Omidsalar, Mahmoud. "Haji Firuz." *Encyclopaedia Iranica*, 2012, 11/5, 551–52. Accessed December 30, 2012. http://www.iranicaonline.org/articles/haji-firuz.

Onley, James. "The Raj Reconsidered: British India's Informal Empire and Spheres of Influence in Asia and Africa." *Asian Affairs* 40, no. 1 (2009): 44–62.

Otsby, Marie. "'There Are in Persia Many Subjects Not Accessible to Female Inquiry': Eurocentric and Cross-Cultural Feminist Nomadism in Lady Mary Sheil's *Glimpses of Life and Manners in Persia* (1856)." In *Feminism in World Literature*, edited by Robin Truth Goodman, 23–40. London: Bloomsbury, 2022.

Oualdi, M'hamed. *A Slave between Empires: A Transimperial History of North Africa.* New York: Columbia University Press, 2020.

Pahlavi, Riza Shah. *Safarnamih-yi Khuzistan; Safarnamih-yi Mazandaran.* Tehran: Talash, 1974.

Parsienejad, Iraj. *A History of Literary Criticism in Iran, 1866–1951.* Bethesda: IBEX, 2003.

Parvin, Nasreddin. "Ettela'at." *Encyclopaedia Iranica*, 1988. Accessed February 5, 2016. http://www.iranicaonline.org/articles/ettelaat.

Payne, Les, and Tamara Payne. *The Dead Are Arising: The Life of Malcolm X.* New York: Liveright, 2020.

Peirce, Leslie. *Empress of the East: How a European Slave Girl Became Queen of the Ottoman Empire.* New York: Basic Books, 2017.

Peirce, Leslie. *Imperial Harem: Women and Sovereignty in the Ottoman Empire.* New York: Oxford University Press, 1993.

Perry, Imani. *Vexy Thing: On Gender and Liberation.* Durham, NC: Duke University Press, 2018.

Perry, J. R. "Aga Mohammad Khan Qajar." *Encyclopaedia Iranica*, 1982. Accessed November 11, 2016. http://www.iranicaonline.org/articles/aga-mohammad-khan.

Polak, Josef. *Persien, das Land und seine Bewohner: Ethnographische.* Vol. 1. Leipzig: Brodhaus, 1865.

Pourtavaf, Leila. "Reimagining Royal Domesticity: Intimacy, Power, and Familial Relations in the Late Qajar Harem." *Journal of Middle East Women's Studies* 16, no. 2 (2020): 165–92.

Princewill, Victoria. *In the Palace of Flowers.* Abuja: Cassava Republic Press, 2021.

Ramizani, Muhammad, ed. *Hizar va Yik Shab.* Tehran: Chapkhanih-yi Aftab, 1936.

Redhouse, J. W. *The Diary of HM the Shah of Persia during His Tour of Europe.* London: John Murray, 1874.

Reilly, Benjamin J. "A Well-Intentioned Failure: British Anti-slavery Measures and the Arabian Peninsula, 1820–1940." *Journal of Arabian Studies* 5, no. 2 (2016): 91–115.

Reyes, Angelita D. "Performativity and Representation in Transnational Blackface: Mammy (USA), Zwarte Piet (Netherlands), and Haji Firuz (Iran)." *Atlantic Studies* 16, no. 4 (2018): 1–30.

Rice, Clara Colliver. *Persian Women and Their Ways: The Experiences and Impressions of a Long Sojourn amongst the Women of the Land of the Shah with an Intimate Description of Their Characteristics, Customs and Manner of Living*. Philadelphia: J. B. Lippincott, 1923.

Rice, Kelsey. "Forging the Progressive Path: Literary Assemblies and Enlightenment Societies in Azerbaijan, 1850–1928." PhD diss., University of Pennsylvania, 2018.

Ricks, Thomas. "Slaves and Slave Trading in Shi'i Iran, AD 1500–1900." *Journal of Asian and African Studies* 36, no. 4 (2001): 407–18.

Ringer, Monica. "Rethinking Religion: Progress and Morality in the Early Twentieth Century Iranian Women's Press." *Comparative Studies of South Asia and the Middle East* 24, no. 1 (2004): 47–54.

Roberts, Dorothy. *Fatal Invention: How Science, Politics, and Big Business Re-create Race in the Twenty-First Century*. New York: New Press, 2011.

Roberts, Dorothy. *Killing the Black Body*. New York: Penguin Random House, 1997.

Rostam-Kolayi, Jasamin. "Origins of Iran's Modern Girls' Schools: From Private/National to Public/State." *Journal of Middle East Women's Studies* 4, no. 3 (2008): 58–88.

Russell, Mona L. *Creating the New Egyptian Woman: Consumerism, Education, and National Identity, 1863–1922*. New York: Palgrave Macmillan, 2004.

Rustayi, Muhsin, and Hussein Ahmadi-Rahbarian. *Kitabchih-yi aʿdad-i nufus-i ahali-yi Dar al-Iman-i Qom, Sar-shumarih-yi jamiʿat-i ahd-i Nasir al-Din Shah (1275 Q)*. Qom: Nur-i Mataf, 1397.

Sabban, Rima. "Encountering Domestic Slavery: A Narrative from the Arabian Gulf." In *Slavery in the Islamic World: Its Characteristics and Commonality*, edited by Mary Ann Fay, 125–53. London: Palgrave Macmillan, 2018.

Sadr-i Hashim, Muhammad. *Tarikh-i jaraʿid va majallat-i Iran*. Isfahan: Intisharat-i Kamal, 1984–85.

Samuels, Ellen. "Examining Millie and Christine McKoy: Where Enslavement and Enfreakment Meet." *Signs* 37, no. 1 (2011): 53–81.

Satrapi, Marjane. *Persepolis: A Story of Childhood*. Paris: Pantheon, 2003.

Sattari, Mohammad, and Khadijeh Mohammadi Nameghi. "Photography Studio of the Naseri Harem in Nineteenth-Century Iran." In *The Indigenous Lens? Early Photography in the Near and Middle East*, edited by Staci G. Schweiller and Markus Ritter, 257–73. Berlin: De Gruyter, 2018.

Savoy, Benedicte. *Africa's Struggle for Its Art: History of a Postcolonial Defeat*. Princeton, NJ: Princeton University Press, 2022.

Schine, Rachel. "Race and Blackness in Premodern Arabic Literature." In *Oxford Research Encyclopedia of Literature*, 2021. Accessed December 6, 2021. https://doi.org/10.1093/acrefore/9780190201098.013.1298.

Schweiller, Staci Gem. *Liminalities of Gender and Sexuality in Nineteenth-Century Iranian Photography: Desirous Bodies*. New York: Routledge, 2017.

Schwerda, Mira. "Amorous Couples: Depictions of Permitted and Prohibited Love." In *An Album of Artists' Drawings from Qajar Iran*, 78–83. Cambridge, MA: Harvard Art Museum, 2017.

Schwerda, Mira. "Death on Display: Mirza Riza Kirmani, Prison Portraiture, and the Depiction of Public Executions in Qajar Iran." *Middle East Journal of Culture and Communication* 8 (2015): 172–91.

Schwerda, Mira. "Iranian Photography: From the Court, to the Studio, to the Street." In *Technologies of the Image: Art in 19th-Century Iran*, edited by David J. Roxburgh et al., 81–105. Cambridge, MA: Harvard Art Museums, 2017.

Sharpe, Christina. *In the Wake: On Blackness and Being*. Durham, NC: Duke University Press, 2016.

Sheehi, Steven. *The Arab Imago: A Social History of Portrait Photography, 1860–1910*. Princeton, NJ: Princeton University Press, 2016.

Sheehi, Steven. "Glass Plates and Kodak Cameras: Arab Amateur Photography in the 'Era of Film.'" In *The Indigenous Lens? Early Photography in the Near and Middle East*, edited by Staci G. Schweiller and Markus Ritter, 257–73. Berlin: De Gruyter, 2018.

Sheil, Mary Woulfe. *Glimpses of Life and Manners in Persia*. London: John Murray, 1856.

Shirazi, Maziar. "A Review of *Tarabnameh*, or, Why Are Iranian-Americans Laughing at Blackface in 2016?" *Ajam Media Collective*. Accessed December 8, 2016. https://ajammc.com/2016/12/07/why-are-iranian-americans-laughing-at -blackface-in-2016/.

Siamdoust, Nahid. *Soundtrack of the Revolution: The Politics of Music in Iran*. Stanford, CA: Stanford University Press, 2017.

Sipiani, Muhammad. *Dibachih bar tarikh va jughrafiyayi sharestan-i Firaydun Shahr*. Qom: Nashriyat-i Idih Gustar, 2012.

Skjærvø, Prods Oktor. "Kayanian." *Encyclopaedia Iranica*, 2013. Accessed April 15, 2020. https://www.iranicaonline.org/articles/kayanian-vi.

Smith, William Gervase Clarence. *Islam and the Abolition of Slavery*. Oxford: Oxford University Press, 2006.

Sobers-Khan, Nur. *Slaves without Shackles: Forced Labour and Manumission in the Galata Court Registers, 1560–1572*. Berlin: Klaus Schwarz Verlag, 2014.

Sohrabi, Naghmeh. *Taken for Wonder: Nineteenth-Century Travel Accounts from Iran to Europe*. Oxford: Oxford University Press, 2012.

Steele, Robert. *The Shah's Imperial Celebrations of 1971: Nationalism, Culture and Politics in Late Pahlavi Iran*. London: I. B. Tauris, 2020.

Stephenson, Lindsey. "Rerouting the Persian Gulf: Transnationalization of Iranian Networks, c. 1900–1940." PhD diss., Princeton University, 2018.

Suzuki, Hideaki. *Slave Trade Profiteers in the Western Indian Ocean*. London: Palgrave Macmillan, 2017.

Tahmasbpur, Muhammad Riza. *Nasir al-Din Shah-i ʿAkkas*. Tehran: Nashr-i Tarikh, 2012.

Tanavoli, Parviz. *European Women in Persian Houses*. London: I. B. Tauris, 2015.

Taqvayi, Naser, dir. *Arbaʿin*. 21 mins. 1970.

Taqvayi, Naser, dir. *Bad-i jinn* (*The Demon Winds*). 22 mins. National Iranian Radio and Television, 1969.

Tarikh-i ʿumumi va Iran. Vol. 1. Tehran: Bungah-i Matbuʿat-i Ilmi va Saʿadat, 1956.

Tawfiq, ʿAbbas. *Tawfiq chigunih Tawfiq shud*. Tehran: Farhang-i Nashr-i Naw, 2019.

Tawfiq, Firuz. "Census." *Encyclopaedia Iranica*, 2000. Accessed August 4, 2015. https://iranicaonline.org/articles/census-i.

Thelwell, Chinua. *Exporting Jim Crow: Blackface Minstrelsy in South Africa and Beyond*. Amherst: University of Massachusetts Press, 2020.

Thompson, Ayanna. *Blackface*. New York: Bloomsbury, 2021.

Thompson, Levi. "Vernacular Transactions: Ahmad Shamlu's Persian Translations of Langston Hughes's Poetry." *Middle Eastern Literatures* 22, nos. 2–3 (2019): 128–40.

Tolan-Szkilnik, Paraska. *Maghreb Noir: The Militant-Artists of North Africa and the Struggle for a Pan-African, Postcolonial Future*. Stanford, CA: Stanford University Press, 2023.

Toledano, Ehud. *As If Silent and Absent: Bonds of Enslavement in the Islamic Middle East*. New Haven, CT: Yale University Press, 2007.

Toledano, Ehud. "The Imperial Eunuchs of Istanbul: From Africa to the Heart of Islam." *Middle East Studies* 20, no. 3 (1984): 382.

Toledano, Ehud. *Slavery and Abolition in the Ottoman Middle East*. Seattle: University of Washington Press, 1998.

Tolino, Serena. "Castration." In *The Encyclopedia of Islamic Bioethics*, Oxford Islamic Studies Online. Accessed December 10, 2021. http://oxfordislamicstudies .com/print/opr/t9002/e0288.

Trouillot, Michael Rolph. *Silencing the Past: Power and the Production of History*. Boston: Beacon, 1995.

Troutt Powell, Eve. *A Different Shade of Colonialism: Egypt, Great Britain, and the Mastery of the Sudan*. Berkeley: University of California Press, 2003.

Troutt Powell, Eve. *Tell This in My Memory: Stories of Enslavement from Egypt, Sudan and the Ottoman Empire*. Stanford, CA: Stanford University Press, 2012.

Turkchi, Fatimih, and Ali Tatari, eds. *Asnad-i banuvan dar durih-yi Mashrutiyyat*. Tehran: Kitabkhanih va Markaz-i Asnad-i Majlis-i Shura-yi Islami, 2011.

Vafa, Amirhossein. "Race and the Aesthetics of Alterity in Mahshid Amirshahi's *Dadeh Qadam-Kheyr*." *Iranian Studies* 51, no. 1 (2018): 141–60.

Vanzan, Anna. "Eunuchs." *Encyclopaedia Iranica*, 2012. Accessed February 6, 2019. https://www.iranicaonline.org/articles/eunuchs#.

Varahram, Farhad, dir. *Siyahan-i Junub-i Iran* (*The Black People of the South of Iran*). 55 mins. DEFC, 2014.

Vaziri, Parisa. "Arbaʾīn and Bakhshū's Lament: African Slavery in the Persian Gulf and the Violence of Cultural Form." *Antropologia* 7, no. 1 (2020): 189–214.

Vaziri, Parisa. "Thaumaturgic, Cartoon Blackface." *Lateral* 10, no. 1 (2021). https://csalateral.org/forum/cultural-constructions-race-racism-middle -east-north-africa-southwest-asia-mena-swana/thaumaturgic-cartoon -blackface-vaziri/.

Vejdani, Farzin. *Making History in Iran: Education, Nationalism, and Print Culture.* Stanford, CA: Stanford University Press, 2015.

Walcher, Heidi. *In the Shadow of the King: Zill al-Sultan and Isfahan under the Qajars.* New York: I. B. Tauris, 2008.

Walker, Tamara J. *Exquisite Slaves: Race, Clothing, and Status in Colonial Lima.* Cambridge: Cambridge University Press, 2017.

Walz, Terence, and Kenneth M. Cuno, eds. *Race and Slavery in the Middle East: Histories of Trans-Saharan Africans in Nineteenth-Century Egypt, Sudan, and the Ottoman Mediterranean.* Cairo: American University in Cairo Press, 2010.

Ware, Rudolph. *The Walking Qur'an: Islamic Education, Embodied Knowledge, and History in West Africa.* Chapel Hill: University of North Carolina Press, 2014.

Wegmann, Thomas. *Persian Nights: Amazing Boutique Hotels and Guest Houses in Iran.* New York: teNeues, 2021.

Wekker, Gloria. *White Innocence: Paradoxes of Colonialism and Race.* Durham, NC: Duke University Press, 2016.

Wexler, Laura. *Tender Violence: Domestic Visions in an Age of U.S. Imperialism.* Chapel Hill: University of North Carolina Press, 2000.

Wiesohofer, Josef. *Ancient Persia.* London: I. B. Tauris, 2001.

Willis, Deborah, and Barbara Krauthamer. *Envisioning Emancipation: Black Americans and the End of Slavery.* Philadelphia: Temple University Press, 2013.

Willoughby, Bam. "Opposing a Spectacle of Blackness: Arap Baci, Baci Kalfa, Dadi, and the Invention of African Presence in Turkey." *Lateral* 10, no. 1 (2021). https://csalateral.org/forum/cultural-constructions-race-racism-middle -east-north-africa-southwest-asia-mena-swana/opposing-spectacle -blackness-arap-baci-kalfa-dad-african-presence-turkey-willoughby/.

Wills, Charles James. *In the Land of the Lion and the Sun or Modern Persia: Being Experiences of Life in Persia during a Residence of Fifteen Years in Various Parts of That Country from 1866 to 1881.* London: Forgotten Books, 2018.

Wingham, Zavier. "Arap Bacı'nın Ara Muhaveresi: Under the Shadow of the Ottoman Empire and Its Study." YILLIK: *Annual of Istanbul Studies* 3 (2021): 177–83.

Young, Alden, and Keren Weitzberg. "Globalizing Racism and De-provincializing Muslim Africa." *Modern Intellectual History* 19, no. 3 (2022): 912–33.

Yule, Henry, and A. C. Burnell. *Glossary of Anglo-Indian Colloquial Words and Phrases and of Kindred Terms, Ethymological, Historical, Geographical, and Discursive.* London: John Murray, 1902.

Zakir Isfahani, 'Aliriza. *Farhang va siyasat-i Iran dar 'asr-i tajaddod 1300–1320.* Tehran: Mu'asisih-yi Mutali'at-i Tarikh-i Mu'asir-i Iran, 2007.

Zdanowski, Jerzy. *Speaking with Their Own Voices: The Stories of Slaves in the Persian Gulf in the 20th Century.* Newcastle: Cambridge Scholars, 2014.

Zekrgoo. *The Sacred Art of Marriage: Persian Marriage Certificates in the Qajar Dynasty.* Kuala Lumpur: Islamic Arts Museum Malaysia, 2001.

Zia Ebrahimi, Reza. *The Emergence of Iranian Nationalism: Race and the Politics of Dislocation.* New York: Columbia University Press, 2016.

Zilfi, Madeleine. *Women and Slavery in the Late Ottoman Empire.* Cambridge: Cambridge University Press, 2012.

Zill al-Sultan, Mas'ud Mirza. *Khatirat-i Zill al-Sultan*, vol. 2. Edited by Husayn Khadivjam. Tehran: Intisharat-i Asatir, 1995.

Zoka, Yahya. *Life and Works of Sani' ol-Molk, 1814–1866.* Edited by Cyrus Parham. Tehran: Iran University Press, 2003.

INDEX

Note: Page numbers in italics refer to illustrations.

enslaved people: as dowries, 46–47, 144, 176n12; enslavers' relationships with, 8, 99–100, 136–37, 144–45, 199nn8–9; in the house of the Bab, 141–43, 200n28; knowledge of Manumission Law (1929), 96; parental rights of, 44–46; as symbols of wealth and status, 98; in Tehran census, 31, 35, 38, 42, 170n19; violence against, 93–94, 133–34, 187n2, 187n5, 198n3

enslaved women: agency of, 138–40; caricatures of, 194n2; as childcare providers, 56–58, 57, 58, 160, 178nn48–49; escape of, 53–54, 177n32; freedom promised to, 27–28, 53–54, 188n6; *kaniz* (term for enslaved woman), 16, 31, 47, 101, 133–34, 170n19, 188n16, 189n18; marriages of, 96, 133–34, 139, 188n5; narratives of, 27–32, 39, 40, 41, 138–40; photograph annotations, 49, 51; portrait paintings of, 157; sale of, 52–53; in the United States, 139; vulnerability of, 27–28, 53–54, 177n33, 188n6. *See also* Khyzran (enslaved woman); Narges (free black woman who was enslaved)

enslavement: architecture reflecting, 37, 45, 105–7, 114, 173n50, 190n41; archives on, 7–9, 10, 13–18; of Baluchis, 103, 104; benevolence of, 22–26, 45–46, 53, 56–59, 61, 100, 138–45, 160, 178n48, 179n49; Blackness associated with, 45–46, 47, 52–56, 59; changing definitions of, 107–8; after Constitutional Revolution, 52–53; denials of, 3, 5, 8, 11, 22, 38, 44–45, 99–102, 114, 133–34, 136–40, 144–46, 150, 151; descendants' narratives on, 13–14, 19, 61, 63–66, 138–42; family complicity in, 136–38, 199nn8–9; forced visibility of, 4, 17–18, 20, 45–46; geography of, 20–21, 29–30, 34, 40, 172n41; in literature, 19, 42, 81–82, 171n25; revisionism, 15, 22, 99, 105, 107–8, 112, 135, 137, 138; social prestige and, 21, 37–38, 45–47, 50, 68–69, 83; United States, 2, 8, 22, 99, 108, 111–12, 136, 139; visibility of, 5, 6, 21, 34–35, 62, 98, 173n59

enslaving children, 5–6, 49, 51–52, 59, 60, 63–65, 64

enslaving families: benevolence of, 22–26, 45–46, 53, 56–59, 61, 100, 138–45, 160, 178n48, 179n49; childcare, 56–58, 57, 160, 178n48, 179n49; children of, 49–52, 59, 60, 63–65, 64; death of, and manumission of slaves, 200n35; denials of enslavement, 8, 44–45, 99–100, 133–34, 136–40, 144–46, 188n5; descendants of, 13–14, 19, 61, 63–66, 136–37, 138–42; disclosures of manumission to freedpeople, 96–97, 138, 200n35; domestic spaces, 45, 105–7,

190nn40–41, 190n44; dowries in, 46–47, 144, 176n12; enslaved children in, 6, 7, 44, 46, 49, 57, 59, 60, 61, 65–66, 143–45; as infallible, 138–43, 199n22; photographs of, 5, 6, 46, 49, 57, 59, 150, 151; prestige of, 21, 37–38, 45–47, 50, 68–69, 83; relations with freedpeople, 96, 98, 150, 174n71, 187n4, 188n5; religiosity of, 144, 145; rights to children of enslaved men, 44–45; violence of, 93–94, 133–34, 187n2, 187n5, 198n3

enslaving women: benevolence of, 56–59, 138–40, 178n48, 179n49; childcare, 56–58, 57, 58, 160, 178n48, 179n49; children as property of, 143–44; maternal femininity, 57; ownership of slaves, 175n5; in photographs, 6, 50, 57, 62, 65

erasure: abolition as, 3, 4–5, 22, 96–99; archival documentation, 8–9, 10, 15–17; of Black children, 5–8, 6; Black Iranians, 22, 150–54, 151; of Blackness, 3, 22, 119, 195n9; demolition of harems, 104–5; denial of slavery, 3, 5, 8, 11, 22, 44–45, 99–100, 102, 114, 133–34, 136–40, 144–46, 150, 151, 160; of ethnic identity, 98–99, 172n41; eunuchs, 15, 22, 25, 89–91, 115–16; history of enslavement, 15, 19, 22, 64–66, 99, 105, 107–8, 112, 128, 135, 138–43, 154, 160, 191n48, 199n24; of Iranian racism with US civil rights movement, 108, 111–12, 193n76; masks, 85, 87, 88, 89, 118; in the media, 133–34; in photograph annotations, 8, 13–14, 16–18, 25–26, 49, 51, 58, 64, 176n18, 176n20. *See also* forced invisibility

E'temad os-Saltaneh, 90

ethnic identity, 2, 34, 98–99, 172n41

Ettela'at (newspaper), 102, 108–9, 110, 111, 191n50, 192nn61–62

eugenics, 125, 196n31

eulogies, 150, 152–53

eunuchs: Abyssinian, 75–76, 77, 78–79, 80; authority of, 21, 68–69, 70, 73–74, 78–79, 82–83, 181n13, 184n43; bequests of, 15, 74, 182n25; Caucasian eunuchs, 15, 75–78, 77, 87–89, 88, 183n39, 185n68; as clowns, 85–87, 88, 89, 185n68; in court photography, 50, 75, 76, 77; deaths of, 67, 74–75, 91, 182n24; facial features, 77, 77–78, 87, 112; forced visibility of, 22, 25, 69–70, 73, 89–91, 115–16; gender identity, 69–71, 77–78, 106, 118, 124, 181nn10–11, 181n13; Georgian eunuchs, 78, 183n39; in harems, 68, 72, 73, 78–79, 81, 104, 116, 181n7; "The King of Kings" (cartoon), 83; in literature, 19, 42, 70–72, 81–82; marriages of, 74, 182n25; names of, 42, 67, 70–73, 81, 172n43; photographs of,

21, 49, *50*, *51*, 69, 73, *75*; physical appearance
of, 77, 78–79, 80–81, 87, 89–90, 115; portraits
of, 86, 87, *88*, *155*, 185n68; racist caricatures of,
79, *80*, 82–84, *83*, 89–91, 118, 120–21, 185n60,
185n68; records of, 73–74, 76, 116; sexuality,
70–71, 118, 124, 181n11, 181n13; treatment of, 34,
75–76, 80–82, 183n30, 183nn32–33

facial expressions, manipulation of, 61, 85, 87, 89,
118, 121, 122
facial hair, 77, 78, 87, 112
family: in American newspapers, 110; intimacy,
45, 72, 106, 175n4, 182n20, 190n40; *khanevadeh*
(family), 21, 43, 45, 59, 106; networks of freed
African women as, 53–54
Farahani, Mirza Mohammad Hosayn, 33–34, 35
Farah Diba, Queen, 95
Farrant, Francis, 31–32
Fath ʿAli Shah, 68
feminism, 138
Feuvrier, Jean-Baptiste, 77, 78, 79
Field, Kendra T., 198n5
films, 112, 119, 131, 133–34, 152, 153, 195n9, 201n10
Firuzabadi, Seyyed Reza, 100, 101
Floyd, George, 140
forced invisibility: of abolition, 30, 37, 99, 153–54;
of Black Iranians, 22, 150–54, *151*; buildings,
96, 105–6, 107, 114, 116, 201n3; of enslaved
children, 63–65, *64*; of enslavement, 3, 5, 8,
11, 22, 44–45, 102, 114, 133–34, 144–46, 150,
151; forgotten names, 8, 13, 14, 21, 67–68; of
freedpeople after abolition, 96, 98–99, 116,
150, 174n71; history of enslavement, 15, 19, 22,
64–66, 99, 105, 107–8, 112, 128, 135, 138–43, 154,
191n48; photographs, 17–19, 45–46
forced visibility: archives, 17–18; of Blackness,
5, 20–21, 29–30, 34, 38, 42, 45–46, 58–59,
115–16; circulation of photographs, 17–18;
contested ownership of photographs, 13,
14, 16–18; of East Africans, 20–21, 30, 34; of
enslavement, 18, 20, 21, 29, 37–38, 45–46, 83,
98, 102; of eunuchs, 22, 25, 69–70, 73, 89–91,
115–16; in photographs, 6, 17–19, 45–46, 49, *51*,
58, *59*, 60, 61, *75*; unburied bodies, 72. *See also*
photographs
freedmen, 44–45, 89, 90, 177n33, 186n71
freedpeople: British government treatment of,
28, 40–41; children of, 44; citizenship for, 3,
98–99; delayed manumission of, 54, 96–97, 138,
200n35; forced visibility of slavery, 99; reloca-
tion of, 96, 98, 150, 174n71; rights to children,

44–45, 177n33; visibility after abolition, 96,
98–99, 150, 174n71
freedwomen, 53–54, 96, 177n36
Fuentes, Marisa, 165n22

gender, 37, 69–71, 77–78, 106–7, 142, 181nn10–11,
190n40, 200n26
Geneva Convention on Slavery (1926), 107
genre of distortion, 23, 56, 134, 137–41, 154, 198n3
geography of Blackness, 20–21, 29–30, 34, 40,
172n41
Georgian eunuchs, 78, 183n39
gholam (term for enslaved man), 31, 35, 98, 102,
133, 170n19, 189n18
gholam Siyah, 35
Gilroy, Paul, 29
girls, 6, 8, 13, 14, 21, 35, 62. *See also* Khyzran
(enslaved woman)
Golestan Palace, 15, 16, 19, 25, 37, 48, 104, 105, 107
Goli Chehreh, 49, *51*
Gomez, Michael, 54
Gone with the Wind, 108, 191n48
Gursel, Zeynep Devrim, 177n24

Habashi, 121
hairstyles, 61, 62, 65, 66
Haji Firuz, 90, *117*; acceptance of, 128, 129–32,
192n58, 198n54; facial features of, 124; history
of, 116, 122; material representations of,
122–24, 129, 196n23; Nowruz holiday, 116, 122,
124, 129, 192n61; in satirical magazines, 123–24,
125; as Siavash, 129–30
Haji Mirza Aghassi, 31–32
Haji Mobarak, 141–42
Haji Naneh (freed Black woman), 53, 54
Haji Nuri, 78–79
Haji Sarvar Khan, *77*, 78
Haley, Alex, 109, 111
Hall, Stuart, 128
harems: disbanding of, 138, 139; eunuchs in, 68,
72, 73, 78–79, 81, 83, 104, 116, 181n7; in Golestan
Palace, 25, 37; guests of, 173n56; memories
of enslavement, 104–5; photographs of, 46,
48–49, 176n17; polygamy, 104–5
Hartman, Saidiya, 18, 89
Harvard University, 17–18
Hassan Khan, 49
Hathaway, Jane, 181n10, 182n27
holiday entertainment, blackface in, 120, 121, 122,
124, 128, 192n61
Hopper, Matthew, 40, 174n71

masks, 85, 87, *88*, 89, 118, 121
maternal femininity, 57
Mecca, 31, 33–34, 173n46
medical racism, 143–44, 200n33
Mesri, Mahdi, 121
Message, *The* (film), 112
Ministry of Finance, 15, 104, 105
minstrel shows: blackface minstrelsy, 21–22,
    90–91, 186n69, 192n61; race, 21, 22, 88–91, 117,
    118, 122; *Siyah-bazi* (playing Black), 21, 22, *88*,
    88–89, 117, 118, 122
Mirza Ahmad ʿAkkas, 87
Mirza Ebrahim Khan, 87, *88*
Mirzai, Behnaz, 11, 170n12, 170n14, 172n44,
    183n29, 188n8
Mitchell, Robin, 173n59
Mobarak (enslaved servant of the Bab), 141, 142,
    144–45
Mobarak (*Siyah-bazi* character), 121, 125, 196n33
mockery, 83–85, *83*, 85, *86*, 115–16, 120–21,
    185n60, 185n63
Mohammad (the Prophet), 112
Mohammad Reza Shah, 22, 99, 113
Mohammad Shah Qajar, 27, 31–32, 105
Moʿin, Mohammad, 107
monkeys, 124–25, 196n31, 196n33
Morier, James, 171n25
mosques, 150, *151*
motherhood, 13–14, 52–53, 56–58, *57*, 138–40, 160,
    178n48, 179n49
Motlagh, Amy, 12, 45, 138, 140, 175n4
Mozaffar ed-Din Shah, 21, 49, 51, 83–84, 87, 139,
    182n26
Muhammad, Elijah, 109–10
Mulla Ahmad, 28
Munes od-Dowleh, 52
museums, 105, 107, 114, 201n3
Muslims, 35, 109–10, 200n26

Najmabadi, Afsaneh, 45, 52, 69, 181nn10–11
names: documentation of, 6, 7–8, 13, 14–15, 49,
    51; of enslaved children, 8, 13, 14, 21, 25, 61; of
    enslaved men, 1, 31, 35, 39, 72–73, 98, 121–22,
    125, 163n1, 170n19, 188n8; of enslaved women,
    39, 49, *51*; ethnic lineage reflected in, 201n10;
    of eunuchs, 42, 67, 70–73, 81, 172n43; family
    names, standardization of, 98; forced invisibil-
    ity of, 8, 13, 14, 21, 67–68; racial aspects of, 8, 14,
    35, 98, 123–24, 131, 172n42, 188n8, 196nn24–25;
    social class reflected in, 8, 14, 72, 73
nannies, 13–14, 52–53, 56–57, *57*, 138–40, 160

Narges (free Black woman who was enslaved), 21,
    52–54, 56, 177n33, 177n36
Naserbakht, Mohammad Hosayn, 130
Nasir ed-Din Shah, 21, 27; assassination of, 51,
    78, 83; court jesters of, 84; eunuchs of, 21, 42,
    69, 72, 75–76, 77, 80; Golestan Palace harem,
    37, 105; Haji Firuz photograph, 116, *117*; photo-
    graph annotations of, 25–26, 49, *51*; photogra-
    phy interests of, 47–48, 77, 80; Teheran census,
    27; travelogue of Mirza Mohammad Hosayn
    Farahani, 33
Nation of Islam, 109–10
Naylor, Celia, 190n44
networks, of freed African women, 53–54
newspapers: censorship, 104; denial of slavery,
    102; on enslavement of women, 52; Haji Firuz
    in, 122; on Manumission Law (1929), 102;
    Nation of Islam, 109–10; on racism in the
    United States, 108–11, 191n50, 193n70; on slave
    trafficking, 104
Nowruz holiday, 116, 122, 124, 129, 131, 192n61

Observer (London), 109, 110
Odumosu, Temi, 17
Olsen, Jack, 111
Ottoman Empire, 11–12, 30, 170n12, 171n25,
    172n39, 177n24
Oualdi, Mʾhamed, 170n16

papier mâché masks, 85, 87, *88*, 118
Perry, Imani, 177n33
Persian Encyclopedia, *The* (*Daʾirat al-Maʿarif*), 107–8
Persian language: *bardeh*, 3, 11, 15, 94, 99, 101–3,
    108, 133, 189n18; *kaka* (racial slur), 35, 123–24,
    131, 172n42, 172n44, 196nn24–25; *Loghat-nameh*
    (dictionary of the Persian language), 107–8; pid-
    gin Persian, 74, 115, 119–20, 130, 131; racism in,
    11–12, 35, 124–25; in *Siyah-bazi* (playing Black),
    120, 121, 122; slavery in, 8–9, 102, 107–8, 124–25;
    translations of American literature, 109, 110, 111,
    191n48, 192n62; Westernization of, 189n18
photographs: annotation of, 8, 13–14, 16–18, 25,
    48, 49, *51*, 58–59, 160, 176n20; of Black Ameri-
    cans, 110, 111, 193n70; Blackness in, 25, 58, 59,
    88–89; circulation of, 16–18, 48, 160, 176n18;
    class differences in, 5, 6, *57*, 60; daguerreo-
    types, 17, 18, 47–48; enslaved children in, 6,
    49, 57, 61, 65–66; eunuchs in, 21–22, 50, *51*, 69,
    75, 76, 79, 80; fashion in, 57, 58; identification
    of individuals, 5–9, *6*; invention of camera,
    47–48; nudity in, 17, 18, 48; positions in, *6*,

photographs (*continued*)

48–49, *51*, 57–58, *57*, *59*, 60, 61, 65, 66; sexual humor in, 85, *86*; visibility of slavery in, 2, 6, 17–18, 45–46, 48–49, *59*, 61, 62–63, 72, 99, 140

pidgin Persian, 74, 115, 119–20, 130, 131

plantation slavery, 2, 8, 99, 108, 136, 139n4, 190n44

playing Black. See *Siyah-bazi*

portraiture, recentering Blacks in, 154, *156*

positions in photographs, 6, 48–49, *51*, *57*, 57–58, *59*, *60*, 61, 65, 66

postage stamps, 111, *112*, 193n78

Powell, Eve Troutt, 54, 166n30, 177n34, 183n28, 195n17

prestige, 21, 37–38, 45–47, 50, 68–69, 83

Princewill, Victoria, 19, 70

race: census categories, 25, 29, 31, 35, 38, 42–43, 98, 170n19; minstrel shows, 21, 22, 88–89, 117, 118, 122; mosque entrances as Black and white, 150; and national prominence, 150–53, 201n10; revisionist narratives of, 99; skin color, 29, 34, 52, 58, *59*, 82, 87, 89, 118, 152

racism: anti-Black stereotypes, 89–91, 115–16, 121–25, *124*, *126*, 128, 196n50; *Bashu: The Little Stranger* (film), 119, 195n9; blackened faces, 122, 123–24, 196n23; categorization of enslaved East Africans, 33–34; clown eunuchs, 85–87, *88*, 89, 90, 185n68; denial of, 3, 10–11, 118–19, 133–34, 146, 165n16, 198n3; eugenics, 125, 196n31; genre of distortion, 23, 56, 134, 137–41, 154, 198n3; *kaka* (racial slur), 35, 123–24, 131, 172n42, 172n44, 196nn24–25; language of, 11–12, 35, 82, 123–24, 124–25, 131, 172n42, 196nn24–25; in magazines, 83, 83–84; monkey caricatures, 124–25, 196n31, 196n33; names, 8, 13, 14, 21, 35, 98, 172n42, 188n8; racial otherness of Black Iranians, 151–52; *Towfiq* magazine, 22, 123–27, *126*, 196n28; United States and, 108–12, 146, 193n76; violence of, 93–94, 108–11, 133–34, 140, 187n2, 187n5, 191n50, 192n62, 193n70, 198n3. *See also* blackface; *Siyah-bazi* (playing Black)

Rahimi-Golkhandan, Shabnam, 184n51

Reilly, Benjamin, 169n10

research methods, 11

revolution (1979), 111, 128–29

Reza Shah: abolition, 3, 90–91, 94, 100; erasure of Iranian slavery narratives, 99, 104; human sacrifices for, 93–94, 187n2, 187n5; manumission laws, 94, 99; Westernization of Iran, 15, 100; wives of, 105

Rice, Clara Colliver, 38

Ricks, Thomas, 42

Roberts, Dorothy, 200n33

Roots: The Saga of an American Family (Haley), 111

Rose Hall Plantation (Jamaica), 190n44

rowzeh-khwan, 149, 152

Royal Persian Paintings: The Qajar Epoch, 1785–1925 (exhibit), 154–60

Samanbar (enslaved child), 143, *145*

Sani' ol-Molk, 71, *158*, *159*, 185n68

Satrapi, Marjane, 193n76

Schweiller, Staci Gem, 13, 176n17, 177n24

Selmi, Mohammad Baqer, 44

servants, 8–9, 14, 31, 37–38, 42, 102, 119–20, 159, 170n19, 173n59

Sevruguin, Antoin, 85, *86*

sexuality, 27, 53, 70–71, 76, 86, 96, 104–5, 118, 124, 133–34, 177n33, 177n36, 181n11, 188n5

Shafaq-e Sorkh (newspaper), 104

Shaherzad (*A Thousand and One Nights*), 71

Shahnameh (epic), 129–30

Shahrbaz (*A Thousand and One Nights*), 71

Shah Siyah, 54–55, 89

Shah Zaman (*A Thousand and One Nights*), 71

Shamlu, Ahmad, 110

Sharaf (newspaper), 37

Sharpe, Christina, 1

Sheehi, Steven, 177n24

Sheil, Justin, 32, 34, 39, 41

Shi'i Islam, 149, 150–52, 179n49, 200n1

Shirazi, Seyyed 'Ali Mohammad (the Bab), 141–43, 199n22

Shokuh os-Saltaneh, 49, *50*

sholi character, 194n7

Siavash (folkloric character), 129–30

Siyah, 2, 20, 22, 29, 32–35, 44, 49, 55, 115, 120–22, 125, 171n22

Siyahan-e Jonub-e Iran (*The Black People of the South of Iran*) (film), 133–34

Siyah-bazi (playing Black): actors, 83–84, 118–23, 130–31, 185n63, 195n10; Afshar, Sa'di, 119–20, 121, 129; black makeup, 119, *120*, 121, 195nn9–10; enslavement characterized in, 118, 121, 194n7; facial expressions, manipulation of, 61, 85, 87, 89, 118, 121, 122; films, 131; history of, 119–20, 130; Islamic Republic on, 128–29, 195n22; minstrel shows, 21, 22, *88*, 88–89, 117, 118, 122; Mobarak (*Siyah* character), 121, 125, 196n33; monkey references in, 196n33; non-Black Iranians in, 118, 120–21; Nowruz celebrations, 116; racism in, 84–90, 115–16, 118, 120, 121, 124, 130–31; sexuality, 86, 118; *sholi* character,